EATING DRUGS

Eating Drugs

Psychopharmaceutical Pluralism in India

Stefan Ecks

NEW YORK UNIVERSITY PRESS

New York and London

NEW YORK UNIVERSITY PRESS
New York and London
www.nyupress.org

References to Internet websites (URLs) were accurate at the time of writing. Neither the author nor New York University Press is responsible for URLs that may have expired or changed since the manuscript was prepared.

LIBRARY OF CONGRESS CATALOGING-IN-PUBLICATION DATA
Ecks, Stefan, author.
Eating drugs : psychopharmaceutical pluralism in India / Stefan Ecks.
pages cm
Includes bibliographical references and index.
ISBN 978-0-8147-2476-7 (cloth : alk. paper)
1. Psychopharmacology—Social aspects—India—Kolkata. 2. Ethnopharmacology—India—Kolkata. 3. Psychotropic drugs—Social aspects—India—Kolkata. 4. Cultural psychiatry—India—Kolkata. 5. Medical anthropology—India—Kolkata. I. Title.
RC483.E25 2013
616.89'180954—dc23
                    2013019859

New York University Press books are printed on acid-free paper, and their binding materials are chosen for strength and durability. We strive to use environmentally responsible suppliers and materials to the greatest extent possible in publishing our books.

Manufactured in the United States of America
10 9 8 7 6 5 4 3 2 1

Also available as an ebook

CONTENTS

ACKNOWLEDGMENTS

How do I say thanks if I should not *say* thanks? One of the first things I learned after arriving in Calcutta was that it is impolite to say "thank you" in Bengali. The expression *dhanyabad* is said to be an equivalent to English "thank you." But *dhanyabad* does not perform the same speech act that "thank you" performs in English. In Bengal, receiving a favor is imagined as part of a conviviality in which the calculative measuring of an exchange is ill-mannered. A favor is either another moment in a long-standing relation or the beginning of a new series of exchanges, whereas "thank you" implies that no further contact is necessary. Hence verbalized thanks transgress what might be called Bengali "baseline communism" (Graeber 2011). But what can I do if I am not allowed to say thanks? At this moment, all I can do is to *acknowledge* my gratitude for all the kindness I have received from so many people over the years.

First, I want to express my gratitude to all the people in Calcutta—doctors, patients, friends—who allowed me to spend time with them and who so generously helped me in the creation of this book. Thank you all for making my times in Calcutta so unique, so enjoyable, and so memorable.

My research over the years was assisted by exceptional people. Jokesh Francis was brilliantly helpful in supporting the research on popular body concepts, on Ayurveda, and on homeopathy. His dry sense of humor made the sheer endless transcribing as much fun as endless transcribing can possibly be. Bonani Roy, from whom I took Bengali lessons, was a treasure trove of knowledge of the language. Arijit Chakraborty was immensely helpful in collecting data on how Calcuttans define depression. Soumita Basu deserves great thanks for being such a cheerful colleague during a later stretch of the antidepressants research. And Jhunu's superb cooking was the best and most metaphor-free mind food I can imagine.

I want to thank all the friends who have made Calcutta a new home away from home: Shanu-di and Damayanti "Dodo" Lahiri; Suhasini

Kejriwal and family; Rajlakshmi Ghosh and family; P. K. Sarkar and family; Manju Sarkar and family; S. K. Mukherjee and family. Special thanks go to Annu Jalais and her parents, Françoise and Leo, who were there from the beginning. My years in Calcutta were blessed by the friendship of Anirban and Rumela Das, whose kindness and support shine through every page of this book. Thanks for the cabbage curry, too.

The intellectual generosity of so many people in Calcutta never ceased to astound me. My thanks go to Partha Chatterjee, Tapati Guha-Thakurta, Debdas Banerjee, A. K. Biswas, Gautam Chakraborty, Shrimoy Roy Chodhury, and Bhaskar Mukhopadhyay. I also want to thank all the members of the *From the Margins* collective for the wonderful conversations.

Distinguished teachers have inspired and guided this book. I am indebted to Chris Fuller and Jonathan Parry for their acumen and for never letting me become a mere medical anthropologist. William Sax has followed the writing of this book through all its stages, and his immense generosity has helped it find its current form. Jonathan Metzl's enthusiasm was, as always, infectious. And I want to thank João Biehl, Lawrence Cohen, and Mark Nichter for their mentorship.

From the first draft of the research proposal to the final draft of the book, I was blessed with the support of friends and colleagues across five continents: Viola Balz, Crispin Bates, Chris Baty, Stefan Beck, Gerald Berreman, Dominique Behague, André Beteille, Aditya Bharadwaj, Christiane Brosius, Janet Carsten, Indranil Chakrabarty, Nancy Chen, Alex Choby, Jacob Copeman, Ivan Crozier, Abhijit Dasgupta, Hansjörg Dilger, Henrike Donner, Denielle Elliott, Georg Elwert, Matthew Engelke, Christoph Emmrich, Richard Fox, Peggy Froerer, Murphy Halliburton, Chris Harding, Ian Harper, Cori Hayden, David Healy, Heather Hindman, Markus Höfner, Elisabeth Hsu, Sushrut Jadhav, Sumeet Jain, Deborah James, Janis Jenkins, Kriti Kapila, Junko Kitanaka, Laurence Kirmayer, Martina Klausner, Michi Knecht, Martin Kunz, James Laidlaw, Helen Lambert, Annette Leibing, Margaret Lock, Rebecca Marsland, Emily Martin, Linsey McGoey, Axel Michaels, Lucia Michelutti, Gavin Miller, James Mills, Mattison Mines, Joanna Moncrieff, Harish Naraindas, Jörg Niewöhner, Michael Oldani, Aihwa Ong, Adriana Petryna, Stacey Pigg, Chris Pinney, Kaushik Sunder Rajan,

Oliver Razum, A. Jamie Saris, Malabika Sarker, Sjaak van der Geest, David van Sickle, Nancy Scheper-Hughes, Ekkehard Schröder, Nikky Singh, Jonathan Spencer, Allan Young, Ayo Wahlberg, Robert Whitaker, Thomas Widlok, Angela Woods, and Dominik Wujastyk. I also want to thank the late Georg Foster for sending me a copy of his *Hippocrates* book after a Sunday Supper at International House Berkeley, way back in 1995.

Kalman Applbaum and Martyn Pickersgill deserve special thanks for being such astute readers of the final manuscript. My editor at New York University Press, Jennifer Hammer, has been phenomenal in her support and lightning-fast turnaround times.

My life and work have been immensely enriched by the vibrant and welcoming atmosphere at Edinburgh University. Special thanks to all my friends and colleagues in Social Anthropology and the School of Social and Political Sciences, who have given me so much support over the years that it took to finish the book. I also want to thank some of the exceptional students that I have had the priviledge to teach at Edinburgh: Cristobal Bonelli, Conny Guell, Laszlo Lajtai, Hanna Mantila, Kate Milosavljevic, Tania Porqueddu, and Phoebe Rose.

This book has been informed by collaborations with a number of outstanding colleagues. I am particularly grateful to Robert Frank for the work we did together on homeopathy. Dr. Frank, you are a great organizer. Many thanks also to my colleagues from the ESRC/DFID–funded project "Tracing Pharmaceuticals in South Asia" (RES-167-25-0110): Soumita Basu, Gitanjali Priti Bhatia, Samita Bhattarai, Petra Brhlikova, Erin Court, Abhijit Das, Ian Harper, Patricia Jeffery, Roger Jeffery, Allyson Pollock, Santhosh M. R., Nabin Rawal, Madhusudhan Subedi, as well as all members of the Centre for Health and Social Justice (New Delhi) and Martin Chautari (Kathmandu).

The debt to my parents, my foremost teachers, is truly too great to be put into words. I wish I could have given a copy of this book to my beloved mother, just to see her smile.

Thank you, Christine, for being there for me throughout the years that I worked on this book. It takes a very special woman to be willing to discuss Indian concepts of digestion over breakfast, lunch, and dinner. Thank you for raising our children, Carlotta and Noah, while I sat in the attic.

Research grants that supported my various fieldwork stays in Calcutta came from the Studienstiftung des deutschen Volkes and the UK Economic and Social Science Research Council. The School of Social and Political Science at the University of Edinburgh supported several shorter research trips and a year-long sabbatical during which much of this book was written.

A few sections of chapter 2 have appeared in an article in *Anthropology and Medicine* (Ecks 2004), some of the ethnographic data discussed in chapter 3 has been used in an article for *Anthropology and Medicine* (Frank and Ecks 2004), and parts of chapter 4 are informed by a range of previous publications (Ecks 2005, 2008, 2010b; Ecks and Basu 2009).

Introduction

"Mind Food"

The first time I heard psychopharmaceuticals described as "mind food" was during a psychiatric ward round in Calcutta. Dr. Roy, one of the city's most illustrious psychiatrists, invited me to join him at the Advaitananda Seva Prathishthan, a general hospital run by a Hindu philanthropic organization. Located in a busy part of south-central Calcutta, the Advaitananda Hospital attracts patients from all over the metropolitan area. Founded in the first years after Indian Independence, the hospital caters primarily to low-income patients, but richer people also come because of the good reputation of its staff. As in most charitable hospitals in India, the spatial boundaries of the Advaitananda Hospital are minimal. Relatives are expected to feed and look after family members while they are in the hospital; hence most wards can be entered at all hours. Most psychiatric clients are seen in the general outpatient department on the ground floor of one of the hospital's wings. In the middle of a large hall are two rows of wooden benches where patients can sit while waiting to see a doctor. Cubicles for consultation form two long rows on each side of the hall. During daytime hours, the outpatient department (OPD) is packed with hundreds of patients and their relatives, as well as nursing staff and medical representatives. Even with open windows and dozens of fans swirling overhead, the hall is always hot and stuffy. Patients of all medical specialties share the floor, so it is impossible to tell who is waiting for what kind of doctor. Beyond the OPD, a few beds in the hospital's upper wards are devoted to acute psychiatric cases. Patients who stay there are only admitted for a few days; the aim is to discharge them quickly because of staff and space limitations. A pool of psychiatrists gives a few hours per week of free service (*seva*), while maintaining for-profit chambers elsewhere in the city. To do *seva* not only improves the doctors' prestige and good karma but also increases their stock of patients and the number of drug prescriptions written. In the OPD, two or three psychiatrists are available in the mornings. Each doctor's shift lasts for about two hours. The doctors practice separately from one another and usually leave immediately after their shift ends. Senior psychiatrists like Dr. Roy also use the hospital as a venue for teaching sessions.

A plump Bengali in his late forties, Dr. Roy regularly gathered an entourage of up to fifteen psychiatrists at these teaching sessions. Most of them were recent college graduates with work experience in India, yet some also had several years' experience in the United Kingdom or in the United States. These doctors came to see Dr. Roy practice because he had a reputation of being one of the most successful psychiatrists in West Bengal. Among his activities was the foundation of an NGO for mental illness awareness, a place where patients come together to talk about their problems in the fashion of Euro-American self-help groups. He was a favorite of pharmaceutical companies, who propped up his activities with money and drug supplies. He was respectfully addressed as "sir" even by doctors who were barely younger than he.

Dr. Roy was very skilled in establishing rapport with patients. He always touched his patients with his hands during consultations (and he often held my arm while I interviewed him). In a hierarchical society where even a handshake between a doctor and a patient is uncommon, Dr. Roy's tactile care was strikingly different. He was also good at talking to patients and in responding to their concerns. He could simplify psychiatric concepts through earthy metaphors that tapped into popular ideas of body and health. Dr. Roy's expression for psychopharmaceuticals was *moner khabar*, Bengali for "food (*khabar*) eaten by the mind (*mon*)." *Mon* and *khabar* are both common words, but the combination of "mind" and "food" in *moner khabar* is a neologism. *Moner khabar* was coined with the intention of making psychotropic drugs acceptable to those hesitant to take them. "Mind food" is a psychiatric *artifice*.

Bengali *khabar* is "food" in the specific sense of a cooked edible substance for everyday human sustenance, as opposed to terms for raw food, spoiled food, or food offered to a deity. The related verb *khaoya*, "to eat," refers primarily to the ingestion of food but also includes other forms of ingestion: "taking medications" (*osudh khaoya*) is indistinguishable from "*eating* medications." *Mon* is the Bengali term for mind, heart, mood, affection, memory, desire, concentration, and subjective opinion. It is etymologically related to Sanskrit *manas* (from *matih*, "thinking"), Greek *menos*, Latin *mens*, and English "mind." In German, the cognate word *Minne* meant "love" and "affectionate memory" in courtly love songs of the Middle Ages. Bengali *mon* is distinct from both the physical brain (*dimak*) and the head (*matha*), and does not have a precise location in the body. When people use the term, they either point to the solar plexus, point to the forehead, or move their hand between both points. *Mon*'s fluid localization between head and heart motivates the English translation "heart-mind" (Desjarlais 1992: 27; Kohrt and Harper 2008), a term coined to reflect that *mon* is not the rational, analytical counterpart to the irrationally feeling body, as in the Cartesian tradition. Although the concept of *mon* (or its equivalents) is not exclusive to Bengali language and culture, it is more commonly used in Bengali than in other Indian languages. *Moner khabar* literally means "food to be eaten by the mind," and cannot be translated into English as "food for thought" or "intellectual stimulation."

Dr. Roy said it was important to make patients understand and accept prescriptions. It was always possible to write drugs without explanation, but he found that a few words went a long way in increasing adherence. *Moner khabar* was a key expression that he used to link psychopharmaceuticals to food. Similar expressions were "vitamins" and "brain nutrients." To patients, Dr. Roy said that the brain needed sufficient food to think properly, just as the stomach needed food to keep the body going. Most people had enough food for the brain, but some had too little. A starved brain made them moody, fickle, and forgetful. These people could be easily helped by extra nutrients from the outside. The pills that he prescribed worked for the mind like extra nutrition worked for the physical body.

Dr. Roy also used "diabetes" and "insulin injections" as parallels, especially toward patients who needed to be on psychopharmaceuticals for a long time. Healthy people could digest sugar without the aid of medicines, but some people needed a regular supply of insulin from the outside to do so. In the same way, some people needed to take drugs regularly to allow the mind to function. "Insulin" made sense to many patients because diabetes is now a widespread disease, especially in the cities. But even "insulin" did not have the same resonance with patients as "food." The meaning of "insulin" was only understood by patients with some level of education. "Food," however, made sense to everyone. As one of Dr. Roy's followers, Dr. Bose, pointed out, "if there's an uneducated person, he will not understand 'insulin.' But *moner khabar* is the most effective. They can very easily accept."

On one of the visits to the inpatient ward, Dr. Roy and his entourage saw a 63-year-old monk of the Ramakrishna Mission. He had been sent to the Advaitananda Hospital by his superiors during a severe episode of "manic depression." When the group of doctors arrived, the swami (an honorific title for Hindu monks) was clad in saffron-colored robes and sat upright in his bed reading a book. Dr. Roy had already been treating the swami for the past several years and was on familiar terms with him.

After Dr. Roy had greeted him and asked about how he was feeling at the moment, the swami said that he was feeling good and that he would prefer to leave the hospital. Asked what he was reading, the monk showed us the cover of a little book by Vivekananda (1863–1902), who founded the Ramakrishna Mission in 1897. (Vivekananda's works are widely available in cheap paperbacks.) The monk read out a passage from "Lessons in Raja-Yoga," where Vivekananda discusses the "force of thought" in relation to health. Sensory perception makes "the particles of the brain fall into a certain position like the mosaics of a kaleidoscope." Conjuring memories of past perceptions means "resetting these particles." As in perception, a state of bodily and mental health is also a constellation of particles, while disease comes from the particles in disarray. Similar to an act of remembering, powerful thought can rearrange these particles in a healthy order: "In case of illness the memory of the ideal of health may be roused and the particles re-arranged in the position into which they fell when healthy." Once the mental work is done, the body will "follow the brain" and get well again. From this supremacy of the mind over the body, Vivekananda extrapolates that medicines, as gross substances ingested from the outside, cannot cure the body without the support of the mind. All that drugs do is to prop up the internal healing process that is ruled by the mind. The best medicines stir up this endogenous healing force: "There is only one power to cure the body, and that is in every man. Medicine only rouses this power."

By reading this passage, the swami wanted to challenge Dr. Roy to a disputation about the powers of the mind over the powers of medicine, but the psychiatrist only smiled politely and told his followers to note the book title and to read it in their own time. He then asked if the swami had been taking his medication as prescribed. With an oblique glance to the group of psychiatrists, Dr. Roy pointed to a line in the swami's medical record that said that he had not been regularly taking his medication (a mixture of drugs, predominantly fluoxetine and lithium) and that this was one of the reasons for the severity of the current episode. After a few more words about the swami's health, he said that it was now fine to leave and to return to Belur Math, the Order's head monastery on the left bank of the Hoogly (Calcutta's largest river, a distributary of the Ganges). Dr. Roy further reminded him that he had a regular shift at a private clinic near Belur Math and that they should keep in touch. But he also urged him to stick to the course of drugs prescribed. "What is wrong with taking drugs?" he asked. The pills were simply "nutritional supplements" for the brain. Just as anyone should take vitamins when normal food was not enough, anyone should take food supplements for the brain when nutrition was deficient. The prescribed medicines were *moner khabar*, and objecting to them was as unwise as objecting to taking vitamin C while having the flu.

When I later asked Dr. Bose, one of the younger doctors around Dr. Roy, about the meeting with the monk, he said that this was an unusually sophisticated discussion thanks to the relative familiarity between the two. That the monk disputed the efficacy of drugs, that he quoted from philosophical tracts, that he spoke about the mind rather than the body, all this was different from typical consultations. But it was typical that Dr. Roy tried to convince the patient to take the prescribed drugs. Compliance was much better if the patient agreed with the doctor's explanation. Part of any successful psychiatric consultation was to make patients understand psychopharmaceuticals in a language that made immediate sense to them, and nothing made more sense to Indian patients than parallels to food. To develop this language was a great skill of Dr. Roy: "What Dr. Roy does—I also follow the same trend—he says that the brain requires particular foods, nutrients." *Moner khabar* was strategically coined by the psychiatrists and is not an expression used in general parlance. As Dr. Bose said, "food"—and the lack of it—nicely illustrated the causes of mental disturbances and the action of psychopharmaceuticals, overcoming patients' stigmatizations and making them more conscientious in their required daily intake. *Moner khabar* was so intuitively convincing because it translated biochemical transactions between brain synapses into food transactions: as Dr. Bose put it, "There are some people who have these nutrients, which help them to speak properly, to express their affects properly. But there are some other persons who don't have these nutrients in their brain, so they cannot do these things properly, so we have to supply them nutrients from outside. Our drugs are like these nutrients."

Although the parallels between food and psychopharmaceuticals were strongly established in the group around Dr. Roy, not all psychiatrists were equally ready to simplify—or dissimulate—psychiatric models for their lay clients. Indeed, in the hundreds of consultations that I witnessed, psychiatrists' explanations of disease etiologies and drug effects were either absent or kept to a bare minimum. Psychiatrists focused on how the drugs were to be taken, for example, whether before, during, or after meals, in the mornings, or in the evenings. Usually psychiatrists did not need to explain more because neither patients nor their relatives asked. Even when psychiatric patients explicitly focused on digestion themselves, the doctors tended to rely on professional authority rather than on echoing lay preconceptions (see Ecks 2010b: 157-58). While *moner khabar* is not an expression actually used by every psychiatrist in Calcutta, it *can* potentially be used by any of them if they want to talk in a language that makes sense to patients.

This ethnography explores how medications, especially mood medications, are understood and used in Calcutta. It starts from biopsychiatric treatments, traverses popular health practices, explores alternative medications prescribed in Ayurveda (the grand tradition of Indian medicine) and in homeopathy (the second most popular type of medicine in Bengal), and finally returns to psychiatry. The key argument is that patients' suspicions of psychopharmaceuticals are based on suspicions of biomedicine's "magic bullet" model of drug effects. Chapter 1 discusses popular notions of health, with a focus on perceptions of how different drugs are digested and on the humoral balance between the "hot" belly and the "cool" mind. Chapter 2 analyzes Ayurvedic practices in Calcutta and shows how, in traditional Indian medicine, food is medicine and medicine is food. Chapter 3 presents Calcutta homeopaths, emphasizing their self-proclaimed ability to target patients' "nerves." The influential position of homeopathy in Bengal helps us to understand lay suspicions of biomedical drugs as expensive, full of toxic side effects, and capable only of superficial "suppression" of illness symptoms. Chapter 4 unfolds how Calcutta psychiatrists position themselves vis-à-vis popular "superstitions" about psychopharmaceuticals, general physicians, practitioners of nonbiomedical treatments, and the pharmaceutical industry. It reveals how psychiatrists try to manage "doctor-shopping" and overcome nonadherence to treatments. It focuses on psychiatrists' perceptions of food, on "Bengali bowel obsession," and on how neurochemical imbalances are likened to humoral imbalances. The concluding chapter returns to "mind food," showing how psychiatrists are both trying to counter nonbiomedical notions of drug effects and the biomedical model of short-term targeted action itself.

An Anthropology of Pharmaceuticals

Why does "mind food" resonate with Bengali notions of mind, food, belly, digestion, and plural medications? The problem explored in this book seems easily described: there are drugs that are meant to make someone feel better, happier, calmer. The doctors who prescribe them believe that they work well, whereas the patients may not be so sure and may try to refuse taking them. The doctors face a dilemma: should they explain the medications in the same medical terminology in which they themselves have learned about them and ensure patients' "informed consent"? Or should they, as far as possible, avoid friction and describe the pills in a manner that makes intuitive sense to patients? In other words, should doctors insist on scientific purity or opt for a persuasive story? To answer this, we must investigate where patients and doctors agree or disagree; how ideas change through persuasion, dissimulation, or deception; and how new metaphors, such as "mind food," are attempts to overcome these divisions. "Mind food" is a form of psychiatric language that appropriates popular discourses to overcome resistance (Applbaum 2006; Kitanaka 2011).

On a primary level, this requires an ethnography of healer/patient relations. Many studies have been written on the topic, some emphasizing successful persuasion (Csordas 2002; Liebert and Gavey 2009), some emphasizing patients' resistance and nonadherence (Pound et al. 2005; Whitmarsh 2009). The encounter between a healer and a patient can be approached as an encounter between different sets of presuppositions (Helman 2007: 122-55). These presuppositions entail, more or less explicitly articulated, what caused the illness symptoms, what would happen without medical intervention, what procedure seems most appropriate, and when an improvement of the problem can be expected. These presuppositions have been analyzed by medical anthropologists as "explanatory models" (Kleinman 1980: 104-18).

Studies of explanatory models usually assume that healer/patient encounters are temporal sequences. First, people perceive illness symptoms; then they try to make sense of the symptoms; then they seek medical help; then a doctor gives a diagnosis; then, on the basis of that diagnosis, treatment is prescribed. However, this temporality risks obscuring what precedes both the illness episode and the clinical encounter. New illness classifications have been disseminated that are reshaping people's symptom recognition, and new drugs are available that promise a cure for ills where there had been none before. Ian Hacking (2007) argues that medical classifications are interacting with what they are classifying. This makes it impossible to determine what comes first: the disease label, the people being labeled as having that disease, the institutions designed to deal with this disease, the body of knowledge that supports the disease label, or the experts in charge. Analyzing the networks formed by humans and nonhumans, Bruno Latour (1987, 1993, 2005) shows that humans do not precede things, either temporally or hierarchically. Medical encounters are not encounters between two human beings only, but also crossings between disparate networks of objects and people. Work on medicalization processes (Conrad 2007; Busfield 2010; Clarke et al. 2010; Metzl and Kirkland 2010) has shown that changing medical classifications and novel therapeutic promises can turn previously "healthy" people into "patients."

The social importance of material things has long been studied by anthropologists (Appadurai 1986; Miller 2005; Henare, Holbraad, and Wastell 2007). Applying a notion of "social biographies of things" to an anthropology of pharmaceuticals, Van der Geest, Whyte, and Hardon (1996: 153) observe the same power of concreteness in medicines: "By applying a 'thing,' we transform the state of dysphoria into something concrete, into some thing to which the patient and others can address their efforts." The materiality of medicines is particularly important in the domain of psychopharmacology, where drugs are a more stable reference point than disease labels (Healy 1997: 56; Lakoff 2002, 2005). This ethnography takes the presence of psychopharmaceuticals as a driving force in medical encounters, in psychiatry, and beyond. Starting with drugs reverses the temporality of explanatory models and reorders the questions to be asked: What are the available drugs for treatment? How does the presence of drugs influence the perceived causes of illness? How does the availability of drugs transform perceptions of illness? A focus on drugs, and the alternative temporality of healer/patient relations that it triggers, is a constitutive move of an anthropology of pharmaceuticals (Whyte, van der Geest, and Hardon 2002; Petryna, Lakoff, and Kleinman 2006; Biehl 2007; Ecks 2008; Jenkins 2010).

At stake in this book are different models of drug effects and how they come into play with one another. These models are often more tacit and amorphous than explicit and clearly defined. They also always rely on comparisons and metaphors. There is no objective and metaphor-free way of describing drug effects: Ayurvedic medicines are said to "balance" bodily humors. Homeopathic remedies are presumed to "stir up" the "vital force." And biomedical drugs ideally work like "magic bullets" that cure a specific disease with specific active ingredients.

Understandings of drug effects are not contained within the boundaries of discrete medical systems. Instead, ideas about remedies can shade into one another, with sometimes paradoxical results. As I will argue, the plausibility of calling psychopharmaceuticals "mind food" relies less on patients' ideas about biomedical psychopharmaceuticals as magic bullets than on a deeply layered combination of biomedical, Ayurvedic, homeopathic, and popular notions. The persuasive power of the metaphor springs from the illusion that "mind food" transcends all contradictions and inconsistencies. My task is to explore why "mind food" makes both immediate sense and, looked at closely, not much sense at all.

Like healer/patient encounters, medical pluralism is another central concern in social health studies, in India and beyond (Leslie 1976, 1992; Cant and Sharma 1999; Sujatha and Abraham 2009; Broom, Doron, and Tovey 2009). Pluralism can be found in various forms across the world, but it is particularly pronounced in India, where biomedicine always had to compete with long-established traditions, such as Ayurveda. Since the 1970s, the Indian government has officially promoted non-biomedical practices, including Ayurveda, Unani, Siddha, Yoga, naturopathy, and homeopathy. Beyond these recognized "Indian Systems of Medicine," many other local and marginal forms of healing are also practiced (Hardiman and Mukharji 2012).

What drives medical pluralism in India is neither state provision of medical services nor even official recognition, but an almost unregulated private market. Practitioners with training from official institutions are working in parallel to many who do not have any certified education (Cross and MacGregor 2010). Public spending on health—including biomedicine and the Indian Systems—has been rising over the past decades but remains extremely low compared to almost all other countries in the world. There is a chronic shortage of facilities provided by the state and a palpable public dissatisfaction with the quality of care. All this further fuels the predominance of the private health market (Jain and Jadhav 2008; Pinto 2011). About 70 percent of all health expenditures in India go to the private market. Private facilities account for around 60 percent of all in-patient and for 80 percent of all out-patient care. Only a fraction of these expenditures is covered by insurance or other forms of reimbursement; the majority is out of pocket (Organization for Economic Cooperation and Development 2011: 37-38). This ethnography of pluralism in Calcutta focuses on what is happening in private doctors' chambers. The fact that the doctors described here are paid directly by the patients adds pressure on doctors to make sense—lest they lose the patients to the competition.

One effect of doctors having to reckon with medical pluralism is that this makes it more likely that they tell colorful stories. Indian doctors find themselves in a highly competitive market. Ideologists of free market capitalism assume that maximum competition leads to maximum transparency (of prices, quality, and so on). The evidence presented in the following suggests, however, that the relationship between therapeutic competition and therapeutic transparency is inversely related. Doctors' fear of losing patients to competitors—both biomedical and nonbiomedical—creates a permanent goal conflict with being truthful, if being truthful risks confrontation with patients, and if confrontation leads to a potential loss of business (see Ariely 2012: 67-96). In the absence of effective regulation of the way doctors must explain diagnoses and treatments to patients, they tend to prefer obfuscation to transparency. Obfuscation takes many forms, and explaining one's drugs in terms of other substances to "make the medicine go down" is one of them. Perhaps a general principle can be inferred from this: whenever medical pluralism and market competition increases, deceptive behaviors by doctors also increase.

Definitions of medical pluralism are contested, including the supposition—as suggested by "pluralism"—that different systems are existing happily alongside one another. But professional biomedicine occupies a hegemonic position that no other stream of healing can ignore. In India, a "doctor" is first of all a biomedical doctor, commonly called "allopath" (see chapter 3). Any other healer would need to be specified, for example as a "homeopathic" doctor. Biomedicine sets the standard for the way doctors look and for how drugs look. The chapters take the boundaries between different medical streams as a starting point, but each of them shows where the boundaries get blurry. I try to refrain from making claims about how medical "systems" in their entirety are related to one another: attempts in this direction usually lead to wrong generalizations. What I try to do, however, is to show where there is friction between different sets of assumptions about drugs and how a metaphor such as "mind food" is able to gloss over crucial differences.

This is a study in the anthropology of pharmaceuticals, but at many moments in the discussion, food comes to the fore: for example, when Ayurvedic "drugs" shade into "food," when medical diagnostics begin with food tastes, and when ritual concepts of subtle nourishment inform popular ideas of drug efficacy. There is a burgeoning anthropology of food and the sensuality of eating (e.g., Sutton 2010). This scholarship shows the many connections between food and other domains, such as power (e.g., Mintz 1996; Bray 1997; Farquhar 2002), religion (e.g., Khare 1992), kinship (Carsten 1997), or memory (Holtzman

2006). The cosmo-political centrality of food in India has long been studied (e.g., Appadurai 1981; Roy 2010), and excellent ethnographic work has been carried out on Bengali cooking in particular (e.g., Donner 2008; Janeja 2010). Psychiatrists who speak of "mind food" establish an explicit connection between food and psychopharmaceuticals. Yet the links between meals and medications discussed in this book are almost all one-sided: while food is used to make sense of drugs, drugs are not used to make sense of food. Metabolic metaphors such as *moner khabar* take features of food and transpose them to the domain of medications, but they seem to have little, if any, influence on what is meant by food. It would, however, be extremely interesting to incorporate pharmaceuticals in anthropologies of food and to see how eating medications might change the way meals are eaten.

Social studies of both patient/healer relations and medical pluralism avoid the question of drug efficacy. Whether a remedy "works" or not is left to medical research. In this book I also stay clear of my own opinions of efficacy. But this does not mean that efficacy gets bracketed. Instead, I represent how drug efficacy is evaluated from a diversity of viewpoints. The chapter on lay perceptions of health explores how allopathic, homeopathic, and Ayurvedic remedies are seen to work. In turn, the chapters on professional healers look at how they try to make patients understand prescriptions. "Drug effects" are treated in the broadest possible way, including how notions of bodily constitution, diagnostic procedures, and different ways of producing and dispensing drugs impinge on perceptions of how they work. Drug effects also raise critical questions of postcolonial modernity, individual autonomy, and ethical authenticity. They also raise fundamental ontological questions about materiality and the relation between matter and the mind.

Since psychopharmaceuticals frame this ethnographic investigation, some remarks on how they are currently evaluated are in order. The efficacy of psychopharmaceuticals, especially of antidepressants, has long been the subject of controversy (Healy 2004; Breggin 2008). There was a time when new medications seemed to herald a new era of treating mental ills through drugs. The drugs not only were easing illness but also were capable of making people "better than well" (Kramer 1992; Elliott 2003). This position now seems untenable. Over the years, evidence against antidepressants has been mounting, and even psychiatrists have announced "the end of the psychopharmaceutical revolution" (Tyrer 2012). As many critics point out, the theory of "neurochemical imbalance," which undergirds and explains the efficacy of the drugs, has never been proven (Moncrieff 2008; Kirsch 2009; Whitaker 2010). Meta-analyses of clinical trial data, including findings that had been withheld by pharmaceutical companies, conclude that antidepressants are no better than placebos for mild and moderate depression (Kirsch 2009). Even more alarming is the allegation that rising prescription rates of antidepressants and other psychopharmaceuticals is the *cause* for the current epidemic of mental illnesses and chronic disability (Whitaker 2010). Psychiatric drugs do have an effect on brain chemistry, but the beneficial effects seem to occur only—if they occur at all—in the early treatment phase. Over longer months and years, the drugs appear to deepen and to prolong suffering. Statistics show that those who never got treated with psychopharmaceuticals have a *better* chance of full recovery than those who did. Assessments of efficacy had systematically neglected the outcomes of long-term exposure (Whitaker 2010: 65). At the very least, there is no reason to believe that biopsychiatric drugs are unquestionably superior to other forms of treatment or even superior to *no* treatment. This book is written from a position of *doubt* about psychopharmaceuticals.

Doubting pharmaceuticals is difficult when the mandate to treat everyone who suffers is taken as the highest goal. All major international health organizations support the widened uses of psychopharmaceuticals, even though the imperative to use drugs is not as clear-cut as in other areas, such as infectious diseases. The basic position of the World Health Organization (WHO) is that there is a worldwide "treatment gap" for mental illnesses, with developing countries staying far behind the developed countries in providing effective treatments to everyone in need. "Scaling up" psychiatric provisions across the globe is the only answer to the rising rates of disease. The latest global treatment algorithms (World Health Organization 2010) recommend "considering" antidepressants for moderate-severe depression together with non-pharmacological interventions such as psychoeducation. Mild depression and unexplained somatic symptoms should no longer be treated with antidepressants. This is a more cautious guideline than those of a few years ago, when SSRIs were recommended as the best first-line treatment (Dawson and Tylee 2001). Given that drug prescriptions are much cheaper and much easier to organize than other services, they clearly remain the default mode of treatment for mood disorders.

Being doubtful is difficult in a biopolitical regime that makes health an unquestioned priority. "Biopolitics" is a concept coined by Michel Foucault to describe a particular regime of power that emerged in the seventeenth century and fully unfolded in the nineteenth century. Biopolitics are engaged with birth, life, death, health, and illness. Foucault (1978) introduced biopolitics under the heading "biopower" (*bio-pouvoir*). Biopower has two basic forms. The first is "anatomo-politics," which is centered on the individual body that is being disciplined, optimized in its capabilities. The other basic form of biopower is biopolitics, which tries to optimize life and longevity through interventions and regulatory controls (Foucault 1978: 139). Biopolitics is always an intervention focused on optimization, with "health" as a moving target on an infinite horizon. These optimizing inventions provide, in turn, legitimacy to political and bureaucratic regimes. Even if states do not always have the right or the obligation to intervene and optimize, and even if the responsibility for health has, in many ways, shifted from states to individuals (Rose 2007), biopolitics remain a pervasive force as a generalized form of governing (Fassin 2009; Raman and Tutton 2010).

A concern with biopolitics raises many questions (Lemke 2011: 117-24): what makes diseases unacceptable and populations "in urgent need of therapy"? Who profits from the promised optimization of health? How are individuals called upon to improve their physical and mental health? If "health" has become the ultimate justification for any intervention, can one even think and act "against health" without sounding deviant (Metzl and Kirkland 2010)? This ethnography of plural medications in India addresses these questions of biopolitics in diverse ways, showing that "health" has many meanings. Its goal is to describe alternatives to a monoculture of happiness encapsulated in biopsychiatric medications (Kirmayer 2002; Ecks 2005; Lock and Nguyen 2010).

Notes on Method

Calcutta is the capital of the Indian state of West Bengal and the cultural and economic center of northeastern India. The spelling of the city's name was officially changed to "Kolkata" in 2001 to emphasize its Bengali pronunciation, yet "Calcutta" remains widely used in English-language publications in India and abroad. More than fifteen million people live in the Calcutta metropolitan area, making it one of the world's most densely populated urban agglomerations. Calcutta is famous for its artistic and intellectual aspirations, as well as for decades of communist and trade union dominance. For thirty-four years, from 1977 until 2011, the Communist Party of India (Marxist) ruled, making it the longest-running democratically elected communist government in history. Once one of the richest and most globally connected cities in the world, Calcutta experienced economic decline throughout the second half of the twentieth century. In the first decade of the twenty-first century, the moderately "pro-capitalist" policies of Chief Minister Buddhadeb Bhattacharya brought an economic upturn. But violent protests against industrial megaprojects, such as a chemical plant in Nandigram (2007) or the proposed Tata Nano car factory in Singur (2006-2008), showed that "pro-people" politics remain a decisive force in West Bengal. This book is based on research conducted in Calcutta during this decade of accelerated yet contested economic liberalization.

The chapters on Ayurvedic, homeopathic, and allopathic doctors are based on interviews and observations of clinical practice. I chose to look at Ayurveda and homeopathy because they are the most established nonallopathic medical streams in Calcutta. Different healing streams are variously present across the regions of India, and for West Bengal and many other parts of northern India, homeopathy is far more popular than Ayurveda or any other nonallopathic system.

All of the doctors discussed here were trained in medical colleges; worked predominantly in private practice; and have had several years of work experience. Nearly sixty doctors from homeopathy, Ayurveda, and psychiatry were interviewed, as well as more than thirty doctors from other branches of biomedicine. Most of the doctors I met were men, which reflects the strong gender bias found in these professions. Almost all interviews were recorded and transcribed. Personal names were altered to ensure anonymity.

The doctors were generally very cooperative. From among the different healers, homeopaths were by far the easiest to approach. It certainly helped that I am originally from Germany, the motherland of homeopathy; and it was not unusual for doctors to point to a portrait of Samuel Hahnemann in their chamber and exclaim something like, "Hahnemann, our God!" Psychiatrists were slightly less receptive, but still very welcoming. The greatest problem with psychiatrists was that they were short of time and rarely willing to sacrifice more than one hour. In turn, Ayurvedic doctors were the most difficult to deal with. It often felt as if I was stumbling into an ongoing turf war among rival lineages of doctors, without me fully understanding where they each positioned themselves. Many of the Ayurvedic *kavirajs* were unwilling to introduce me to other colleagues under the pretext that that they did "not know anyone else."

Research on popular ideas and practices was mostly conducted in southwest Calcutta, a mixed residential and commercial area. The majority of residents in this part of the city are Bengali-speaking Hindus. Some tracts of southwest Calcutta had been settled since before the eighteenth century, but it was only with the arrival, in enormous numbers, of Hindu refugees from East Bengal (now Bangladesh) between the 1950s and the 1970s, that the area received its current architectural form (Kundu and Nag 1990). Most people who live in southwest Calcutta are lower-middle- and middle-class people who partly work in local businesses, partly in the offices of central Calcutta. There are a number of *bustees* (slums) throughout the area, most of them Hindu, some of them Muslim. The male residents of the *bustees* engage in various types of informal wage labor. Many of the *bustee* women work as domestic servants in local middle-class households.

Nevertheless, this is an ethnography of Calcuttans more generally, rather than an ethnography of people in a specific neighborhood (De Neve and Donner 2006). No doubt, convenient access to a physician is a factor in people's health-seeking behavior. But in a metropolis like Calcutta, mass transportation tends to decouple access to physicians from place of residence. Patients often travel all over the city to see a doctor whom they trust, and many doctors practice in up to three different locations across Calcutta. One of my longest conversations with a psychiatrist took place over several hours, when we were sitting in his car and driving to one of his charitable clinics in a district outside of Calcutta. During participant observation in different clinics, I usually saw patients from different areas of Calcutta, as well as patients from other parts of Bengal, from neighboring states, and even medical tourists from Bangladesh. The "bigger" the doctor, the further the distance a patient is willing to travel. For psychiatry, which is still stigmatized, the need to travel outside one's own neighborhood was an advantage.

I found that getting Calcuttans to talk to me was not difficult. People were curious about what I was doing and always open to talk. "Health" was seen as an obvious and worthy field of research for someone from Europe. Moreover, Bengalis hold academic research in high esteem. I never had any problems in getting people to spend time answering my questions, even people who were busy with their working lives. Calcuttans are proud to say that their city is not as "mechanical" and hurried as Delhi or Mumbai, and that people still take time to sit and chat whenever they feel like it.

For research among Calcuttans, I combined long-term participant observation with interviews. Participant observation was mostly unstructured. Day-to-day observations and serendipitous conversations were recorded in a diary. Besides everyday encounters, I conducted unstructured and semistructured interviews. Overall, I followed the rules of "nonprobability sampling" (Bernard 2002: 180-202), which is better suited for cultural interpretations of *how* things are done than methods that emphasize how *often* they are done.

The data include a set of ninety-five interviews. From among these, seventy-nine were with Bengali informants and sixteen with people from other ethnic groups. Seventy-eight interviews were with Hindus, fourteen with Muslims, and three with Christians. Fifty-six interviews were conducted with men, twenty-nine with men and women together (e.g., husband and wife), and ten with women only. Bengali language was most common in these interviews, but several were also recorded in English and in Hindi. For translations from Bengali and Hindi, I worked with an assistant, Jokesh Francis. As with the doctors, I have anonymized all personal names.

In terms of socioeconomic class, roughly thirty-one of the interviews were conducted with lower-class informants, forty-eight with lower-middle-/middle-class informants, and sixteen with upper-middle-/upper-class informants. When Calcuttans speak about "class," they mostly make blanket distinctions between "the rich" (*bara lok*, "big people") on one side and "the poor" (*garib lok*, "poor people") on the other. Depending on the speaker and the context of the conversation, the lines between these two groups can shift strongly. For example, a lower-ranking white-collar government employee appears as a *bara lok* to a slum dweller but as a *garib lok* to a member of the upper classes. The distinctions that are drawn here between lower-, lower-middle-, upper-middle-, and upper-class are fluid. As an approximation, "low" means that people can hardly scrape a living, are staying in rickety houses, and have enjoyed no or only rudimentary education. "Middle-class" people live in decent brick-built houses, have completed formal education, and have a reasonable amount of disposable income. "Middle-class" includes the *bhadralok* ("respectable people"), an ideal type of a cultivated white-collar employee that emerged in the nineteenth century (Donner 2008; Janeja 2010: 27-36). Difference between "lower-middle" and "upper-middle" is only one of degrees. In terms of economic standing, for example, lower-class people have no or only a few luxury goods such as washing machines or cars, whereas upper-middle-class people have several of these items. Lastly, "upper-class" people have been through many years of English-language education and enjoy the same living standards as people in Western Europe or North America.

Capturing popular perceptions of mind, body, and different medications is challenging. Summarizing decades of research on folk medicine, George Foster (1994) underlines its methodological difficulties: "To attempt to formulate the principles underlying health beliefs and practices is somewhat akin to fitting together the pieces of a gigantic jigsaw puzzle" (1994: 21). Other aspects of culture, such as religious rituals or daily work, tend to be routinized and observable as discrete events. Yet illness episodes can only be observed in a fraction of the population, hardly ever from beginning to end, and their episodic character tends not to be molded into routines. To shift one's attention to the (relatively) public and routine behaviors in doctor-patient encounters does not, of course, solve the problem of studying understandings held outside clinical settings. Hence ethnographic research on popular perceptions must rely on what people say, and what they say takes more often the form of passing remarks than of coherent illness narratives. Moreover, anything that relates to health and "the body" is often only tacit know-*how*, instead of explicit know-*that* (see Bloch 1998; Dreyfus 1991; Taylor 1995; Thompson, Ritenbaugh, and Nichter 2009).

To analyze data that are largely linguistic, fragmentary, and about tacit know-how, I relied on analysis methods developed by cognitive linguists, who showed that metaphors pervade not only everyday language but also everyday thought and action (Lakoff 1987; Lakoff and Johnson 1980). The body is the existential ground of culture (Csordas 1994), and metaphors are "the body in the mind" (Johnson 1987), condensing elementary bodily experiences of spatial orientation, shape, taste, and physical texture. Sensory experiences of the body motivate systematic "image schemata," or *gestalt* structures, with which the world is described. Both popular and scientific thought can be analyzed as a compound cluster of metaphors (see Blumenberg 1999; Bachelard 1967). Metaphors are "good to think with" because they make abstract ideas concrete and create consensus through sensual simplicity. Given that metaphors change more slowly than actual practice (e.g., we still speak of someone who is overcommitted as having "too many fires burning"), a close study of metaphors also enables us to detect the traces of half-forgotten traditions. For local speakers, metaphors can be grasped easily and appear to make thinking effortless (Danesi and Perron 1999: 183). To systematically collect and analyze metaphors in this way has been done by many cultural and medical anthropologists over the past decades (e.g., Desjarlais 1992; Kirmayer 1993; Parry 1985, 1991; Nichter 1989; Mukharji 2009).

Metaphor analysis is also akin to current thinking in transcultural psychiatry. In a literature review on the cultural emergence of somatic syndromes and their place in the new edition of the American Psychiatric Association's *Diagnostic and Statistical Manual of Mental Disorders* (DSM-5), Kirmayer and Sartorius (2007: 835) argue that notions of "culture-bound syndromes" are outdated and should be replaced by "cultural idioms of distress." Also drawing on cognitive linguistics (e.g., Kövecses 2000), Kirmayer and Sartorius point out that bodily experience, language, and culturally shared illness narratives co-constitute each other. What have, so far, been described as "syndromes" are not discrete disorders but "culturally prescribed modes of understanding and narrating health problems and broader personal and social concerns" (2007: 835). To speak of *idioms* of distress emphasizes the communicative dimension of suffering: what seems like an exotic complaint might simply be "a way to express dissatisfaction with living conditions, legitimate difficulties in performing social roles, and allow the individual to seek outside help" (2007: 835). Metaphors are one of the best entry points into these expressions.

1

Popular Practice

The Belly and the "Bad Mind"

"If the Belly Stays Cool, the Head Stays Cool"

The first principle of Bengali body concepts is that the belly is the somatic center of good health. The basic Bengali term for belly is *pet*, which signifies "stomach," "belly," and, in women, also "womb." Bengali has terms for the various organs that are contained in the belly, such as *yakrit* ("liver"), *pliha* ("pancreas/spleen"), or *antra* ("intestines"), but *pet* is most encompassing and most widely used. The belly is so vital for health because it is like a kitchen where food is cooked and refined. *Pakasthali*, the "place of cooking," is a Sanskrit word for "the belly." *Thali* here stands for "place," and *paka* means both "digesting" and "ripening." Another Sanskrit word for the belly-as-kitchen is *jatharagni*, the "digestive fire." *Mandagni*, the "slow fire," is indigestion. According to Jonathan Parry, "the digestive process is itself represented as a matter of cooking—or re-cooking—food in the digestive fire of the stomach (*jatharagni*)" (1985: 614; Barrett 2008: 134). The expression *surya grantha* ("sunbelt") underlines that the belly is defined by heat. Heat, cooking, sun, fireplace: all these concepts are united by heat. The belly cooks food, but it also "cooks" babies: the gestation of embryos in the female womb is a form of slow cooking. A formal word for "belly" is *udar*, which can be traced to the Indo-European root *udero*, which also informs Greek *uderos* and Latin *uterus*, both meaning "abdomen" or "(lower) belly" (Mallory and Adams 1997: 2). To cook food to perfection, the fire must neither be too high nor too low. Heat is good, but it must not be excessive. Bengalis focus on humoral moderation and balance. A "burning" stomach is a clear symptom of disease. Likewise, too much cold imperils the fetus, while too much heat can lead to a premature birth.

For Bengalis, health depends on the proper alignment between the belly and the mind. In this alignment, the belly is a "hot" source of energy that needs to be controlled by the "cool" sovereignty of the mind. A peaceful and controlled *mon* is seen as a precondition for a healthy life. When you are not worried about anything, when you keep your mind concentrated, you will always be healthy. The symptoms of a cool mind are a shiny, radiant face; success in any sphere of life where one chooses to excel; and the ability to transcend petty worldliness altogether. Conversely, there are dire consequences for the whole body if *mon* is disturbed, distilled in the saying "if the mind is bad, the body is ill" (*mon kharap lagle, sharir kharap lage*). A jumbled *mon* can be the source of any disease: fever, headaches, high blood pressure, diabetes, obesity, deranged hormones, heart stroke, or drug addiction. In popular etiology, *mon* does not cause these problems directly, but it is the hot belly let loose that imperils health.

In turn, mental power (*moner jor*) can overcome all ills. When the heat of the stomach is under control, the mind can stay under control as well. At its simplest, this is expressed in the Bengali saying *bhudi thanda thakle, mudi thanda thake* ("if the belly stays cool, the head stays cool"). *Bhudi* means "a fat tummy." It appears commonly together with *mudi* (a colloquial form of *mudo*, "head") in the expression *mudi-bhudi*. To keep the whole body healthy and whole, mind and belly must be aligned and properly balanced. Keeping the mind healthy will keep the belly healthy, and vice versa. A Calcutta woman explained this as follows: "*Bhudi thanda thakle, mudi thanda thake.* If food properly is digested, all health will be good. Also: If someone is hungry, he gets irritated. He gets annoyed quickly. His mood changes. When appetite is satisfied, the mood cools down."

For good health and lucid thinking, the belly must not be allowed to overpower the mind. An aphorism attributed to the Hindu saint Ramakrishna (1836-1886) lists *udar* with the anus and sexual organs as the third constituent part of a *tribhumi* ("three-partite land"). For Ramakrishna, most people's thoughts never rise up to the divine, never get beyond the borders of these "three lands" governed by the gross desires of eating, sex, and excretion. Sarbani Ma, a female guru in the Kriya Yoga tradition, whom I once interviewed in her ashram on what she thinks about psychopharmaceuticals, said that drugs could only ever act temporarily. Conversely, true peace came from changing one's inner attitude to the outside world: "Depressed people are misguided, they don't know the other side of life, they go with the material life." The mind must rise upward: "All ego problems come from the lower self. The lower self rules the mind when the mind becomes attached to it. But when the mind is attached to the higher self, then it washes the lower self, and all good qualities come when a person practices yoga, all diseases will go, insomnia and mental disorders."

Calcuttans are not specific about how a disturbance of *mon* produces illness. That too strong outside disturbances and too many worries make you sick is taken as an obvious fact that needs no further justification. One explanation I heard about the "inside machine" used a peculiar combination of religious ideas and chemical production: eating was like doing worship. If there is no concentration on the act, there cannot be good results. If the mind is not peaceful, no saliva will be produced. No gastric secretions will flow; the liver will not give its juices. Only if you concentrate your mind on the meal will digestive *rasa* be produced in the intestines. Urine and stool will be separated from the subtle matter, which goes into the blood. If the mind is deeply disturbed, one cannot digest anything. Only with the concentrated mind can the machine inside do its work.

Many South Asianists, above all the ethnosociologists, emphasize that popular Hindu notions of the body are monist, and not dualist as in the Cartesian West (e.g., Marriott 1976, 1989). Since "all is one," there is no fixed boundary between the inner and the outer, and personhood is "fluid" (Daniel 1984). Ironically exaggerating the difference between Western "bounded bodies" and ethnosociological descriptions of Indian "fluid bodies," Lawrence Cohen notes that stereotypical Westerners suffer from constipation, whereas Indians suffer from diarrhea: "they let everything out. They survive the heat, but at the cost of any attention to boundaries" (1998: 23). The main reference for

the ethnosociological interpretation of Indian personhood is the philosopher Adi Shankara (eighth–ninth century CE), who consolidated
the doctrine of Advaita Vedanta. In his version of nondualism, *atman*
(soul) and *Brahman* (eternal reality) are one; differences are illusions.

Bengali Hinduism is strongly influenced by Tantrism, and the worship of the black goddess Kali is more popular here than in most other
regions of India. The mythical imagination of a nondualist cosmos is
also colored by the cult of Kali. When I once asked Mr. Mukherjee, a
Brahmin pundit, about the meaning of the Sanskrit term *vishvato-
mukhah*, the "mouth of the universe," he explained that it expresses the
divine destruction of the world at the end of time. *Visva* means "universal," and *mukha* means both "face" and "mouth." As the "universal face,"
the Supreme Being (Brahma) is looking into all directions, into the past,
the present, and the future. *Mukh* is also "mouth," and Kali takes on the
twin roles of creator and devourer of time. From Her mouth, everything
is created, and at the end of time, Her mouth eats up everything again:
"Out of Her mouth, She creates. And then . . . [*moves his hand to his
open mouth as if he were eating food*]." This was a mythological image to
illustrate the philosophical insight that all physical matter is the product
of mind: "Mind precedes and creates matter. So if mind is the creator of
matter, and matter is nothing but a particular transfiguration of mind,
then this entire universe is nothing but mental." Anyone who engaged
in deep meditation realized that everything is *maya*, an illusion, and that
the entire universe is a creation of the mind. Mother Kali eating up the
entire universe was a vivid image for a timeless philosophical truth of
the unity of *atman* and *Brahma*: "Ma Kali is not gulping any matter. She's
gulping the transfiguration of mind," explained Mr. Mukherjee.

Not all Bengali Hindus are able to give the same scholarly explanation of why Ma Kali swallows up the world, but nondualism is undoubtedly the most widely shared philosophical position among them. Such
nondualism does not mean, however, that they do not see a separation
between mind and body, as is often suggested. Nondualism is popular in Bengali Hinduism, but there is no firm belief that the mind and
the body are made from the same "substance codes." The model that
I extracted from dozens of interviews looks as follows: (1) Mind and
body are separate entities. (2) Mind and body interact with each other.
(3) This interaction should be hierarchically structured: it is a good

interaction when the mind is in control over the body; it is a bad interaction if the body is in control over the mind. (4) To control the body,
the mind must be disciplined, steady, and calm. If it is disciplined, it can
control the body. If it is undisciplined, it loses control over the body.
(5) Ideally, the body is controlled by the mind, whereas the mind is not
influenced by the body. (6) If the mind is in control, anything can be
eaten. It will not have an impact on the mind. (7) Only if the mind is
weak will the qualities of food have an influence.

Popular Bengali ideas of mind/body relations are shifting amalgama-
tions of different philosophical ideas that are logically coherent only if
they are kept apart. For example, in the Sanskrit canon, *mon* is only
one among many levels of mind and consciousness. In the Upanishads, and also in later philosophical streams such as Samkhya, Yoga,
and Advaita Vedanta, *mon* is distinguished from *cit* (consciousness).
The mind is influenced by sensory perceptions, whereas consciousness
transcends them as illusions. The states of the mind are linked to food,
drink, and outer experiences, whereas consciousness remains a witness,
pure and unaffected (Gupta 2003: 34). In the Katha-Upanishad—written after the fifth century BC and the most famous in the canon—the
mind *(manas)* appears in the metaphor of a chariot (Katha Upanishad
3, 3-4). The *atman* (individual soul) is compared to a passenger. The
chariot is the physical body. The intellect *(buddhi)* is the charioteer. The
horses are the organs of sense perception. The outside objects passing
through perception are likened to the path on which the chariot travels.
The mind is the rein that controls the horses (the senses). When the
charioteer keeps the rein tight, he can steer the passenger to perfection;
when the charioteer slackens the rein, the horses veer off course. In this
depiction of the mind, the definition of perfection is neither coolness
nor stillness, but firm control. Cool stillness is the perfect state of *buddhi* and *atman*, but not of *manas*.

At the least, this passage from the Upanishads shows that Indian
concepts of the mind should not be reduced to an opposition between
either dualism *or* monism—if one looks closely, many subtle shades of
unity and difference in between the mind and the body can be discovered (Halliburton 2009). One of the senior psychiatrists I interviewed
in Calcutta, Dr. Gangopadhyay, also said that there was a spectrum of
opinions about mind/body relations. Based on his experience, he felt

that nondualism was more common in the cities, whereas rural people tended toward a clear dualism between body and the mind. In his consultations with patients, he shunned any discussion of this question. If challenged, he replied that the body is material and perishable, whereas the soul is immaterial and imperishable. The mind (*mon*) was part of the body and separate from the soul (*atman*): "*Mon* is *in* the brain. It is a qualitative manifestation of biochemicals. Serotonin and brain chemicals are not mind. But the manifestations that they effect, that is mind." The soul always remained untouched by the materiality of the mind, as well as by any medications that might be taken. To locate the *mon* in the body and not in the soul helped avoid alienating patients who strongly believe in the transmigration of souls: "Your mind definitely dies. *Mon* dies, but *atma* goes on. Everyone will say that body and mind are separate, that is a deep philosophical belief in our culture."

Bengalis might tend to be monists philosophically, but in everyday conversations, *mon* and belly are antagonists. Where the belly exerts an animal-like agency, *mon* brings the person closer to the gods. The belly desires to be filled and to be fed, but the mind aims to take in as little as possible. Where the belly is moving and heating, the ideal *mon* is still (*mon thaka*) and cool (*mon thanda*). Where the belly constantly threatens a person's self-control, the *mon* is the part of the body that can bring self-control. The belly as a hot, undisciplined, and greedy part of the body can only be brought under control by a cool and restrained *mon*.

The "Bad Mind" (*Mon Kharap*)

Mon is so often mentioned in everyday conversations because, among other reasons, it expresses personal opinion: *amar mone hay* simply means "I feel" or "I think." When one "makes mind" (*mon kara*), one clarifies one's goals. When one convinces others of one's own point of view, one succeeds in "winning" their minds (*mon paoya*). A lasting impression on others is achieved when one "draws a line in the mind" of others (*mone dag kata*). Or one can "melt" (*mon gola*) the mind of others with sweet words. To say "that depends on your *mon*" (*eta tomar moner bepar*) is a catch-all phrase for individual preference. For Bengalis, it depends on your *mon* whether you believe that the gods accept your sacrifices, or whether you feel drawn to one deity more than to others. It depends on your *mon* whether you find one political party more convincing than another. It depends on your *mon* whether some drugs work better for you than for others. To cite the orientations of *mon* when discussing the eating habits of different castes and religions is regarded as a marker of enlightened tolerance. For example, even if most Hindu Bengalis reject eating beef (because cows must not be killed for food), many pointed out that impurity only results when the mind believes in impurity. And it depends on your *mon* whether the evil eye exists and exerts a harmful effect or not.

The cool mind *(thanda mon)* and the hot belly are opposed to each other. When the mind begins behaving like the belly, trouble starts. For example, the mind can be "on fire" and heat up, but that reflects a serious disturbance. When the "mind's fire" *(moner agun)* burns, the person feels grief, worry, and all kinds of negative emotions. The mind's fire that burns slowly like the dried shell of the coconut *(moner agun dhiki-dhiki jvale)* is a mind that smolders after an emotional insult. *Moner agun* can also express passionate feelings for another person. In contrast to the "belly's fire," which can easily be sated with a good meal, the "mind's fire" is hard to extinguish. A Bengali saying identifies the body with the belly and holds that the body's fire can be put out, but the mind's fire cannot *(sharirer agun nibhana yay, kintu moner agun yayna)*.

The belly is a physical container, whereas the mind is without a fixed place in the body and without strict boundaries between an outside and an inside. Hence it is problematic when the mind also acts like a deep and dark container. *Moner kali*, the "mind's blackness," stands for destructive urges within. A person who appears to harbor evil thoughts can be asked to "open" this obscure container and let his words and feelings come forward *(mon kholo!)*. Someone with a dark mind can be urged to speak directly "from the mind" *(mon theke bala!)*. Once the mind (as container) opens up, it can become "clean" again *(mon parishkar)*. Like the "belly's word" *(peter katha)*, the "mind's word" *(moner katha)* also denotes secrets hidden away from others in the dark chamber of the mind. In contrast to *peter katha*, however, the *moner katha* is not nasty gossip, but one's true feelings. Similarly, to feel affection may mean to give a place in one's mind *(mone sthan daoya)*. When these emotions are harbored in secret, the truth needs to come out sooner or later.

When the mind loses its cool and start to heat up, confusion results. Concentration is lost when the mind starts to wander. At once, the person becomes "unmindful" (*anmona hay yaoya*). Even if the mind "stays," it remains vulnerable to disturbances. It may start to "shake" under pressure. It may "become small" (*mon choto haoya*) when it feels inferior toward others. Tensions and depressing feelings may cause "mind's pain" (*moner byatha*) and, eventually, make it "break" (*mon bhanga*). A broken mind can lose all interest in the world (*udashi mon*). At its worst, the broken mind becomes a "dead mind" (*mon mora*), when the person feels no joy or hope. The broken mind is "cold": not in the sense of "cool" sovereign control but in the sense of inertia and death.

The "mind becoming bad" (*mon kharap haoya*) is the closest equivalent in Bengali for the psychiatric concept of developing unipolar depression—without ever being synonymous with it. *Mon kharap* features in questions that doctors can ask about depressive symptoms. If a psychiatrist wants to ask a Bengali patient about feelings of depression, she might ask if the mind is not feeling well (*mon bhalo lagchena?*) or if the mind is feeling bad (*mon kharap lagche?*). *Mon kharap* is related to other negative affects, such as anxiety (*dush cinta*), sadness (*dukkho*), and hopelessness (*nirasha*).

To get a sense of how *mon kharap* is related to other bodily and mental states, I conducted a neighborhood survey (Ecks 2005). Using a semistructured questionnaire, I randomly contacted twenty women and twenty men and asked them about a range of problems that psychiatrists commonly associate with depression. All of the forty respondents were Bengali Hindus, most of them from lower- or lower-middle-class backgrounds. The questionnaire did not mention the term "depression," and instead of starting with "mental" problems, I began by asking about physical illness (*sharir kharap*), appetite, and sleep, before gradually moving on to moods. Each open-ended answer was probed with a scale to capture the severity, asked as "a little" (*olpo*), "much" (*beshi*), and "very much" (*khub beshi*). I also included a few questions to capture whether *mon kharap* is a "medical" problem, and where people would go to seek help if they experienced it. The questionnaire was similar to those used in "cultural epidemiology" (e.g., Weiss 2001; Chowdhury, Chakraborty, and Weiss 2001). In contrast to that of cultural epidemiology, my aim was not to quantify the prevalence of mental health problems in a local community but to gauge how the notion of *mon kharap* is related to other physical and psychological problems.

In the survey, *mon kharap* was one of the most often mentioned problems. From among forty people interviewed, twenty-four said that they had been experiencing *mon kharap* in the past month. Most common was anxiety (twenty-eight), followed by *mon kharap* and physical illness (each twenty-four) and *gastric* (twenty-two). The least common replies were for difficulties making decisions (fifteen), restlessness (thirteen), and lack of appetite (seven). Fourteen people said that their *mon kharap* was either "much" or "very much" severe. *Mon kharap* was the most commonly reported problem of a more severe type, along with anxiety (also fourteen). *Mon kharap* was also in the cluster of problems that were reported with the highest level of severity (*khub beshi*): four out of forty said that their experience of *mon kharap* was most severe, along with anxiety and indecisiveness. In comparison, physical illness was mentioned by three respondents as "very much" serious. After *mon kharap* and anxiety, other issues experienced in the preceding month with a severity of either *beshi* or *khub beshi* were physical illness (twelve), lack of concentration (twelve), feeling no joy (eleven), sleeping badly (ten), being unable to make decisions (ten), exhaustion (nine), hopelessness (eight), *gastric* (seven), restlessness (six), and lack of appetite (four).

The fourteen people who reported *mon kharap* as more serious ("much" or "very much") also reported the following problems as more serious: anxiety (ten), physical illness (ten), sadness (nine), lack of concentration (nine), indecisiveness (nine), no joy (eight), exhaustion (six), hopelessness (six), restlessness (five), sleeplessness (five), *gastric* (five), and lack of appetite (three). In fourteen cases, respondents said that they had experienced *mon kharap* and *gastric* together in the past month on all levels of severity. Although *gastric* troubles were mentioned by more than half in total (twenty-two), only six of them said that their *gastric* was bothering them "much" or "very much."

Another way of capturing popular Bengali notions of *mon kharap* was to ask about the most effective forms of relief. It is a well-known phenomenon that different labels for illness are correlated with different hierarchies of resort (Kohrt and Harper 2008). Relatives of a sufferer could label the same symptom constellation either as "depression" or as *mon kharap*, with each label suggesting a different healing response. People using the psychiatric label "depression" do not only seek biomedical help; yet using the "depression" label in the household makes resort to biomedicine more likely than if a nonmedical label is applied. This hypothesis was confirmed in the neighborhood survey: *mon kharap* did not entail a mandate to contact a biomedical doctor. Instead, the most commonly mentioned relief was prayer to deities: twenty-seven out of forty people said that prayer lightens a *mon kharap*. Other religious practices were also frequently mentioned: visiting a temple (*mandir*) was recommended by sixteen people, reading religious books (e.g., the *Bhagavad-Gita*) by nine people. Practices aiming primarily at calming and focusing one's *mon* that are not necessarily religious were also prominent, especially withdrawing oneself (twenty-one), trying to think positively (seventeen), meditating (six), and doing yoga exercises (four). The popularity of praying and of going to religious places was not matched by the popularity of religious specialists: Hindu pundits or Muslim *maulvis* were only recommended by four respondents, faith healers by only two (compare to Weiss et al. 1988; Halliburton 2009). Drawing on social togetherness was also seen as soothing for a *mon kharap*, especially family support (nineteen) and help from friends (fourteen). Regulating one's food intake was most prominent in relation to fasting (fifteen). Changing one's diet was mentioned by five respondents, home remedies (*totka*) by only one. Resort to professional healers was rarely seen as an appropriate way to deal with *mon kharap*. More of my respondents recommended visiting an astrologer (seven) than visiting an allopathic doctor (five) or going to talk to a pharmacist (four). That going to a "mental health doctor" (*manushik rog daktar*) could help with a *mon kharap* was affirmed by only two out of forty people. To contact a homeopath with a *mon kharap* made sense to four people, but Ayurvedic healers were not mentioned by even a single respondent. My questions about medical help for a *mon kharap*, be it from an allopath or other kind of healer, were often greeted with bemused surprise: "What has a doctor got to do with *mon kharap*?" one lower-class woman replied. This attitude is not born of an outright stigmatization of *pagoler daktar*—"madmen's doctor," as psychiatrists are popularly called. Instead, there was a genuine conviction that *mon kharap* cannot be treated with biomedical drugs.

Ill-Tempered Bodies

The opposition between "cool" mind and "hot" belly is based on a humoral worldview. Humoralism is not special to India but also predominated in Europe, the Middle East, and eastern and southern Asia until at least the nineteenth century. From then it came to be slowly supplanted by the new paradigms of specific etiology and cellular pathology (Sigerist 1961; Nutton 1993), summarized by Paul Ehrlich's (1854-1915) idea that drugs work like "magic bullets" that only target one specific pathogen and leave the rest of the organism unaffected. Yet humoralism remains buoyant in popular physiologies (e.g., Helman 1978). It is what Claude Lévi-Strauss (1966) would call a "wild" way of thinking. In the *pensée sauvage* of humoralism, everything is similar or different from everything else, and causal relations are constructed on the basis of oppositions and resemblances. For example, if garlic is "hot," and if states of emotional agitation are also "hot," then the conclusion is drawn that eating garlic leads to agitation. In humoralism, there is no separation between medicines for the body and medicines for moods—they are always the same.

Humoral thinking is widespread in different cultures around the world, but its exact formulation varies strongly among different cultural regions, social groups, and individuals, or even within individuals in different contexts. Some differences are immediately visible. For example, Greco-Roman medicine describes four basic elements of the cosmos: air, fire, water, and earth. Each natural element is characterized by a combination of hot/cold and wet/dry: air is hot/wet, fire is hot/dry, water is cold/wet, and earth is cold/dry. The four bodily humors are classified with the same scheme: blood is hot/wet, black bile is cold/dry, yellow bile is hot/dry, and phlegm is cold/wet. The four constitutional types follow the same logic: sanguine people have a predominance of blood, melancholics have too much black bile ("melancholy" means "black choler"), choleric types have too much yellow bile, and phlegmatic people too much phlegm. This version of humoralism, based on the Hippocratic Collection dating to the fifth century BC, was the most influential stream of European medicine for centuries.

By contrast, Indian Ayurvedic humoralism is based not on four but on three humors (*tridosha*) called *vata, pitta,* and *kapha.* According to the *Sushruta Samhita* (1.21.9), *pitta* is derived from a combination of water (*apah*) and fire (*agni*). *Kapha* is associated with earth (*prthivi*) and water. *Vata* arises from a merger of *akasha* (ether) and *vayu* (air/wind). Because of the threefold structure of the *tridosha,* they do not lend themselves as easily to a twofold classification as Hippocrates' four humors do. *Pitta* tends to be hot and *kapha* to be cold, while *vata* is in between. Yet as the principle of movement, *vata* is more hot than cold.

Humoral thinking is always open to new associations. The popular Bengali term *gas* (pronounced "gash") is a good example of this. *Gas* amalgamates Ayurvedic humoralism with several other theories of digestion. *Gas* can denote the "exhaust fumes" generated by the internal fireplace. Just as there is no fire without smoke, there is no digestion without *gas.* But Bengali *gas* is also related to other medical theories. Calcutta gastroenterologists see *gas* as a linguistic confusion between *gas* and the Latin combining form *gastro,* meaning "related to the stomach" (Ecks 2010a). Bengalis' conflation of two separate concepts confirmed the overattribution of illness symptoms to the belly. Headaches were an often-used example among Calcutta gastroenterologists, as in this explanation from gastroenterologist Dr. Daw:

> They don't know that *gas* comes from the Latin word for stomach, *gastro* . . . the complaint about *gas* includes bloating, farting, but goes way beyond it . . . so they say: "*Gas* goes here [*points to head*], here [*points to hand*], here [*points to leg*]. *Gas* going everywhere and causing problems." Migraine is very common, but people don't believe that it is purely a head problem, they are convinced it is caused by *gas.*

In the history of biomedicine, the word *gas* was first derived from Greek *chaos* by the seventeenth-century physiologist Jan van Helmont. "Gas," in van Helmont's sense, is a kind of guiding spirit, distinct from the element of air. *Gas* is not a byproduct of digestion, but a vital catalyzer of digestive fermentation. The Ayurvedic idea of *vata,* which is the wind element among the body's three humoral forces, is akin to van Helmont's gas, yet without the spiritualism. It is because of uncontrolled *gas* that Bengalis attribute the source of pain to the belly: "all pain comes from the belly" (*peter bhetar theke byatha ase*), as a popular saying goes.

Humoralism sees similarities everywhere, and so finer differences between humoral theories are difficult to spot. George Foster (1994) argues that different forms of humoralism can be best compared when they are traced to their primary dimension: the opposition of "hot" and "cold," which he saw as the most pervasive idea in the global history of medicine and "the longest-lived of all scientific paradigms" (1994: 204). Much research in medical anthropology is devoted to hot/cold classifications and their relation to popular healing practices (Rubel and Hass 1996: 118-20), especially in East and Southeast Asia (e.g., Laderman 1991; Unschuld 1992) and in Latin America (e.g., Foster 1994). All ethnographies that look at South Asian medical traditions mention the hot/cold system at least in passing, and many put it at the center of ethnomedical research (e.g., Beck 1969; Carstairs 1957; Daniel 1984; Lindenbaum 1977; Nichter 1989; Pool 1987; Lamb 2000). Hot/cold classifications remain common in Calcutta, too.

The basic Bengali term for "hot" is *garam*, and the term for "cold" is *thanda*. They have at least two meanings: one refers to measurable temperature, the other to perceived bodily effects. The hot/cold classifications in question here are not a phenomenology of outer objects but a phenomenology of physical experience. Actual temperature and bodily experience can relate to each other in four ways. First, thermal and metaphorical are in congruence: sunlight is both hot in temperature and metaphorically hot in its perceived effect on the body. Second, thermal and metaphorical values are contradictory: in South Asia, cold coffee is thermally cold but metaphorically hot. Third, an entity can be "neutral" in terms of temperature but metaphorically hot or cold. For example, biomedical tablets do not have a "temperature" as such, but are considered "hot." Last, some entities do not have fixed "hot" or "cold" values. For example, wind and ambient air are neither statically hot nor statically cold (see Hsu and Low 2008).

Anything can be classified as "hot" or "cold," but food is the most important area of application. A controlled intake of food is a technology of the self that laypeople use to keep healthy. Elaborate recommendations about the right kind of food for the right kind of person, eaten at the right time and at the right place, testify to this. In Calcutta, typically "hot" foods are meat, egg, garlic, onion, mango, and ginger; "cold" foods are boiled rice, yogurt, cucumber, papaya, and banana. These items are widely cited in the literature on Bengal (e.g., Jelliffe 1957), and on Hindu South Asia at large (e.g., Michaels 1998: 201-2).

In a classic ethnography of a Tamil village, E. V. Daniel (1984: 187) analyzed how hot/cold classifications are used in lay taxonomies of illness. For the Tamils, most illnesses are caused by an excess of heat. From among the twenty-six most common illnesses, respondents identified twenty-five as heat related, and only one as cold related, hence "heat is far more likely to be implicated in causing bodily disorders than cold" (1984: 187). This is similar to humoral traditions in Southeast Asia (Laderman 1991), but markedly different from Latin America, where most illnesses are cold related (Foster 1994: 69).

Similar to the Tamils, Bengalis also see bodily balance as more easily disturbed by an excess of heat than by an excess of cold. Diseases are primarily retraced to digestion, and digestion is more prone to an excess of "hot" *pitta* and *vata* (middling, but tending toward "hot"). In Calcutta, I found that common illnesses are not as overwhelmingly "hot" as in the Tamil village studied by Daniel. For example, it is often said that too much "cold" food can lead to a "cold" stomach and put one's health at risk. An excess of "cold" is diagnosed when the stool contains a large amount of mucus, signifying too much of cold *kapha*.

"Cold" food should never be taken too quickly. An excessively hot state must be cooled, yet this cooling process should be done with care, otherwise a shock may result that can be more harmful than the excessive state it is supposed to counterbalance. Not only an excessive deviation from the healthy median is dangerous but also any sudden change, no matter which direction it takes; Foster (1994: 34) calls this the "temperature differential."

Hot/cold illnesses and hot/cold weather are immediately linked. For example, a Calcutta man explained that *gastric*, as Bengalis call the generic form of digestive disturbance, happens more during the hot season: "The trouble comes from the climate. Everybody has it [*gastric*]. If the weather is hot, then the secretion of *pitti* becomes more, and then the body becomes even hotter. That's why one must never stay on an empty stomach in hot weather, because that will further increase *pitti*." Hot conditions usually have a "drying" effect, cold conditions a

"moisturizing" effect. Consider, for example, the health recommendations in a Bengali almanac (*panjika*) for the month of *vaishak* (April–
May; Skt. *vaishakha*), one of the hottest of the year:

> In this month the sun will be very hot. For this reason, the land and the
> ponds will be very dry, people will suffer from a lack of water and from
> the reduction of fat. Because of the reduction of fat, the animals will get
> tired and weak. Hence, in this season, ghee, milk, and lots of *carbohy-*
> *drates* are to be taken. Especially barley mixed with sugar, with water
> added, made into syrup; it will be good when you take this syrup in the
> month of *vaishakh*. Papaya, green coconut, watermelon, seeds of the
> palm tree, lemon, butter, buttermilk, and green mango syrup are used to
> get rid of tiredness. Too much exercise, too many stimulating things, too
> much sunlight, too much salt, and bitter-tasting drink are prohibited.
> After having lunched, it is necessary to take rest, in an area with plenty of
> air. At night, sleeping in an area with plenty of cool air is good for getting
> rid of tiredness and weakness. (*Panjika* 2000: *Dinapanjika*, 5)

These recommendations for seasonal self-care are based on the
observation that the heat of the sun dries both the land and the bodies
of humans and animals. The main symptoms of this process of desic-
cation are described as "weakness" and "tiredness." Hence it is recommended to take food that is watery and fatty to increase cooling *kapha*.
Papaya, green coconut, watermelon, and lemon all contain water and
have a cooling effect. Ghee and butter build up fat. Milk and butter-
milk replenish both fat and water. Barley, sugar, mango syrup, and palm
seeds refuel lost energy. In turn, it is advised to avoid food that would
exacerbate the heat of the sun. Salt is seen as risky because it can drain
the body of water. In this passage, "bitter-tasting drink" seems to be a
euphemism for alcohol, which is extremely heating. In terms of bodily
exercise, it is counseled to take it easy (sweating is desiccating) and to
ensure good ventilation (fresh air is moisturizing).

Bengali humoralism also considers lunar influences. Along the lunar
cycles, different health problems are more likely to occur, with the full
moon and the new moon phases being the riskiest. During these times,
whoever is easily influenced by lunar phases is advised to take only light
and dry foods, and anything that is not too hard to digest. Fish, meat,

and eggs must be avoided. One Bengali woman told me, "We fast on full and new moons to avoid feeling heavy. Best is only to take drinks and fruits, but nothing made of rice, that's too heavy." The moon influences health because the body is a container of fluids such as water and blood. The Bengali expression is *sharirer ras*, "the body's juices." The "link" (*yog*) between moon phases and the body is one of gravitational attraction. During a full moon, the attraction of the moon is strong, hence fluids go "up," and feelings of dizziness, mental excitement, or sleeplessness result. During a new moon, the gravitational force of the moon is at its weakest, hence body fluids sink "down" into the lower parts of the body, causing trouble in all of its lower parts. Such changes of gravitational force can exacerbate existing illnesses. For example, a popular proverb holds that *purnimar yoge, jvar bare* ("during full moon, fever rises").

In Bengali slang, the belly is also called, in English, a "machine," a "factory," or an "engine." "Everything goes inside the engine" or "if your machine works properly, there is no gastric" are ways of talking common among younger people. Machine metaphors share most features of the idea of the belly as hot kitchen. In both places, raw materials enter, are processed, and are delivered. Both images imply heat and transformative energy. The idea of the belly as an engine has two connotations. People can eat whatever they like and still stay healthy, whereas others fall ill even when they only eat the healthiest food, because the *engines* of different people do not run equally well. At the same time, leaving the belly empty for too long produces symptoms of nausea, all sorts of aches, and an excess of *gas* that causes damage.

Modernity is the "machine age," and Calcuttans also see many links between overheated bellies and living in one of the world's most polluted cities. The linguistic category of all types of health risks associated with modernization and urbanization is the English term "pollution." Certain spaces are considered as particularly "polluting" in this sense: the urban slum (*bustee*), for example, is an inherently unhealthy environment, and any food taken there is hazardous for anyone who is not accustomed to it, not just because of the food but because of the whole "atmosphere" (*jal haoya*, literally "water and air"). The quality of water is widely considered questionable. Even people who are not able to filter or boil their water are aware that one has to be cautious.

Gastric troubles and air pollution are linked. Air is a substance ingested like food. The term for "eating," *khaoya*, does not refer only to food but includes drinking and smoking as well. For example, *cigarette khabe?* means "will you ingest/smoke/eat a cigarette?" Sooty air "blackens" the stomach. Mrs. Chatterjee, a middle-class patient with chronic digestive disturbances, told me that her condition was caused by all the smoke in the air "covering the glands" in her stomach and "blocking" the regular secretion of digestive juices. In this way, air pollution disturbs the power of the stomach to cook the food that enters it. Mr. Tiwari, a middle-class man, related the prevalence of the *gastric* in Calcutta to a lack of "oxygen" in the polluted air. He held that the stomach works like a combustion engine: "burning" the food-fuel properly requires a great amount of oxygen. Yet oxygen is rare in a polluted city like Calcutta. He believed that village air is full of oxygen, whereas Calcutta air contains only "17 percent oxygen." With such a grave lack of fresh air, it was little wonder that most of the food that enters the stomach is not fully cooked in the internal fire, but remains lying there, rotting, slowly becoming rancid, emitting foul gases. The microcosm of the body mirrors the macrocosm of the decaying city: "It's like garbage on the streets. If you leave things in the stomach, it ferments, and then hurts. It pollutes the blood. The *oxygen* that we take through the lungs is not sufficient to fight the bad effect of the *gas*."

In humoralism, bodily spheres and cosmic spheres are governed by the same principles. There is no strict difference between the inanimate and the animate. Changes in the environment have an immediate effect on the body; for example, the sun heats both the land and the body. In humoral medicine, every health recommendation has at least two sides, one for positive action and one for avoidance: for example, to counter the desiccating effects of heat, one should take food that replenishes water and avoid food that drains water.

The Moody Belly

The belly is a container—a void waiting to be filled. Many Bengali words for the belly stress its perennial emptiness. *Gahavor*, an elegant term for a cavity, is used in relation to insatiable hunger. *Khadol* is a colloquial expression that portrays the belly as a deep hole. Most metaphors of the belly describe it as full or empty, as filled or emptied, and as either holding on or letting go. Most of my Bengali respondents found the combination of the container image with that of the cooking stove sufficient to capture the physiology of *pet*.

Whatever is ingested into the belly disappears from sight. Hidden away, the belly's contents are not shared with anyone else—whatever goes inside of it belongs to the person alone. Obscurity gives the belly a negative moral coding: filling one's own belly stands for individual egoism and selfishness. In turn, filling someone else's belly is an expression of caring altruism and selflessness. In Bengali, belly metaphors mix up body and emotion to the point where they become indistinguishable.

To "eat one's belly full" (*bhara pet*) is one of life's most satisfying feelings. Caring for others is to give them all the food they need to feel content (the English words "satisfy" and "content" are also derived from "filling up"). One says that one "feeds someone the belly full" (*pet bhariye khaoyano*). This aspect of Bengali hospitality oscillates between generosity and force-feeding. After a meal, the ritually asked question is, "Have you eaten your belly full?" (*pet bhare kheyecho?*). The proper reply is, "Yes, I have eaten my belly full" (*hyae, pet bhare kheyechi*). A related set of metaphors is also based on the perceived connection between maternal care and the belly as womb. To raise a child with much affection is to raise it "in the belly, on the back" (*pete pithe*). A boy-child who is particularly dear to the mother is her "belly's boy" (*peter chele*). When a child turns out to be a nuisance to the mother, he becomes her "belly's enemy" (*peter shatru*).

The "belly as god" is a comic metaphor close to the excessive "Rabelaisian" belly described by Mikhail Bakhtin (1984). *Pet puja* ("belly worship") means that someone puts personal satisfaction before the satisfaction of the gods. *Pet puja* is so widely used that even pan-Indian advertising draws on it. In 2009, fast food giant McDonald's ran a TV spot that showed stone images of a human abdomen being worshiped like a Hindu god. Ecstatic crowds danced around the belly idols and chanted "*pet puja*." The notion of viewing self-centered eating as a sacrilegious act against the gods can be retraced to concepts of sacrifice first formed in the Vedic era. Charles Malamoud (1989) points out that Vedic religion (ca. fifteenth to fifth century BC) considered *all* food transformed by fire as belonging to the gods: "To eat cooked food is equal to taking something from a meal consecrated to the gods" (Malamoud

1989: 48; my translation). Modern Hinduism has seen deep transformations, but some ideas stayed constant; the power of fire to transform everyday food into a sacred offering is one of them. Popular Hinduism retains the belief that all food comes from the gods and should only be taken in honor of the gods. All human existence becomes a form of debt (Graeber 2011: 56-57). Thus to do *pet puja* and to put one's own human belly in place of a god is a sin. Because of the ever-present suspicion of sin, *pet puja* is an effective joke for the pleasures of eating.

The belly sustains life. But to "keep the belly going" (*pet cala*), one must fill it regularly. Food, as the essential product of daily work, stands metonymically for economic survival. "Empty belly" (*khali pet*) is a common expression for hunger. A "light" or "thin" belly (*pet patla*) cannot hold anything. Like a bag made out of weak fiber, it threatens to tear and lose whatever is inside of it. The metaphor implies either a weakness of the body or a weakness of character. It may mean that the person suffers from sensitive bowels and frequent diarrhea. It may also mean that someone is unable to keep a secret. Persistent diarrhea thins a person's body, up to a point of emaciation when the belly "does not hold the clothes" (*pete kapar thakena*).

"Belly burning" (*pet jvala*) denotes intense hunger. If someone is asked why he does humiliating work for small pay, he could answer that it is "for my belly's burning" (*peter jvalay*). In popular belief, the navel is the only part of the body that is not destroyed when the corpse is burned in the funerary fire. The idea seems to be that the navel is that part of the body that defines bodily identity over time. It is the navel from where the embryo starts to grow, and from where the newborn is cut off from his mother. Hence the expression "hunger makes my navel burn" (*khide nari jvalche*) expresses utmost hunger.

Filling the belly is deeply gendered. For example, men traditionally get more expensive food (e.g., fish) than women. If little food is available, the male members of the family will receive more or even all of it. In poorer families, if there is only one piece of fish to go around, the male head of the family eats it. Men also tend to get more of all other items, including rice. The popular rationale for this hierarchical distribution of food is that the man must be strong enough to work and to fill his family's bellies. The preference for males also includes the children. Next in line in the distribution of food are the male children. Boys are usually more spoiled. In order to get them to eat as much as they can, they are told "Treasure, eat!" (*sona, khao!*). By comparison, girls may be told not to make a fuss and to "swallow!" (*gelo!*). As I have witnessed in neighbors' houses, the boys in the family were usually hand-fed by the mother to make them eat as much as possible. Girls were also hand-fed in the first years of their lives, but boys tend to be hand-fed for much longer, sometimes well into their teenage years. In one of my neighbors' houses, I have even seen a boy in his early twenties being hand-fed by his mother while he reclined on a chair and watched a Bollywood movie. Neither the boy nor his mother felt any embarrassment that an outsider like me was looking on. Food that is given by one's mother's hand is supposed to be more tasty, more nourishing, thus better for the stomach.

Food is the fruit of labor, and it is common to ask about someone's job, "What are you doing to keep your stomach going?" (*tomar pet cale ki kare?*). Work that only pays as much as a meal for one person costs can be called "belly food" (*pet bhat*). In this expression, as generally in Bengali, cooked rice (*bhat*) means "food" in general. Like "bread" in Western culture, "rice" is Bengal's cultural superfood (Greenough 1982), standing as a metonym for all types of food.

To earn one's living, one must be prepared to suffer trouble and pain. Hence, to "eat one's belly [full], the back tolerates [anything]" (*pete khele pithe soy*); that is, even the hardest work is worthwhile if it pays in the end. To criticize somebody for leading a slothful life at the expense of others, one could ask, "Are you not having any belly worries?" (*tumi peter cinta karana?*). Those who "swallow without worrying" (*gelar cinta nei*) are people who are using up other people's fruits of labor without contributing themselves. As filling the belly takes priority, other aspects of life may suffer. When I once asked an elderly Muslim man why Calcutta's Muslims tend to leave school earlier than Hindus, he replied with a proverbial question (in Hindi): *pahela parega yah pet bharega?* ("will you first study or fill your belly?").

Securing one's daily livelihood and "filling the belly" go together. If only a limited amount of food is available, filling one's own belly means that someone else's belly goes empty. Anthropological accounts of pre-capitalist ideologies highlight the "limited good" as central to moral reasoning (e.g., Dundes 1992; Foster 1965). In popular Hinduism, life itself is a limited good that can only be had if other beings (humans, animals, plants, souls) are deprived of it (Parry 1982: 74). In Foster's (1965) discussion of this topic, the ideology of the limited good exists typically in peasant economies where resources seem fixed and output static. By contrast, capitalism is based on an ideology of limitless growth. If resources are ever increasing, filling one's own belly does not hit someone else's belly.

Bengali metaphors of the belly are based on an ideology of the limited good; hence filling one's belly can attract other people's envy. One cannot avoid filling one's belly, but one must be careful not to do so in a greedy way, and not to take more than what is needed. If the belly's inherent and insatiable desire for food cannot be suppressed, it should at least be controlled by modest display. But the belly cannot shake off its hunger, driving the person to egoism. Eating and digesting become metaphors for destructive behavior. In Bengali, eating and the belly are core metaphors of all low, self-centered, and antisocial tendencies.

The close link between eating/digesting and destructive selfishness is not unique to Bengali culture but also appears in many ethnographies of other societies. In *Coral Gardens*, Bronislaw Malinowski (1935) describes yams house rituals of the Melanesian Trobrianders that aim to "close" people's bellies. Without these rituals, people's craving for food would know no bounds and would devastate the community. Franz Boas's fieldwork data on the Kwakiutl (Pacific coast of Canada) show the mouth as a symbol of bestiality and destruction. On the basis of Boas's notes, Walens (1981: 14) writes, "the mouth and the things it does are representations of the bestial, antisocial, destructive aspects of human nature, which must be constantly guarded against, constantly obviated. People must either turn these primal forces to their advantage, or they must suppress them through the proper performance of social interaction." Bengalis also perceive individuals' uncontrolled eating as a danger to the community. Gluttony is a deadly sin associated with the belly. A person who is called a "belly everything" (*pet sarbasva*) is someone who greedily devours endless amounts of food. The belly is a bottomless pit, a big black hole that can only be filled temporarily.

Taking away someone else's work is an act of aggression. To have this happen to oneself is equal to having one's "belly killed" (*pete mara*), or to have one's "food killed" (*bhate mara*). Competitors in the workplace who take away one's job by foul means are "eating it up" (*cakri khaoya*). The boss who fires one can also be said to have "eaten" one's employment. To counter such aggression, one could tell someone, "Don't kick my stomach!" (*amar pete lathi merana!*). This means "Leave me alone, don't take away my livelihood." Feeding oneself and one's family is usually portrayed, by Bengalis of all social classes, as a daily struggle for survival. In this struggle, earnings must be made by any means necessary. Therefore, "for your belly, what are you capable of doing?" (*peter janye ki karte paro?*) is a question that can be directed at someone who is suspected of being involved in crime.

Eating is destroying, and many sayings express irreparable damage in terms of eating. "That's eaten up" (*ei kheyeche*) means that an object is destroyed or that a great opportunity was missed. If a husband (*svami*) dies a premature death before his wife (*bou*), she gets blamed for having "eaten" him (*svami khaoya*). Bad boys who seduce a good boy to alcohol and drugs may be accused of "eating" his good character (*caritra khaoya*). To "eat head" (*matha khaoya*) has several shades of meaning. Friends who have a bad influence on a girl are said to "eat" her head. The mother who excessively pampers her child is also said to "eat" the child's head. It once happened that my questions about the stomach annoyed a respondent enough for her to ward me off by saying, "Don't eat my head!"

The overheated furnace of the hungry belly builds a link to the belly as a site of aggressive emotions toward other people. Anger is "hot," and the sight of someone who evokes hatred or jealousy "makes the belly burn" (*pet jvala kare*). Alternatively, one could say that "bile begins to burn" (*pitti jvala*). Feeling one's bile going "hot" (*pitti garam hay*) means "to go mad." The type of madness expressed here is always one that is connected with loud anger and aggression.

While aggression toward others is a symptom of a "burning" belly, experiencing aggression against oneself leads to the opposite feeling, namely, a "chilling" of the body; while anger is hot, fear is cold. There are plenty of sayings in English that also connect the feeling of chill to feelings of fear, but many expressions are peculiar to Bengali. To say "the belly's cooked rice has become raw" (*peter bhat cal haye geche*) denotes a person's extreme shock and bewilderment. Strong fear can be so "chilling" that even rice that has already been cooked in the belly turns "uncooked" again. To "shit raw rice out of fear" (*bhoye cal hage*) pushes this to its comic extreme. Another saying holds that fear may lead to a disturbance of one's liver (*pile camke yaoya*). For example, a boy who has to "eat" the scolding of his father gets his liver perturbed (*babar dhamak kheye cheletir pile camke geche*).

Greed for money is typical of modernity's corrupting influence on morality, and several Bengali expressions combine money and eating in this way. Government officials who siphon off black money are accused of "eating bribes" (*ghush khaoya*). Money that has gone into the digestive system is money that somebody has unrightfully taken and spent, so that it cannot be recovered anymore. Someone who borrows money (*taka*) and later refuses to pay it back gets chided for having "digested" it (*taka hajam kare phela*).

Other forms of antisocial behavior associated with the belly are treachery, duplicity, and secretive conduct. All these metaphors also belong to the image schema of belly-as-container. What all of them emphasize is that the belly's content is invisible, and that whatever is inside it is hard to bring back into the shared open space. For example, many expressions portray the belly as the place where secrets and bad intentions are hidden. Not to know what is "inside [someone else's] belly" (*peter bhetare*) means that one does not know what he is thinking. If one conceals one's true desires, one has "hunger in the belly, coyness in the face" (*pete khide mukhe laj*). The "belly's word" (*peter katha*) is knowledge not shared with anyone else. If somebody thinks "in the belly belly" (*pete pete*), that is, deep inside the belly, he is thinking in a deceitful, cunning manner. The English expression that somebody is "two-faced" has an equivalent in the Bengali expression "in the belly one [thing], in the mouth/face another [thing]" (*pete ek, mukhe ek/ mukhe ar*), that is, his mouth/face tell one thing, but deep inside, the true intentions are different. If someone's belly is "swelling" (*pet phala*), this may mean that she keeps a secret she can hardly contain, a secret that threatens to burst out into the open.

The similarity between digestion and pregnancy reappears in ideas about jealousy. A Bengali proverb brings these themes together in an inimitably crass yet graceful way: *Kha kha kha, lo tui, pete na thute / Sha sha sha, lo tui, shatin na javalate*, which means "Eat! Eat! Eat! Hey, you! [As long as] the belly doesn't hold / Shag! Shag! Shag! Hey, you!

[As long as] the co-wife doesn't trouble you." In this proverb, food and sex, digestion and pregnancy, become impossible to differentiate. Two image schemata inform this proverb: having sex is eating, and gestating is digesting. The "you" of the proverb is a young wife. She is told to "eat" as long as the belly does not "hold." "Eating" here means having sex with her husband. She should enjoy it as much as possible as long as she is not pregnant. Once the belly "holds," the husband will lose interest in her and abandon her in favor of another wife (*shatin*). Given that *shatin* signifies the second wife in polygynous marriages that were common in Bengal well into the twentieth century, the abandonment of the woman is not one of divorce and separation, but of sexual attention. The idea that the belly is a container brings the domains of sex and food together. The comic effect of the proverb comes from putting as identical the two openings of the belly-container: the mouth and the vagina.

Greedy, destructive eating also underlies popular beliefs about the "evil eye" (*kharap cokh*). Ideas and practices around the evil eye are a well-documented theme in anthropology, both in India and in other parts of the world (e.g., Carstairs 1957: 197; Dundes 1992; Fuller 1992: 238-40; Rubel and Hass 1996). The concept of life itself as a "limited good" is the key to understanding the evil eye. Greed makes one person envious of another's health, beauty, children, possessions, or social status. Unspoken or even unfelt impulses of greed can have a harmful effect on the person who is envied. According to Alan Dundes (1992), the evil eye does not harm by penetrating a victim's body like a bullet. Instead, the evil eye *takes away* the "good" from one person and transmits it back to the person with the evil eye. Since the evil eye is not just about visual looking but also about an actual transfer of substances, the psychoanalytic anthropologist Géza Róheim interprets the devouring glance as a form of "evil mouth." The evil eye does not just look at an object of desire but "swallows" it like a hungry mouth: "The oral quality of the evil eye is evident. In French we have the saying 'Devorer des yeux,' in Hungarian 'His eyes are bigger than his mouth,' i.e., he desires more than he can manage" (Róheim 1992: 217). Regarding beliefs about the evil eye in rural Tamil Nadu, Clarence Maloney (1976) observes that stomach aches are often attributed to the evil eye. Consumption of food outside of the house puts a person at risk of the evil eye, especially from those who are hungry: "A hungry look at someone's food may make the eater sick or give him diarrhea. Therefore, a poor or hungry person should not see one eating, nor should one eat in the presence of others without giving them some of the food" (Maloney 1976: 106).

In Bengal, evil eye beliefs are pervasive among all ethnic and social groups. In an early ethnography of rural Bengal written in the 1920s, Biren Bonnerjea (1927: 130-44) devoted the bulk of his chapter on popular medicine to the evil eye. In Calcutta today, evil eye beliefs are still common, not only in relation to health but also in relation to career success. A direct connection exists between the evil eye and digestive illness. A popular saying exists that accuses the glance of "greedy" people of causing gastric trouble: *O khub lobhi, pet kharap habe* ("He is so greedy, bad stomach will happen"). The "eye's hunger" (*cokher khide*) stresses a link between the eye and the hunger for other people's goods. One of my respondents, a Bengali in his sixties, confirmed that digestive health and the evil eye are linked, but many also said that not all people are equally susceptible to its perilous influence. If one is weak in mental power, the evil eye can strike; if one is strong in mental power, it has no effect. References to the strength of a person's *mon* made it hard to distinguish between gastric troubles that are directly caused by the evil eye and those that only strike because someone *thinks* he was hit by a greedy glance. For instance, when I asked a 25-year-old engineer about the link between the evil eye and gastric troubles, he replied,

> That depends on your *mon*. If you think this while you eat in front of someone and you have stomach pain, then you'll have a pain. If you do not think in this way, you will not have [stomach pain]. If you eat on the road, if the food is bad, then you have stomach pain. If you keep your mind free, nothing will happen. If you keep your mind free, and eat poison, it won't affect. If you think you'll die, you'll die. But if your mind is free, nothing will happen.

Summarizing evil eye beliefs in popular Hinduism, Chris Fuller (1992: 239) finds that "complete skepticism is rare." Calcuttans believe that the evil eye exists but can be warded off by mental self-control. The superiority of self-control has two versions. One, only those people who are of weak mind can be affected by the evil eye. Two, only those people who are weak in mind *believe* in the existence of the evil eye in the first place. That is, a mere belief in the evil eye is a symptom of mental weakness. Hence it is every (mature) individual's responsibility to ward off the evil eye either by being mentally strong or by not even believing in it.

Keeping the Mind Religiously Cool

Mon kharap is the opposite of keeping the mind "peaceful" (*moner shanti*), "cool" (*thanda mon*), or "still" (*mon thaka*). A peaceful, cool, unmoving *mon* is the best precondition for achieving whatever one sets out to do, be it staying healthy, passing an exam, or coming closer to the gods. A "single mind" (*ek mone*) can be achieved through *sadhana*, a spiritual practice of uniting the individuated self (*jivatman*) with the highest Self of Brahman (*paramatman*). As a Bengali man put it, "If you concentrate, do *sadhana*, you achieve a 'single mind' [*ek mone*]. You get *mental satisfaction*." A cool, concentrated *mon* brings one into the realm of the superhuman, where anything is possible, as this Bengali man explained:

> It all depends on the *mon*. Your mind power (*moner jor*) is stronger than anything (*sab theke bara*). The *mon* is very important, it's the greatest thing (*anek bara jinis*). Suppose I sit here and think that I'll go to New York: *I* am sitting here, but my *mon* is gone there! If your *mon* is good, everything is good.

Moner shanti resonates with wider themes in Hinduism. Achieving control over one's mind and various forms of meditative withdrawal from the world are a central element in all strands of Hinduism (Michaels 1998: 347-77). Virtually all the major figures of modern Hinduism emphasized control of the mind as a path to enlightenment, freedom, and true happiness. The exact technique that is used for meditation may be different for each person, but the goal is roughly the same. What is essential is that the mind becomes still. As much as the *mon* expresses personal opinion, it does not belong to an individuated self. The differences between "religious" and "secular" ways of cooling and focusing the mind are impossible to define in a Hindu framework. Withdrawing oneself, thinking positive thoughts, meditating, and doing yoga exercises are all effective for bringing peace to a *mon kharap*, but their success lies in transcending the self.

The *Bhagavad-Gita* teaches that realizing one's duty in life and performing one's work well, while disowning the fruits of the work, constitute one of the best ways of achieving liberation: "With soul detached from everything, with self subdued, [all] longing gone, renounce: and so you will find complete success, perfection, works transcended" (Gita XVIII.49). Shartok, a pharmaceutical sales representative I met while waiting in a GP's office, said that "doing one's work to one hundred percent, disregarding success or failure, leaving everything up to G.O.D., not worrying about it" was his main way of dealing with life's pressures. "G.O.D." stood for "Generator, Operator, and Destroyer." He also recommended meditation, a balanced diet (no oil, no fat, no spices), physical exercise to "release endorphins," good sleep, good sex for "hormonal balance," visiting calming temples such as Dakshineswar, and reading religious books. Shartok had been thinking about mental peace ever since he failed to win entry into medical college, ending his dream of becoming a doctor. The company that he represented did not manufacture antidepressant drugs, but he said that he knew enough about them from other medical representatives. He was certain that depression could never be treated pharmaceutically. These drugs might help through an acute phase but would never solve problems in the long run.

If performed with a concentrated *mon*, everyday prayer can keep the mind cool (*mon thanda rakha*). In Hinduism, "prayer" primarily means to concentrate (*dhyan*) on the image of a deity and to mutter mantras at the same time. This form of prayer commonly includes giving an offering, even if it is only a flower or the scent of incense sticks. Hence, the lines between prayer and *puja*—worship of a deity at a domestic shrine or at an outside temple—are fluid (see Fuller 1992: 57-105). The explicit purpose of *puja* is to give satisfaction to the deity. But just as important are comfort and peace (*moner shantana*) for one's own self. Cause and effect are blurred and depend on individual and caste beliefs. For example, from an orthodox high-caste point of view, doing *puja* for instrumental gain is condemned (Fuller 1992: 72), but there are different opinions about what "instrumental gain" is. Whether or not a peaceful mind should count as instrumental gain is open to debate. Moreover, praying and performing *puja* gives mental satisfaction. Yet it is not clear whether this mental satisfaction comes from concentration itself, or whether peace of mind is a blessing granted by a deity. A prayer done well is already proper "labor" (*karma*) done for a transcendent cause. This is how a male devotee of the goddess Kali, affectionately called Ma (Mother), sees the link between prayer and divine grace:

> If you really think while you pray and you concentrate in your prayer that today I'll talk to Ma Kali, if you really have faith and you really concentrate [*dhyan*], you will get the fruit [*phal*]. If you ask God to give, you also have to give something. If you want to get work done, without work you can't expect to get a result. First you give *proper labor* to Ma Kali, only then will you get the result.

Another way of looking at the question is through the ideology of the "limited good." Praying for business success is instrumental because, in a world of limited goods, the fulfillment of this wish harms others. By contrast, aspiring to have a "single mind" (*ek mone*) gives personal satisfaction without anyone else suffering. Hence few Bengalis see a problem in "instrumentalizing" prayer to achieve peace of mind for oneself, not least because a still mind realizes unity with the All of Brahma and, therefore, is not one's "own mind" anyway.

More equivocal is the question whether *moner shanti* can be achieved by ritual action such as *puja*. In my neighborhood survey, twenty-seven out of forty people said that a *mon kharap* can be eased by prayer. But only sixteen said that going to temples helped. Seeing Hindu priests was only recommended by four people—reaffirming Mandelbaum's (1966) argument that priests are not usually expected to cure specific ailments. Even if these numbers are not representative, they tally with popular perceptions otherwise expressed. Here I want to focus on the question of whether eating food offered to a deity can also calm the mind.

Eating *prasad*—the leftovers of a food offering to a deity—is regarded as a powerful remedy for any mental or physical problem. It is also common to take medical drugs in the spirit of *prasad*: if one thinks of one's favorite deity and then eats the medicine, it is bound to be more efficacious. Understanding how Bengali Hindus conceive *prasad* is important for understanding relations among physical matter, food, the mind, and divine power. *Puja* rituals performed daily at temples (*mandirs*), as well as all the major domestic *pujas*, include a phase when food is put in front of a deity's idol and is thereby transformed into *prasad*, the blessed leftovers of the deity's meal. "Feeding the deity" (*naivedya* in Sanskrit) is a standard part of *puja*, but not essential. Other forms of showing respect (*upacara*) to the divine include invocation, installation, feet washing, welcome, mouth rinse, bath, clothing, girdling, unction, flowers, frankincense, lighting, salutation, circumambulation, and dispersal. There are also forms of *puja* where only five, three, or fewer elements are enacted. It is even possible to give *manasika puja*, which occurs only in one's own mind and without outward action (Michaels 1998: 265-70). Among all these elements of *puja*, however, feeding has attracted the most attention among South Asia scholars, because food transactions are fraught with significance in relation to caste hierarchies and gender relations (Babb 1982; Fuller 1992; Sax 2009). Even beyond the Hindu context, the proposition that humans can *physically* feed gods is not easy to understand in any religion.

The orthodox way of conceptualizing the transformation of food offerings into *prasad* among Bengalis—both lay and priestly—is that the idol of the deity is filled with divine power. To please the deity, one needs to treat Her like a high-status human being, which means that the idol needs to be dressed in fine clothes, be bathed, and also be offered good food. After the food is placed in front of the idol, the doors to the inner sanctum are closed and the deity is given time to eat (in domestic *puja*, a blanket is placed before the idol to shield it from the devotees' eyes). During this time, the deity ingests the food and infuses it with divine potency. Once the deity has finished eating, the leftover *prasad* is distributed among devotees for them to eat and, thereby, to ingest Her power. Eating *prasad* is one form of establishing immediate contact with the divine. The power of *prasad* is fully mobile. *Prasad* is always eaten after the *puja* is formally over, and it retains its potency even if it travels elsewhere and is given to other people. By contrast, the moment of seeing eye to eye with the deity (*darshan*) cannot be contained and transported elsewhere.

This orthodox interpretation of *prasad* is shared by a majority of Bengalis whom I met, but definitely not by everyone. When I asked people if the gods truly eat the food presented to them, many affirmed that this is first of all a "religious belief" and a "guideline for life." The sources of this belief are "tradition," "olden times" (*purana yog*), "what our parents say," or "what Brahmins say." More to the point, the deities ate the food because, if they did not, it would be foolish to offer anything. Millions of people were offering food to millions of gods every day, and it was impossible that they could all be wrong. As one Bengali man explained in view of Kalighat temple, "Why close the door? Because Ma Kali eats. If She doesn't eat, why would they close the door? We believe this 101 percent. Hundreds of thousands of people are going to visit Ma Kali, what for? Everybody is not a fool." To please the deity can bring eternal merit, immediate blessings, or at least a sense of mental satisfaction of having done something that transcends the self.

Believers tell many stories about what miracles can happen when a *puja* is done well, but also about what can go wrong. For example, a Bengali woman told me an anecdote about a local Brahmin pundit, Shyam-ji. This pundit was a staunch devotee of Ma Kali. Every night between midnight and two o'clock, he performed *puja* at his house. Every night he would make sure to reach his home in time for the ritual. One day, the pundit was engaged to perform a marriage ceremony at a hotel. His patrons assured him that the ceremony would be over well before midnight so that he could stick to his nightly routine. Yet this time, the groom and the bride got delayed, and the *puja* had to be shifted back into the night. When Shyam-ji realized that he could not be home in time, he phoned his wife to ask her to give *puja* to Ma Kali on his behalf. But Shyam-ji's wife fell asleep watching TV and failed to give the *puja* as demanded. Then, in the middle of the wedding, the pundit involuntarily mixed up the Sanskrit mantras proper for a wedding with those for funerary rites. His assistant saw that something was wrong and asked the pundit what was happening. At that point, he realized his mistake and stopped. He rushed out of the hall and called his wife on his mobile phone because he knew that Ma Kali was disturbing him. His wife woke up and admitted that she had not done the *puja*. The pundit shouted at his wife that Ma Kali needed the *puja* immediately. Half an hour later, the pundit felt in his *mon* that Ma Kali had accepted the *puja*. He calmed down and continued with the ceremony.

The eyes are an important source of evidence. Some people say that they have not seen with their own eyes that the goddess eats, and so it might not be true that she eats. Anyone who claimed to have seen deities eat was lying. Others said that Brahmins see gods eat in their dreams, and that saints such as Ramakrishna truly shared meals with Ma Kali. The power to see a deity eating could be translated into questioning human visual powers. Not everyone has the same powers of sight: those who performed meditation and *sadhana* could see things that average people could not.

The power of the eye reappeared in relation to the way the gods partake of the offered food. Some say that the food is physically eaten, even if only the smallest portion of it: "Just one pinch will be gone," one man said; "the goddess eats an atomic portion," said another. Others said that the gods do not eat the food with their mouth but that they only look upon the offering. Such looking is already equal to eating. That *human* eyes can eat explained why the deity is shielded from onlookers while taking the food: "After offering the door is closed because of the bad eye (*kharap cokh*). No one should stare at that food, no one should give bad eye to that food that has been offered."

Skeptics declare all this to be superstitions and "inventions by Brahmins." Several said that the statues of the gods were "just mud" and that blind faith in religious superstitions explained why India is so backward. When foreigners heard about Hindus putting cooked food in front of mud idols, they were appalled: "People who come from outside and see what is going on, they are shocked that a statue made of mud is being praised." One of the most down-to-earth arguments I heard is that humans are greedy and only ever want to receive blessings from the divine, but not offer anything themselves. A goddess that *really* ate would *not* be worshipped: "Ma Kali does not eat the food. If a mud statue starts eating the food, they would not offer rice, fruits, fish. I mean, if She would actually eat it, that is too expensive, no one could afford it! They could at best give sugar drops."

Those skeptical of the skeptics said that it is a healthy attitude to have faith rather than to analyze everything by scientific standards. Taking for granted that deities eat the food presented to them accepts that *puja* allows humans to worship the divine in an approachable form (*ruup*). The eating deity is one among many true manifestations of the divine, and to offer worship by serving tasty food is good for one's own peace of mind.

"Inner Heat" and the "Cool Mind"

The notion of *sadhana* opens a paradox: that the "cool" mind is produced by *tapas*, which is "heat." In the Hindu tradition, one of the principal means to expiate transgressions of the cosmic order is called *tapas*, which the Sanskrit scholar Sylvain Lévi describes as "burning splendor radiating from a body mortified by asceticism" (1966 [1898]: 23; my translation). *Tapas* signifies both the *act* of "performing austerities" and the *effect* of this act, which is the generation of "inner heat." If a transgression has defiled an evildoer, *tapas* has the power to purify him by "burning away" the "stains" of his deeds (*Laws of Manu* XI.242). All expressions for the nature and effect of *tapas* are derived from the root metaphors of burning fire and beaming brightness. Purity (*shuddhata, shuci*), in the widest sense, is what is light, glowing, mobile, subtle. By contrast, pollution (*ashauca, ashuci*) is what is dark, damp, and inert, what weighs down. In order to pass from the condition of pollution to a condition of purity, *tapas* or *tapasya* is performed. The performance of austerities can also be understood as a process through which one is able to reach a higher level of energy and purity. To generate *tapas* means, literally, to *cook* oneself until all impurities are burned away.

In principle, all beings have the potential to create inner heat, whether they are gods, humans, animals, or plants. Just as all of them, even the lowest ones, have "internal consciousness and experience [of] happiness and unhappiness" (*Laws of Manu* I.49), *tapas* can be created by all (*Laws of Manu* XI.235-41). Since *tapas* pervades the whole cosmic order, it also potentially transcends caste differences. Yet depending on a being's position in the caste hierarchy, the methods of generating *tapas* are different. One way to increase inner heat open to all beings is proper conduct and service according to one's innate duty. Praise of service and respect for one's own duty (*svadharma*) are a cornerstone of Hindu philosophy and one of the main arguments unfolded in the *Bhagavad-Gita* (III.35): "Better do one's own duty, though void of merit, than to do another's well."

The idea of *tapas* can be retraced to the oldest Vedic sources (Kaelber 1979, 1989). In one of the *Rig Veda*'s creation hymns (X.129), *tapas* brought the universe into being: "Darkness was hidden by darkness in the beginning; with no distinguishing sign, all this was water. The life force that was covered with emptiness, that one arose through the power of heat [*tapas*]." Heat can create anything, or it may lift a soul to a high state of energy by destroying lower forms of embodiment. In a funeral hymn (*Rig Veda* X.16.4), the god of fire is beseeched to both destroy the dead man and lift him up to heaven: "Let your brilliant light and flame burn him. With your gentle forms, O knower of creatures, carry this man to the world of those who have done good deeds." The gods may also use *tapas* for purifying destruction. In their fights against the demons, *tapas* is one of their lethal weapons (see *Rig Veda* II.23.14, IV.4.1, VIII.23.14).

Post-Vedic texts emphasize that *tapas* is an innate ability of *all* living beings. While *tapas* is used in the Veda to destroy impure demons, the *Dharma-Shastras* focus on the destruction of impurity and evil. The source of heat is now *within* the agent; thus the fire god Agni is not directly invoked any longer. The predominant use of *tapas* is not creation, but inside purification. This is often described as the "interiorization" of the sacrificial fires (see Eliade 1975; Biardeau and Malamoud 1976; Heesterman 1993; Kaelber 1989). Hinduism shifted from outward ritual to inward purification, and with it came an increasing emphasis on humans being able to burn up their own impurities through austerities: "*Tapas* then comes to assume its most prevalent meaning: self-imposed austerity, asceticism, mortification, or penance" (Kaelber 1979: 198).

Since the era of the Upanishads, the supreme good to be achieved in Brahmanical Hinduism is liberation from *dharma* and its obligations. The notion of *moksha* signifies the deliverance from the cycle of rebirths. *Moksha* leads to the union with the "ultimate reality" of Brahma. If this supreme condition can be described at all, it would be best imagined as boundless energy or unlimited potential. Given that even the gods are subjected to the cosmic order, achieving *moksha* is even superior to divinity. Ultimate freedom is gained when the last traces of impurity are destroyed. When the flames of *tapas* have completely burned the body of the renouncer, his corpse is considered to be equal to a heap of ashes. The achievement of *moksha* is still practiced in Hindu death rites today: instead of the corpse of the *sannyasin* being cremated on a funeral pyre, it is only immersed in a river (Das 1992: 123; Parry 1994: 184), because no burning is necessary.

The radiant heat of *tapas* continues to have a place in popular notions of the mind (Barrett 2008). For example, for Deepak, a Hindu pundit in his late thirties, the performance of austerities created a spiritual power that transcended normal human powers. Deepak came from a high Brahmin caste and made a living from performing *pujas* for clients (*jajmans*). He lived together with around fifty other relatives in a traditional joint family household; many of his relatives were also working as pundits. Asked if there is a lot of demand for *pujas* these days, he answered contentedly, "We all have good food, full stomach, no problem."

For Deepak, the power of *tapas* was evident in the mantras that he had learned (Michaels 1998: 252-54). Just as there were different mantras for different rituals, there were different mantras for different diseases. The power of mantras was obvious because "two hundred years ago there was no medicine," and so all that people had at their disposal were prayer and *puja*. He told me how he is also called in medical emergencies:

> Suppose someone falls sick, if anybody has problems, if anybody is serious and is in hospital, and doctor have given up, and when doctors give twenty-four hours' time, then I can keep the patient alive for forty-eight hours. So much confidence I have, I can turn twenty-four into forty-eight hours. What mantra I'll do, there is *power* in that mantra.

Mantras could also save people who attempted suicide: if someone tried to poison himself, the right mantra, well performed, could delay the onset of death: "You take a poison, then you ask me to stop it, a poison such as cyanide, if the poison affects after half-hour, the mantra I do, with that mantra it won't affect for six hours. It will affect only after six hours."

Deepak went on to explain why mantras were so powerful: an effective mantra was based on long and strenuous research, just as biomedical pills were. A mantra was nothing other than a highly compacted research product, like an over-the-counter pain killer such as Saridon (a combination of propyphenazone, paracetamol, and caffeine):

> For small things like headaches, people take Saridon from the shop. Such a small thing—the cost is only one rupee—for such a big pain. They take the medicine so that it works, they don't know how the medicine was made. Scientists did research for that medicine, they did so many things to make a small medicine. Like that, mantras have also has been made.

Pundits, Brahmins, *Rishis*, they went to the jungle for *tapasya*, they do *tapasya* for many years, and then they got the power.

He further said that he himself did not have to undergo *tapasya* because others had done the hard work already. All he had to do was to learn the mantras. Just as there was no need to spend years of one's own life on making a tablet of painkillers, so it was unnecessary to reinvent the power of mantras.

Many of the ways of keeping the *mon* cool that people mentioned in my survey on *mon kharap* are entailed in the notion of *tapas*. Fasting, prayer to deities, visiting temples, reading religious books, withdrawing oneself, thinking positively, meditating, and doing yoga are all performances of *tapasya*. Hence, one answer to the question why biomedical drugs seem an implausible choice to treat a *mon kharap* is that the "inner heat" of *tapas* cannot be easily transferred from one being to another. Psychopharmaceuticals might be the fruits of strenuous labor, but swallowing them cannot be a substitute for one's own efforts.

Finally, how can the paradox of "cooling" the mind through "heat" be resolved? One answer lies in the difference between hot energy *stored* and hot energy *dissipated*. For example, *tapas* is a major theme in the mythology of the god Shiva as "erotic ascetic" (O'Flaherty 1973). Through long *tapasya*, Shiva stores up immense amounts of energy (synonymous with semen) in his forehead, only to dissipate all of it when having sex with his wife, Parvati, or when getting enraged by others disturbing him. When Shiva keeps cool and still, he keeps the radiant energy of *tapas* together, and when he starts moving, the energy dissipates and everything around him heats up. Coolness can only be maintained by stillness. The same idea is encapsulated in Bengali popular notions of *mon*, which has to stay still to retain the stored energy. Another possible answer is that the popular Bengali definition of *mon* is an amalgamation of different philosophical ideas that are logically coherent only if they are kept apart. Where Sanskrit philosophies distinguish *manas* from *atman* (soul) or *buddhi* (intellect), the popular Bengali term *mon* condenses several levels into a single opposition between *mon*, soul, and intellect on the one hand, and the sense organs and the body on the other.

The final answer is that such philosophical and theological complexities do not bother most Bengalis. When probed for an opinion, they would say that all of this is *tomar moner bepar*—up to your own *mon*.

Choosing between Remedies

Mon is held to be the ultimate source of decisions about medical therapies. Choices among allopathy, homeopathy, Ayurveda, or other forms of healing are described as the *mon*'s internal decisions, often even beyond conscious reflection. The extent to which one "takes to" a particular doctor, or a particular kind of medication, depends on the unconscious workings of the *mon*. As one Bengali man in his thirties put it,

> If I look at the doctor, he is my doctor, I'm having a problem, his medicine works for me. If *you* go, it won't suit you. If I suggest you to go to my doctor, he'll suggest you medicines. But for you, the medicine doesn't work [*kaj karena*]. You may be ill, but just to think of your doctor, or to see him, and you become well.

Although it is not always clear why one's *mon* has certain preferences, it is vital to heed them. Drugs and doctors require various amounts of faith (*visvas*) to accomplish their healing effects. Allopathy is usually seen as relatively neutral to faith, homeopathy and Ayurveda need more of it, and religious healing work is strongly dependent on it. The belly also needs to be consulted to see whether a medicine can be digested without problems.

Differences among medicines are discerned by different frames of temporality. On the level of epochal periodization, the most obvious choice for "modern" medicine is biomedicine, whereas Ayurveda is "traditional." Religious healing is outside of time for those who strongly believe, and "traditional" for those who would not bet their lives on it. Homeopathy occupies a peculiar position: it is sometimes seen as "timeless" quackery that was as wrongheaded in the late eighteenth century as it is today. But it is more common to see homeopathy as *more* modern than "modern medicine," because it is cheap, free of side effects, and suited for chronic and long-term problems. The most prevalent idea about homeopathy in Calcutta is that it is a kind of *hyper*modern alternative to biomedicine. As one Bengali woman in her sixties remarked, "Our grandparents took Ayurveda, we take allopathy, the younger generation chooses homeopathy." Epochal periodization is important, but in Calcutta it is not as important as other frames. Pragmatic evaluations overrule questions of tradition or modernity. Sometimes people say that homeopathy is now more famous than in earlier times, that Ayurvedic doctors are worse than in the old days, or that allopathy now has fewer side effects. But I have never heard anyone say that they went to an allopath because that was the "modern" thing to do, or that going to an Ayurvedic healer was motivated by a love for "traditional" knowledge. There is only one small exception to this, which is that richer people joke about psychiatrists as a "modern" fad.

The temporality of drug effects in the body surpasses epochal considerations. The main distinction is between "slow" (*deri*) and "fast" (*tara-tari*) medicine. In all my conversations about this topic, people conceptualized the speed of recovery by comparing allopathy to homeopathy: allopathy is the best "quick" medicine, whereas homeopathy is quintessentially "slow." Closely related to the fast or slow action of drugs is another type of temporality: suitability for acute or chronic illnesses. Allopathy was the best "quick" medicine for "quick" illnesses. For chronic conditions, better suited were softer alternatives, but only for small problems that are not life-threatening. Homeopathy and Ayurveda are widely regarded as better choices for long-term drug consumption.

The speed with which different medicines work is experienced through dietary changes imposed by various healers. One advantage of allopathy was that its drugs worked independently of what one ate, so that dietary changes were unnecessary. This was juxtaposed to Ayurveda, where medicines were never given without dietary advice. Mr. Biswas, an elderly Bengali, told me about how he had suffered from chronic constipation fifteen years earlier. He first went to an allopath, but the medicine did not work. Then he went to a *kaviraj*, who did not even prescribe a remedy, but only put him on a dour diet of bread and milk for two months: "For a Bengali like me, that was very difficult." After two months, the Ayurvedic healer finally gave him a medicine that purged undigested waste from his body: "all the dirt came out" (*sab moyla beriye gaeche*). Since then, his digestion had never troubled him again. Homeopathy was somewhere between biomedicine and Ayurveda when it came to cumbersome dietary regulations. Not all homeopaths insisted on food avoidances, but for some Bengali patients I talked to, homeopathy was too arduous to be a viable alternative to allopathy. Mangla, a low-class woman, explained, "I don't like homeopathy. If you take allopathy, it works fast. Homeopathy works very slowly. And they ask you not to eat this, not to eat that. For this reason, I don't take homeopathy."

Even poorer people who otherwise do not speak English use the term "side effect." Allopathic medicine is said to be *khub kara*, "too strict." The idea is that allopathy's "chemical" and "synthetic" drugs create a "shock" to the body that lingers on for weeks or months later. This "shock" is understood as a primary side effect of any drug that acts "fast" (Nichter 1989). By contrast, homeopathy is seen as "not strict" *(kara nay)*, "light" *(halka)*, and "soft" *(naram)*. Ayurveda's "herbal" and "natural" drugs were safe, but homeopathic remedies are regarded as least hazardous. Side effects are mostly framed in explicitly humoral terms: allopathic drugs are "heating" the body and are making it "dry" *(koshe)*. The typical symptom for this heating and drying effect is constipation and deep yellow urine. Allopathic drugs are perceived to be so heating and desiccating that doctors routinely prescribe cooling tonics to be taken along with pills and tablets. The tonic Liv.52 by Himalaya Ltd. has been one of India's top ten best-selling medicines for decades. The most prominently displayed products in every Bengali medicine shop are the bottles of liver and digestive tonics (a sample of products found displayed on one shelf: Aristozyme, Cyaptin, Cypon, Digeplex, Estozyme, Gastracid, Gastril, Globiron, Heptaglobine, Livagod, Livomer Z, Livoluk, Livosin, Liv-R, Lysicon-V, Parazygen, Redizym, Tefroliv Forte, Trisoliv, Wino Brona, Zest).

Besides tonics, another way of softening the blow from allopathic drugs is to lower the prescribed dosage. When I interviewed the Bengali support staff in a charitable clinic run by a German NGO, they said that the German visiting doctors always used too high dosages. The bodies of Calcutta slum dwellers were weaker and smaller than European bodies, and hence unable to cope with heavy doses. They therefore saw it as their duty to dispense lower doses than what was written on the prescriptions; for example, they gave antibiotics at only half the dose prescribed by the German doctors. Asked if the visiting doctors knew about this, they said that they never said anything because this would lead to "unnecessary" conflicts. The same logic of lowering doses or of avoiding allopathy altogether is applied to anyone whose overall resistance is too low to digest allopathic medicines, especially children and older people.

Explicit discussions about the quality of different drugs are surprisingly rare. Drug efficacy tends to be subsumed under general headings such as "good" or "bad" medicine. When people are asked if one type of medicine is better than another, the usual way of responding is to talk about personal experiences. Most common were stories in which taking a *non*biomedical drug had better results than expected. For example, people talked about episodes when they, or a family member, had tried several remedies in vain, and then at last a homeopathic or an Ayurvedic drug worked wonders. Here is a typical narrative by Bhanu, a Bengali man in his midthirties:

> I had a swollen gland, some years ago, and for that I took so much [allopathic] medicine. Then I took homeopathy. In just three days, the gland disappeared. That gland had become so big. The allopath said I had to go for an operation. I got scared. Then I went to a homeopath, he gave three days medicine . . . on the third day, the gland burst. I thought it would take much more time.

The most dramatic narratives relate to the wondrous effects of religious healing. One temple that Calcuttans often mention for its miraculous healing powers is Tarakeshwar, located sixty kilometers northwest of Calcutta. Thousands of people travel there each day to worship a form of Shiva. The temple is famous for dream healing: people with chronic diseases come to the temple to undergo several days of fasting, until Shiva appears to them in a dream and tells them what task they have to perform to get well. The temple also has a pond where one can wash one's sins away. In an annual ritual, devotees fill sacred water from Tarakeshwar into brass pots balanced on bamboo rods and walk barefooted back to Calcutta. The therapeutic powers of this pond transcended scientific rationality. One middle-aged man described the Tarakeshwar pond (*pukur*), which was built in the nineteenth century, in its current state:

> There's a *pukur*, it is more than one hundred years old, from British times. My generation, and the old generation, we all know about it. That

pukur is very dirty. But if anyone falls sick, they go there and take a bath, and they get well. So many scientists have been there, they tested the water, and they said that no one should take bath there.

A retired government clerk, Mr. Dasgupta, told me how his son had been born with a congenital heart defect. He and his wife usually had him treated at a government hospital, but after a doctor told them that their son was bound to die soon, they desperately tried other healers. One of them was an Ayurvedic *kaviraj*, and the Dasguptas were happy when their son kept reasonably well for six years afterward. When the son was again in hospital and the doctors had already given up, two of Mr. Dasgupta's friends rushed to Tarakeshwar to pray to Shiva on behalf of his son. They had started off from Calcutta late in the day and it was practically impossible that they could reach the temple before its gates were shut for the night. But for no evident reason, everyone they met on their path helped them. For example, a policeman stopped a van bound for Tarakeshwar and put the men on it. At the exact moment when the friends gave *puja* to Shiva at Tarakeshwar, his son suddenly rose from his Calcutta hospital bed and said he wanted to go home: "The doctors couldn't believe it, but he was fine." After this miracle, the son lived for another three years, but then could not be helped for longer and died.

Although Tarakeshwar is particularly potent, any daily *puja* at any site can work the same healing wonders. Eating *prasad* (the leftovers of a food offering to a deity) is regarded as a powerful remedy for any disease. It is also common to take medical drugs in the spirit of *prasad*: if one thinks of one's favorite deity and then eats the medicine, it is bound to be more efficacious. Of course, it depends on one's *mon* whether *prasad* actually has such powers.

Paying for Medicines

Bengalis say that, for buying the necessary medicines, "one does not see the face of the money" (*paisar mukh dekhle hayna*), meaning that one must be prepared to spend all it takes to get healthy. A woman in her fifties, who lived on alms given by Kalighat temple visitors, compared her family's expenses on medicines with expenses on food. In big cities, food could always be found, even if only leftovers thrown into the bin by other people. But spending money on drugs was a must, because one's very life depended on it:

It's important to spend money on medicine. We have to save our life. If my husband earns fifty rupees [approx. one U.S. dollar] and medicine costs fifty rupees, what do I do? I buy the medicine! Nothing is bigger than life [*jibon theke bara kicchu nei*]. I would buy medicine first, to save my life. Food, I can go anywhere and get it.

Allopathy is universally seen as the most expensive treatment option. Private allopathic doctors' fees were on average the highest in the market and the drugs were more expensive than drugs from other healing streams. Also, allopaths are known to always prescribe several remedies at a time, instead of single remedies: liver and digestive tonics are often accompanied by more pills for, for example, pain relief. One Bengali man underlined that his own family doctor was an unusually good doctor because he never prescribed more medicines than were truly necessary: "Our doctor only prescribes the medicines needed, so nothing is wasted."

If an unperturbed *mon* is important to keeping oneself healthy, anxieties about medical treatment costs should be avoided whenever possible. This results in doctors often not telling seriously ill patients what is going on. For example, Bimol, a middle-aged man whose father suffered from cancer, told me how the doctor had explained the diagnosis only to him, not to his father. Both the son and the doctor agreed that there was no point in telling his father the truth. His father would only get mentally "tense" (*cinta pare yabe*), and this would further weaken him. The family could not afford the treatment, which cost ten thousand rupees [$180]. The son had already asked his employer for a loan, but that request was rejected. He also tried to borrow money from relatives, but Bimol had failed in that as well. Since his father was deeply religious, it was best to let him go to the temple every day and not do anything else about the cancer: "Everything is in God's hand" (*sab thakurer hate ache*).

For Ayurveda and other forms of healing, people have no consensual opinions about costs. The usual frame for cost comparisons is, again, the difference between allopathy and homeopathy. Where allopathy is expensive, homeopathy is cheap. Homeopaths' consultation fees are seen as lower than those of allopaths. Above all, the remedies are cheap.

Different homeopathic manufacturers charge different prices, with remedies imported from Germany or the United States being twice as expensive as Indian domestic products. But even premium-priced homeopathic remedies still cost less than what an average allopathic drug costs. Many people told me that homeopathy was once cheaper than now, but remained cheap in comparison to allopathy.

Money is the chief reason why an allopathic quick fix would be preferred to a homeopathic slow cure. Even if many Calcuttans agree that a course of homeopathic medicines, conscientiously followed over a long period of time, can give lasting improvement, they feel that it takes too long. Poorer people suffer most from "time famine": they have to go out and earn money from day to day. Some people in safe employment can take time off to get well, but most have to "buy time" with drugs (Vuckovic 1999). Even if homeopathic medicines were cheaper to buy than allopathic ones, the loss in daily earnings could not compensate the difference. Neel, a male shop assistant in his forties, calculated the relative costs of allopathy and homeopathy:

> We are workers, so it's not possible to wait for the medicines to work in "their" time. If we don't work, we won't get paid. We want our illness to go away soon, and we want to start working again and looking after our family. Homeopathy takes time. It is not expensive, but it takes time. That's why we don't go for it. We go for allopathy, it is fast and quick. Allopathy is a good medicine. There and then it works, right as you take it.

Another daily laborer, Bapin, described himself as a "working guy" (*kajer chele*) who needed to be back on his feet as soon as possible. Allopathy had the power to make one join work again immediately, but it could never give a permanent cure. That homeopathy is so "slow" was a necessary consequence of the medicine removing not just superficial symptoms but the very "root" of the sickness (*ei rogta shekar theke ber kare dey*). Whereas homeopathy went to the root, any symptom suppressed with allopathy would inevitably recur:

> Homeopathy takes its time. That doesn't work for me, because I'm a working guy, I have to get well soon, so I take allopathy. We want immediate result. [*Ever used homeopathy?*] I used homeopathy. It's not bad. If

you take it properly and in time, if you follow the rules, then it works better than allopathy. Allopathy gives cure for some days only. If you take homeopathy, it will take out the illness from the body, the illness won't come back again. But in allopathy, again after some time it will come, you will have the same problem. That's the difference between allopathy and homeopathy.

Money also features in reflections on the addictive potential of different drugs. Many people I talked to were concerned that they had become addicted to allopathic drugs. Mr. Bandhyopadhay, an elderly Bengali man with a long history of asthma, said that he never wanted to become a "slave" to medicines:

> I should not get immune to any kind of medicine, that's my view. Too much leads to immunization. If you take it for ten years, no effect. In Calcutta, people think: "I've been to that doctor, I've bought that medicine, so I should live on medicine." Whether it's acting positively or not. What it does in the body, they don't know. If I start taking medicine, I'm a slave to that medicine. People take too many medicines, that's of no use . . . if you walk around Calcutta, you see people queuing all around to buy medicine. People like eating medicines more than eating vegetables [*laughs*].

Such principled rejection of pharmaceuticals is rare, but unease about their harmful long-term effects is widely shared. An addictive potential is only attributed to allopathic drugs, never to homeopathy or to Ayurveda, even though the mentality of resorting to remedies even for small illnesses would apply to them as well. Being a slave to drugs was a drain on both one's physical vitality and one's finances.

Self-Medication

Financial constraints make self-medication common in India (Das and Das 2005). To avoid paying for a doctor, people consult relatives or neighbors who have a reputation for knowing about pharmaceuticals. For example, a wage laborer in his midtwenties told me that a piece of paper from a trusted neighbor was all he needed:

If anything happens, I take a tablet right from the shop. [. . .] If I go to the doctor, he charges one hundred rupees [$1.80]. Why should we go to a doctor? We don't earn that much. I go and ask some good people, who have knowledge, they write down on a paper what medicine I should get from the shop.

Among all the various drugs offered in India, allopathic drugs are easiest to get. Instead of going to an allopath for a prescription, one can go directly to the pharmacist. Most Calcuttans self-medicate with drugs bought from shops, not only with over-the-counter products but also with prescription drugs. If one knows what drug to take, there is no need to spend money and time on a doctor. Local lay knowledge of drugs is cut loose from the control of doctors. Almost all drugs can be bought from any medicine shop without a prescription from a licensed doctor.

The open boundaries of allopathic drugs retailing allow the phenomenon of "floating prescriptions" (Ecks and Basu 2009). This term is used by medical professionals to describe how knowledge of drug prescriptions starts to "float" among patients, shops, licensed and even unlicensed prescribers. In India, prescriptions written by a doctor always stay with the patient. When a retailer fills a prescription, he neither keeps the original paper nor leaves a mark on it to indicate that the drug was already dispensed. This makes it possible for patients to get drugs as often as they want. Prescriptions contain the patient's name and the date of the consultation, and so it would be easy for retailers to deny filling prescriptions that are older than, say, a few weeks. In practice, however, prescriptions stay with the patients, and are used over and over. Indeed, not even a written prescription is required: patients commonly bring emptied blister packs or bottles to shops and ask for a new one of the same kind. They might also ask for "the green (or white, or blue) tablet" that they received last time. When patients show old prescriptions to other doctors, the doctors learn not only about patients' medication histories but also about the prescribing styles of other doctors. This, in turn, makes certain drugs the "established" treatments and individual brands "trusted" (see Brhlikova et al. 2011).

In recent years, the spread of cable TV has expanded the reach of direct-to-consumer marketing for over-the-counter drugs. Statements such as "what they show on TV, for headache and other problems, I take that" are common in Calcutta. Yet the Indian state does not allow TV or print marketing for prescription drugs.

More important than structured advertising are word-of-mouth recommendations. This form of "floating" prescriptions starts within households and the immediate neighborhood (*para*). Bengalis usually take medicines in plain view of other family members. I have often observed in friends' houses how, after breakfast or dinner, a small basket containing all the drugs currently used by different members of the family is passed around, and everyone takes whatever he or she needs. In this context, people discuss the advantages and side effects of the drugs they are taking, and might even suggest to a relative or a guest to try one of them if he or she has a similar set of symptoms. In India, "phamily" patterns of pharmaceutical uses (Oldani 2009) emerge without prescriptions.

Household self-medication is also common with homeopathy. In Calcutta, as indeed in most of India, the foremost homeopathic practitioners are not professional doctors but laypeople. Homeopathic remedies lend themselves to self-medication because they are seen as cheap, free from side effects, and without risk of overdosing. They were also heat-resistant and long-lasting. Since they did not have expiration dates, they could be used for years on end after purchase. The "homeopathy chest," which contains a set of common homeopathic remedies, is a stock item in many Bengali middle-class homes. The phenomenon of "self-instructed part-time practitioners" of homeopathy is also mentioned by Charles Leslie in his 1970s survey of Indian medical practices (1976: 359), and it appears that domestic uses of homeopathic remedies are just as popular today as in earlier decades. Mr. Datta, a pharmacist in a homeopathic medicine shop, even felt that the homeopathy chest was becoming *more* popular: "The homeo-chest is even more common today than earlier. People have a kit in their home with thirty to forty different medicines. Some people make their own kit according to their choice, then come and buy specific medicines." Visiting Calcutta houses, I was occasionally offered a quick dose of homeopathic globules for a bit of cough and cold or for a light fever, usually by elderly ladies. These wooden boxes with small glass bottles are, for many, an abiding memory of their childhood medication histories. Any common illness could be soothed by a few sweet globules made of milk and sugar.

Self-medication beyond the supervision of a licensed homeopath has been a characteristic trait of Indian homeopathy since its beginnings in the nineteenth century. In their history of Indian homeopathy, David Arnold and Sumit Sarkar (2000: 43) underline that it was homeopathy's "do-it-yourself appeal" that led to its quick adoption in India. One of the most famous part-time practitioners of this kind was Rabindranath Tagore (1861-1941), the national poet of Bengal and the first Asian to win a Nobel Prize in 1913. According to Bagchi's (2000: 8-15) "medical biography" of the writer, Tagore taught himself the principles of homeopathy from books, as was (and is) the fashion among members of the Bengali elite. Tagore started to promote the medicine as a rational and cheap alternative to allopathy. Soon, throngs of people came to him for medical treatment. On some days he gave medicines to more than 150 patients free of charge. On his trips to the remote areas of Bengal, Tagore carried a homeopathy chest with him to dispense medicines whenever needed. At Shantiniketan, where he had founded an experimental school and university, Tagore also taught homeopathy to other professors. Among his patients was Amita Sen, mother of Amartya Sen, another Nobel Prize winner from Bengal. Tagore's faith in homeopathy had clear limits, however. Similar to Gandhi, he believed that true health could only be achieved through a healthy, balanced life. Even if homeopathy could not always cure disease, at least it did not cause financial ruin. For Tagore, homeopathy was only the lesser of two evils: "homeopathy kills a life, but allopathy kills both life and financial resources" (Tagore, quoted in Bagchi 2000: 14).

One of my Bengali neighbors, Mr. Sarkar, was one of these self-educated homeopaths. He told me about how he had been "converted" to the homeopathic "faith" several years earlier. His wife had suffered from a bad inflammation of the eye. They went to several different allopathic doctors, but nothing worked. At last, they consulted a homeopath, who gave only one single globule. The first few days after taking the homeopathic remedy, his wife's eye became worse, and some of his relatives were almost on their way to "beat up" the homeopath, but then the inflammation went away, never to return. Mr. Sarkar then decided to learn the basics of homeopathy himself, and has been treating people close to him ever since. For example, he said he cured his domestic maid's foot from chronic pain. He knew that homeopathic remedies

have personalities: "Arnica, for example, is very orderly, like someone who even on his death bed would straighten the blanket." For Mr.
Sarkar, homeopathy made sense because "everything is in the mind."
Personal likes and dislikes of different foods and different climates were
also in the mind. They are "lower-grade mental symptoms," as opposed
to "higher-grade symptoms" such as mental aptitude or recurrent
dreams. Once a patient has given himself up in his own mind, he may
live on for a while out of sheer organic stubbornness, but no doctor
could save him.

When it comes to Ayurveda, few people in Calcutta had a clear
idea about how to distinguish professional prescriptions from house-
hold-based self-care. This confusion was so great that I hardly ever
got a straight answer about "Ayurveda" in the sense of the professional
practice, as opposed to remedies that people concoct themselves. Bengali language allows distinguishing between *khabar*, which is food for
everyday nutrition, and *pathya*, food dedicated to healing. *Totka* is
the label for home remedies that are either based on recipes handed
down through generations or are learned from published books. It was
common that one of my questions about "Ayurveda" would first be
answered with examples of homemade *totka*. As Mr. Bhadari, an allopathic shop owner, said, "I've never been to a *kaviraj*, but we use four
or five *Ayurvedic medicines* in my house. We prepare them ourselves.
Haldi [turmeric] and milk mixed together for cough and cold; boiled
tulsi pata [Holy Basil leaves] for good sleep during a fever." *Khabar*,
totka, and *pathya* are all governed by considerations of their "heating" or "cooling" properties. A *totka* against "hot" child diarrhea is, for
example, a "cold" mix of boiled green bananas and yogurt. Since both
bananas and yogurt are everyday food items, this preparation is only
distinguished from *khabar* by the intention of making the child well
again.

Hot/cold considerations are supplemented by other classificatory
schemes. For example, several *totkas* for "hot" digestive problems are
not "cold" as such, but are able to "control" the stomach's humoral
imbalance in other ways. Two popular remedies against *ambol* ("sourness" or acidity) are mixtures of *amla* (Indian gooseberry) with either
joyan (caraway seeds) or *haritaki* (Terminalia chebula). These remedies
reduce excessive sourness. The classification applied here is that of the

six "tastes" (*svada*). Reminiscent of Ayurveda's six *rasa*, the six tastes are, in Bengali, *teto* (bitter), *kosh* (astringent), *jhal* (pungent, spicy), *tak* (sour), *nunta* (salty), and *misti* (sweet). For controlling excessive heat in the stomach, bitter and astringent foods are effective. The bitter leaves of the *neem* tree, for example, are commonly recommended during the hot season to keep excess heat under control. Yet opinions about how to classify the six tastes in terms of hot/cold vary widely. For example, *neem* leaves are more often seen as cooling than as heating, but there was no common view of this. Contradictions are often solved with reference to dosage: if taken in moderation, bitter things are cooling. If taken in excess, they are heating.

2

Ayurveda

"You Are the Medicine"

"No problem, it's just acidity": A *Kaviraj's* Illness Narrative

Dr. Sengupta and I first met at his house on the southern outskirts of Calcutta. He was seventy-five years old at the time. We sat cross-legged on the veranda. His wife served tea and traditional Bengali sweets. Dr. Sengupta always preferred to speak in Bengali, as this allowed him, he explained, to speak in more precise terms. He practiced Ayurveda in the third generation, following the tradition of his father and grandfather: "From small I saw how they were being made at home. My father never bought anything from outside, he used to make his own medicines by hand. I used to help my father." Dr. Sengupta said he wanted to become a *kaviraj* not just to continue the family line but also because he witnessed what healing miracles his father could perform. Many patients arrived in hopeless conditions, but "my father made them stand." While showing me around his garden, where he cultivated herbs for use in his medicine, he stressed how important it is to have one's own garden and to be able to correctly identify medical herbs by seeing, touching, and smelling them. He also talked fondly of his son, who had trained at one of Calcutta's Ayurveda colleges. Our conversations during the day were punctuated by a few long-time patients dropping in. They all had been in treatment with Dr. Sengupta for many years, as had many of their relatives. Dr. Sengupta knew most of them and asked about how they were doing. His patients addressed him as if he were a senior family member, their *jheta moshai* (father's elder brother), or their *baba* (grandfather): "I treat them like my family members, and they do the same with me." Everything looked like an idyll of classic Ayurveda—until Dr. Sengupta started to talk about the cancer in his esophagus.

From his childhood days, Dr. Sengupta had suffered from a mild pain in the stomach. The pain always went away when he ate something, so his family thought this was nothing too serious, just a common *gastric*. The problem persisted throughout his adult life until, when he was sixty-five, the pain became unusually strong, and he felt that something more severe was happening. For a second opinion, he first turned to one of his colleagues, also an Ayurveda practitioner, but did not get a new diagnosis: "He said, no problem, it's just acidity." His colleague discussed his dietary regimen with him, yet did not prescribe any medicines. The pain persisted, and Dr. Sengupta turned to another *kaviraj*, who diagnosed an "enlargement of the liver." Still dissatisfied, he decided to go for investigations at a private center for gastroenterology. After a series of tests, including ultrasound, x-rays, an endoscopy, a biopsy, and "barium swallowing" for visualization, the gastroenterologist who treated him found a cancerous growth in the esophagus. Dr. Sengupta was referred to a private hospital near his residence in southern Calcutta for "ray treatment." One month later, he had to do more tests, and it was found that the tumor had almost disappeared. Yet Dr. Sengupta's pains persisted, as did his difficulties with swallowing food. From a friend he heard about an excellent private center for cancer treatment in Mumbai, and decided to go there for another check-up. The Mumbai doctors confirmed the initial diagnosis of cancer, and also found that it had not been removed. Dr. Sengupta then went through lengthy chemotherapy, and was finally told that he had been healed. The pain during swallowing continued, and he went back for tests; he was told that everything was fine but that he should come back to Mumbai every six months for check-ups. When I returned to Calcutta and tried to contact Dr. Sengupta a few years later, I learned that he had passed away, aged eighty-one.

Throughout our conversation, Dr. Sengupta used the English term "cancer." When I asked if there is an Ayurvedic term for this, he said that Bengalis sometimes called it *karkar*, and that the proper Sanskrit term was never used. He also hesitated when I asked him what the Ayurvedic explanation for the outbreak of the cancer might be. Earlier on in our conversation, when I inquired about the prevalence of "gastric" complaints among his patients and the reasons for it, he laughed and said that "greed" (*lobh*) and uncontrolled eating were the reason for it: "90-95 percent have that! [. . .] The reason for these troubles is greed (*lobh*). Greedy people get that. Without greed, there is no stomach problem." In regard to his own cancer, he did not mention this argument again. He suggested that even if his earlier pain in the belly might have been related to some dietary fault, the cancerous growth in his esophagus probably had nothing to do with it. In any case, no one knew for sure the reasons for cancer, not even allopaths.

The costs for the treatment were high. Dr. Sengupta could only afford the treatment because he had basic health coverage through the pharmaceutical company that he worked for at the time. Shortly before being diagnosed with cancer, Dr. Sengupta had started to work for East India Pharmaceutical Works Ltd., a West Bengal government undertaking, which had hired him to develop a line of Ayurvedic remedies to be produced alongside their biomedical generics. At the company, Dr. Sengupta helped to turn Ayurvedic recipes of his father and grandfather into medicines for mass manufacturing. One of these products, Cyclovarin, a capsule for use against menstrual pain, is still marketed today. When I visited the factory at Behala, a suburb of Calcutta, the marketing director proudly told me that the herbal products were more profitable than the allopathic generics business. Before his employment with East India Pharmaceutical Works, Dr. Sengupta had worked for three decades for the State Pharmacopoeial Laboratory and Pharmacy for Indian Medicine (SPLPIM) at Kalyani, a northern suburb of Calcutta. There he had also been engaged in the development and marketing of Ayurvedic drugs. But in his own chamber, he preferred to give medicines that he had prepared himself. Patients also demanded his preparations, rather than "market medicine." To help him make the medicines, Dr. Sengupta employed two compounders. Despite having spent much of his professional life in pharmaceutical companies, Dr. Sengupta was mostly negative about the changes that this had brought to the discipline. Younger doctors were less able to make their own medicines, and instead relied on prescribing factory-made products: "Ayurveda is going down, it's getting spoiled. It's not like before. Ayurveda doctors don't have a grip on the subject anymore. Now these doctors turn this medicine into a business."

To counter certain side effects of the cancer treatment and to avoid a relapse, Dr. Sengupta took Ayurvedic remedies, among them turmeric, neem (*Azadirachta indica*), and *ashvagandha* (*Withania somnifera*). For him, the cancer was an opportunity to experiment on his own body with formulas for anticancer treatments. He also imagined using his insights for mass-produced drugs, but only if he could run trials with at least one hundred patients, which could not be taken for granted in Ayurveda. If no proven Ayurvedic remedies were available, either for cancer or for other diseases, he would never hesitate to send patients to an allopath for treatment: "If I can't do it, I send them to allopathy. You cannot ignore allopathy, it is so important, it's compulsory. Especially for emergency cases. I have never got a single patient referred from allopathy, not one. But I have sent many patients to allopathy." According to Dr. Sengupta, the strength of Ayurveda lay in treating chronic conditions of the stomach, liver, heart, brain, and joints.

Despite his feelings of not being fully cured, Dr. Sengupta said that the biomedical approach to cancer was largely effective. But he also felt that his strong mental power was essential for recovery: "Now I'm better. I have will power (*moner jor*). I am not afraid of cancer. I was not afraid when I was diagnosed with cancer." Such mental power could not be achieved through medications, only through proper use of the mind: "It's self-hallucination." He said that he saw an increasing number of "psychological" patients. Most of their complaints were *vayu rog*, that is, diseases caused by an excess of the "air" humor. He preferred not to confront his patients with a psychological diagnosis: "If I told them, they would think: 'Oh, this doctor cannot diagnose properly.'" Instead, he diagnoses a physical problem and prescribes a placebo. With some younger patients, it was possible to be more frank: "I say: 'You have a psychological problem, you don't have to take medicine.'"

Dr. Sengupta's illness narrative is unique, but it also reflects how Ayurveda is changing in India. Ayurvedic knowledge used to be passed down from one generation to the next, and Dr. Sengupta was proud to follow the family tradition. Now, most of the training his son received was in a government-run college. Ayurveda used to be "the Sanskritic, literate system that received royal patronage" (Wujastyk 1998: 30), the health counsel appointed to the king's court (Zimmermann 1987). The Bengali name of the Ayurvedic doctor, *kaviraj*, the "king of the verse," still echoes this claim to sovereign status. But today, Ayurveda is relegated to an inferior place, by allopathy across India and by homeopathy in West Bengal. Ayurvedic diagnostics used to be couched in Sanskrit and to a lesser extent in vernacular terminology, but is now usually a hybrid of English and Sanskrit. The English biomedical term "cancer," for example, was used by Dr. Sengupta despite his reservations about using English. Such change toward biomedical terminology is pushed by the dominant presence of biomedical diagnostic laboratories. Ayurveda used to claim expertise in all fields of medicine, including surgery, as is evinced by the detailed discussion of surgery in the *Sushruta Samhita*, one of Ayurveda's three canonical texts. But acute, life-threatening diseases such as cancer are now immediately referred to allopaths, while Ayurvedic physicians focus on chronic and non-life-threatening conditions. Dr. Sengupta never claimed that Ayurveda could cope with his cancer, and the herbal remedies he experimented with were meant to complement, rather than substitute for, biomedical interventions. This kind of tense accommodation of Ayurveda to allopathy has been documented by many anthropological studies (e.g., Nichter 1989; Langford 2002; Naraindas 2006). Relations between the Ayurvedic physician and his patients used to be on a reciprocal basis, and the notion of kinship ties still speaks to this. However, the rise of mass-manufactured Ayurvedic remedies—a rise that Dr. Sengupta was professionally promoting—is part of a continuing shift toward capitalist commodification through pharmaceuticalization (Banerjee 2008). In the following, I examine in more detail how these shifts are perceived by Ayurvedic physicians in Calcutta.

An Embodied Cosmology of Digestion

Ayurveda underwent many transformations, but the centrality of food and digestion remained a constant. Diet, digestion, and "clean bowels" were discussed in all the consultations I observed between Ayurvedic doctors and patients. Questions about digestion were a routine part of the diagnostic process, and recommendations about diet and the maintenance of daily routines were part of the therapy. When asked about the most frequent complaints that the patients come with, most of the doctors mentioned gastric complaints. In my interviews, I asked what is most important for health. All of them answered that digestion was always a starting point. Many doctors went into great detail about the nature of *agni* (fire), how digestion relates to the *tridosha* (three humors), or why keeping a healthy routine is necessary for health.

The importance of food and its proper digestion puts responsibility for health into the hands of the individual. Illness not only results from the inherent qualities of food but also depends on how the food is ingested. Proper timing is vital. Just as too much wood thrown at once into the fire weakens it, so does untimely and excessively "greedy" eating weaken the digestive fire in the belly. Eating and digestive hygiene were determinants of health over which people had most control, and with which they could achieve most for their own well-being. Ayurvedic care for one's digestion is a vital "technology of the self." To disregard the belly's internal cooking procedures imperils one's life. According to Caraka (ca. 200 CE), the "three pillars of health" are "food, sleep, and a chaste life" (Wujastyk 1998: 67). What Michel Foucault observed for the humoral medicine of Greco-Roman antiquity, namely, that medicine proposed "a way of living, a reflective mode of relation to oneself, to one's body, to food, to wakefulness and sleep, to the various activities, and to the environment" (Foucault 1986: 99), also holds true for Ayurveda (Ecks 2004). In Vagbhata's compilation (ca. 600 CE), the section on daily regimen ends with a poignant counsel for health care as a practice of self-care: "'My days and nights are passing by: what kind of person have I become?' A person who is always mindful of this will never taste suffering" (Wujastyk 1998: 262).

Calcutta *kavirajs* are not too bothered with the exact anatomical locations of digestion. *Agni* was always located in the belly, but some emphasized the "stomach," some the "liver," and some the "gall bladder." Anatomical vagueness notwithstanding, all the doctors agreed that good digestion is of central importance for good health: "Everything depends on the stomach: your ears, eyes, hair. If you upset your stomach, your *whole system* will be upset," said Dr. Barat. Views such as this appeared in all interviews. The doctors also spoke of digestion as a kind of heat or transformative fire in the belly. The images of "fire" and of "centrality" motivate the major metaphors for digestion. In keeping with the image of fire, a common metaphor for the belly was that of a "kitchen," in which the food is first cooked and then distributed to all parts of the body: "For a proper stomach, you need good digestive power (*hajam kara shakti*). In Ayurveda language, we say *agni*. How we cook our rice, with the fire, in the stomach we also have that type of fire," Dr. Sengupta explained. Like the household kitchen, the body's kitchen always had to be cleaned after cooking: "You must keep the kitchen clean. If the kitchen is clean, there is no problem," maintained Dr. Bhattacharya.

The Ayurvedic physiology of digestion has been discussed extensively, by scholars from both India (e.g., Dwarakanath 1967; Majumdar 1971; Ray 1937) and Western countries (e.g., Alter 1999: 52-55; Zimmermann 1987: 159-79, passim). Also, any textbook on Ayurveda will contain a longer discussion of digestion. From among the vast literature available, one of the most lucid is the commentary on the Ayurvedic Sanskrit canon by Dhirendra Nath Ray, a Calcutta *kaviraj* who wrote in the 1930s. According to Ray's *Principle of Tridosa in Ayurveda* (1937), digestion is a process in which ingested food is "cooked" and successively turned into finer and finer substances. The principle of cooking is heat, and so digestion depends on the proper working of the internal fires. There are altogether thirteen digestive fires within the body (1937: 90): seven *dhatvagni*, five *bhutagni*, and one *jatharagni*. First among these thirteen fires is the *jatharagni*, the first to receive food. The other internal fires come successively into play after the *jatharagni* has separated the seven different *dhatu* ("tissues") and five different *bhut* ("elements"). The digestive fire is one of four fires in the cosmos, along with "terrestrial" fire (e.g., burning wood), "celestial" fire (e.g., lightning), and "mineral" fire (e.g., the luster of gold). The principle of bodily fire is *pitta* ("bile"), one of the three *doshas* that govern all bodily processes. *Pitta* is associated with the belly, but is also present elsewhere in the body. Indeed, digestion is "located" all over the body. Moreover, the other two *doshas* are needed for digestion: *vayu* (wind) makes it possible that food and the various digestive products are moved from one place in the body to the next, and *kapha* (phlegm) softens solid food by moisturizing it (1937: 92). Still, the heat of *pitta* remains the defining aspect of digestion. The goal of digestion is to turn the "nourishing" parts of food into the seven bodily "tissues," the *dhatu*. From food, a finer substance called *rasa* is produced. From *rasa* comes blood, from blood comes flesh. Flesh is turned into fat, fat into bones, bones into marrow. The last and finest *dhatu* is semen (Sanskrit *sukra*; its female form remains ambiguous; Ray argues that it is *artava*, the ovum). In all stages of digestion, three parts are produced: the tissue itself, the "food" that "feeds" the next higher tissue, and a waste part. Each *dhatu* "nourishes" the next higher up the hierarchy of refinement: "Thus the *Rasa Dhatu*, derived from the digested food, serves as a food for blood, blood is food for flesh and so on; and in this way the normal condition of the body is continually kept up" (1937: 125). The only exception is semen, which is so refined that is does not have a waste part: "Just as no dross part comes out of the gold that has been burnt a thousand times" (1937: 127), so semen is pure essence. Incidentally, the fact that semen is the most refined *dhatu* led to the erroneous reduction of *dhat* to "male semen" in much of the psychiatric literature (Mukharji 2009: 218; Rashid 2007).

As can be glimpsed from Ray's discussion, Ayurveda pays little attention to the anatomical basis of digestion. The texts are only interested in the fluid transformations of the internal cooking process, and not in the functions of specific organs. The parts of the body only appear as temporary receptacles of the various juices and fluids. Only through the influence of allopathy's obsession with anatomical geography have Ayurvedic writers been pressed to be more precise about the distribution of labor among different organs, but these retrospective rationalizations remain vague. What counts is not organic function but "the opposite, namely, a medicine of properties and virtues, a medicine of metamorphoses" (Zimmermann 1987: 167; Wujastyk 2009: 206).

As a "medicine of virtues," Ayurveda emphasizes the aesthetically pleasing products of the digestive process: even if excrement results from it, digestion is first of all an alchemical *enhancement* of food. Only digestive disturbances, such as the improper cooking of food or the internal accumulation of dross, lead to aesthetically unpleasing results. The perfect belly turns food not into excrement but into the gold of semen. Gaston Bachelard (1967: 175), a philosopher of science, proposes that a metaphorical immediacy exists between digestion and all forms of alchemy: "It is above all in the practice of alchemy that the myth of digestion is extolled. One cannot help being astounded by the countless metaphors derived from digestion" (my translation).

If the belly is the place from where the nourishment of all tissues of the body flows, it becomes clear why proper digestion is so important for overall health. Bad digestion is the root cause of all problems: if *rasa* does not nourish the blood, all parts of the body are immediately affected. If blood does not nourish the flesh, one will suffer from weakness, and so on. One *dhatu* feeding the next one higher up is a chain: if one link is missing, the next higher up cannot be formed. That also means that sexual problems are primarily digestive problems, because semen is a product of digestion (Obeyesekere 1976). The same holds true for mental troubles: a disturbance of the mind can always be located in a fault of the *tridosha*.

Jonathan Parry (1989: 513) observed that the ideology of Hindu caste hierarchy is founded on a cosmology of flux: "Hindu society has often seen itself as engaged in an endless battle against impending chaos and disintegration, of which the ever-present danger of a disintegration and degeneration of the actor's own person is the most immediate and apprehensible manifestation." Instead of "normal" health, there is a wide spectrum of possibilities (Das 2010). Joseph Alter (1999) argues that Ayurveda is not focused on "curing illness" but on achieving "super-health." He suggests that the true Ayurvedic concept of health got obscured by biomedical ideas of "normal" health. In biomedicine, disease is a deviation from normal health, and the task of medicine is to restore the patient to a state of normality. If this idea is applied to Ayurveda, the misleading idea results that normal health is defined by the *tridosha* being "in balance," that disease is an "imbalance," and that the task of Ayurvedic medicine is to restore normal, balanced humors. But, as Alter points out, Ayurveda does not have a concept of "normal" balance: each person's *prakriti* (constitution) is different; no one ever has a perfect balance of all three humors; and the *tridosha* are always in flux. Alter sums up the Ayurvedic philosophy of "metaphysical fitness" as "a radical, often forceful, always struggling mode of metabolic, humoral body-building and cosmic self-improvement—a quest for equipoised perfection in an inherently and naturally imperfect world" (Alter 1999: 45). While Ayurveda may not support an idea of "normal" balance, it undoubtedly thinks about disease as caused by "too much" or "too little" heat/cold, moisture/dryness, and so on. Alter overstates his case, however, when he claims that the *entire* notion of "balance" is an alien import into Ayurveda from biomedicine.

Cosmic Decline

What Alter (1999: 45) describes as Ayurveda's "inherently and naturally imperfect world" must be seen expanded by notions of cosmic time. Ayurvedic physiology has a bipolar view of health: extreme optimism and extreme pessimism always lie close to each other. Optimism and pessimism are temporal: they are both about how the future compares to the past. My conversations with Calcutta *kaviraj* doctors always veered toward the way the discipline's present state compares to its past and its future.

These temporalities wavered between historical time and cosmo-mythical time. A pessimistic view of the possibility of achieving "super-health" can already be found in the Sanskrit texts, which deny that excellent health is achievable in this day and age. Already in the sixth century CE, Vagbhata pointed out that people's digestion is inevitably faulty: "People in this degenerate modern age have poor digestion, they are short, and they lack strength" (Wujastyk 1998: 312). Caraka contains an intriguing reading of the cosmological myth of the four world ages, which interprets the gradual decline of the cosmos from the Golden Age downward to the current age of the *kaliyuga* from the point of view of Ayurveda (Wujastyk 1998: 84). In the Golden Age, Caraka tells us, humankind was as full of energy as the gods, extremely pure and of broad powers. Their eyesight was so powerful that they could see the gods, and everything that the gods can see, with their own eyes. The fall from grace and the decay of the cosmos came, according to this Ayurvedic text, through greed and overeating:

> But as the Golden Age waned, some well-supplied people received too much, and because of that their bodies became heavy. Because of this corpulence, they became tired. From tiredness came apathy, from apathy accumulation, from accumulation, ownership. And ownership led to the appearance of greed in that Golden Age. Then, in the Silver Age, greed led to perfidy, from perfidy came lying, and from lying proceeded lust,

anger, pride, hatred, cruelty, violence, fear, suffering, grief, worry, impetuosity, and so on. Then, in the Silver Age, [. . .] people's bodies began not to be as well-maintained as they used to be by their diet and lifestyle, both of which were losing one quarter of their goodness. Their bodies, besieged by fire and wind, were soon under attack by disease, fever, and so forth. Then, living creatures gradually lost their vitality. (Wujastyk 1998: 85)

In each of the four cosmic ages, one quarter of perfection is lost. In the *kaliyuga*, the current and last of the four ages, almost none of the perfection of the earlier times has been preserved. In other words, world health is cosmically doomed. For Caraka, human bodies have, from birth onward, less goodness than is necessary for good health. The food they are eating is deficient, and they are prone to even worse habits of greedy eating than their ancestors. Poor digestion, short bodies, and short life spans amalgamate into an all-pervading decline of individuals and society at large. Mental health is part of this atrophy: greedy eating and destructive thought patterns go together. Ayurveda postulates an immediate relation between the "outer" world and the "inner" world of the *prakriti*. If the outside is complicated, then the patient's constitution will also be complicated. If the outer world is spoiled, the inner world will be spoiled as well.

Caraka-style images of perdition appeared prominently in Ayurvedic doctors' reflections on India's incomplete transition to modernity and future possibilities of health. All the doctors I talked to considered the modern era as one of degradation and decline. Pollution pervaded water, air, and soil, spoiled digestive powers, and confused people's minds.

Dr. Bhattacharya, a seventy-year-old physician from an old Ayurveda family (a university chair in Ayurvedic medicine at Banaras Hindu University is named after his grandfather), elaborated on the theme of cosmic and human decline. According to him, the authors of the Ayurvedic canon warned against the noxious effects of environmental pollution. The definition of "pollution" they developed was complex enough to be applied to the modern-day situation, since not only the "physical" environment was taken into account but also sociopolitical factors, which Dr. Bhattacharya called "human pollution":

In the classic texts of Ayurveda, since thousands and thousands of years ago, our *Rishis* [mythical sages] warned the people about pollution of water, air, sound, smell. And last but not least human pollution, what modern science is thinking about now. If water is polluted, what are the possible diseases that may come? Two: If air is polluted, what are the possible diseases? Third, stinking smells are injurious to the nerves. Fourth, they have told: tremendous sounds affect nerves. Fifth: Human pollution. Whenever the king, the top person, the top of the administration, becomes corrupted, the lower workers also become polluted day by day. From the top to the lowest, all the people become corrupt. Society itself becomes polluted. That leads to complete destruction. Caraka has told so.

Based on an idiosyncratic combination of Caraka and Einstein, Dr. Bhattacharya developed his own maxim to understand the world: "I tell you my formula: $e = mc^2$." "E" stood for "environment," "m" for "man," and "c^2" for the immense importance of "cultural concepts." For him, environmental degradation was caused by overpopulation and by a culture of exploitation. As for Caraka, the root of all degradation was "greed," which Dr. Bhattacharya defined as abuse of nature (*prakriti*) in the broadest sense. Humans could live happily if they based their daily routines on the principles of nature: "She is the best philosopher, the best friend, the best guide." When people started to exploit nature "by means of force, by means of machines," they started to dig their own graves: "Fifteen civilizations have already been wiped out from this world, all for greed."

The current era was the most exploitative so far. Nuclear bombs and genetically modified food ("everything hybrid!") were typical of human greed. Human pollution also showed itself in social unrest: "Everywhere is murder, nepotism, corruption, despotism." The current age was that of the *goondaraj*, the "rule of bandits." Violent clashes between Hindu and Muslim mobs were part of the picture. The distance between the rich and the poor was increasing day by day, while generosity was decreasing. Dr. Bhattacharya also accused modern medicine of having a share in this. The fees charged by allopathic doctors were too high for poor people, and the doctors were distorting people's beliefs about health and healing. Earlier, people knew that warm water with *tulsi*

leaves was a good remedy against a cold. But now the doctors were telling the patients that ideas like this were wrong, and were making them
pay for expensive synthetic drugs instead. Advertising deepened public
confusion: "Newspaper, television, computers, all the channels, all force
you to take capsules." Greedy politicians, in India and elsewhere in the
world, helped to promote allopathy's wicked schemes.

Dr. Bhattacharya went on to explain how pollution and digestion are
related. Along with coughs and colds, breathing troubles and allergies,
most of his patients complained about bad digestion. Water pollution
was one of the immediate causes. Not only was the water polluted by
bacteria and toxins, but it was also "too hard" for the stomach, especially
water from deep tube wells that were drilled to accommodate millions
of people. Social class influenced how much a patient was affected by
this. The rich could afford water filters and bottled drinks, whereas the
poor drank untreated water. Yet the rich also suffered because of their
artificial lifestyle and an excess of "hot" food: "Some people nowadays
take four eggs a day! But this energy is not spent through movement
or work. There's too much within, and soon the explosion will come."
The younger generation suffered from stress. Worst off were children
subjected to too much academic pressure. Religious affiliation also had
an effect on health. Dr. Bhattacharya thought that Muslims were particularly vulnerable to disease because they were eating too much *tamasik* (impure) foods, such as beef: "Their whole nature becomes *tamasik*,
their tolerance is less, irritable, patience is less, high alert!" Earlier generations of Hindu Bengalis followed a cool, wholesome diet, but nowadays, they were eating as much meat and fried foods as Muslims: "Bengalis have also become *tamasik*. Their bodies have become toxic."

Human pollution resulted in *kavirajs* not being able to use the full
scope of Ayurvedic treatments. For example, *panchakarma*, which aims
at a thorough purging of impurities from the patient's body, could not be
applied as fully as in the past (see Zimmermann 1992). Bengali bodies
were too weak to cope with the kind of heavy purges prescribed in the
old texts. When purges were administered at all, they were administered
only with the lowest possible force. Although patients were weakened
through the corrupting influence of modernity, their bodies were more
in need of a thorough clear-out than ever before. "Purifying the body is
essential. Make him simple, *then* treat him. Then the medicine will work

very elaborately, very swiftly. If the system is cleared, the medicine will be absorbed." The lingering side effects of allopathy were difficult to deal with without a purge. Ayurvedic drugs *would* work in a pure and simple body, but in the modern, complicated, polluted body, they are weak.

No one could escape the overwhelming toxicity of the environment. There is no clean water, no clean air, no protection against noxious smells and deafening noises. There is no protection against overpopulation and the incompetence of politicians. And Ayurvedic physicians have lost confidence in their own expertise: "Whatever we say, we don't believe. Whatever we believe, we don't do." In an era of decline, Ayurvedic medicine could not thrive. Allopathy could overpower other medical traditions because it exploited people's ever-declining health and everyone's futile yearning for cures. Yet the curing powers of Ayurveda are declining along with the decline of nature. Dr. Bhattacharya held that, quite simply, Ayurvedic remedies could not fix the ills modernity had unleashed.

A Visit to the Head Office

In the *kavirajs'* metaphorical language, the centrality of digestion was compared to good governance. For example, one physician likened the stomach to Calcutta's Writers Building, the labyrinthine headquarters of the West Bengal State Government: "The stomach is like Writers Building: it affects everything," said Dr. Kar. Petitions and official documents enter Writers Building, disappear for a while from view, and eventually reemerge stamped and transformed. Likewise, the belly takes in food and redistributes it. If Writers Building works too slowly, accumulates "undigested" files, and makes mistakes in their redistribution, then the whole state of West Bengal will be badly affected. If Writers Building is corrupt, lazy, and incompetent, then everyone will suffer (Calcuttans see Writers Building as a symbol of Kafkaesque bureaucratic ineptitude). Another doctor compared the liver to the body's "head office" (using the English term), on which the proper functioning of the "branch offices" depended: "First thing we have to see: How is your *head office?* If your head office is *fit,* your *branch offices* will also be *fit. Your head office is the liver,*" explained Dr. Datta.

That the liver is described as the "head" office, rather than the brain or mind, fits with Ayurveda's primary focus on metabolism. In turn,

"psychological" symptoms tend to be traced back first to digestive problems. This has been documented in many ethnographies. For example,
Mark Nichter (2001) shows that Ayurvedic physicians (*vaidyas*) in Karnataka treat patients' complaints about stress, tension, and the fast life of
modernity foremost as a disturbance of digestion. Throughout his study,
digestive "dis-ease," above all indigestion, emerges as the main problem patients present to the *vaidyas*. Indigestion is, for Nichter, "both a
central trope for defective modernization, as well as a bodily response
to environmental (physical as well as social) degradation and change"
(2001: 102). In one case (Nichter 2001: 89-92), a Brahmin patient who
is being treated by an allopath for chronically high "BP" (hypertension)
comes and complains about indigestion, *gas*, lack of appetite, mental
weakness, and sleeplessness. The patient feels that these are side effects
of the medicines he is taking, and he asks the Ayurvedic healer to give
him herbal remedies to boost his digestive power. Since the patient also
complains about various psychosocial tensions, such as his difficulties marrying off his daughter, Nichter suggests that the patient could
also have been treated as a psychosomatic patient. Instead of giving
medicine, should not the social and economic affairs of the patient be
changed? In response to Nichter's question, the *vaidya* responds that
Ayurveda sees the patient's stomach trouble as the "root cause" of all the
patient's other troubles. Nichter quotes the *vaidya* saying that any psychological problem first needs a digestive treatment: "To break the cycle
of undigested food and undigested, uncontrolled thoughts, I must first
treat the stomach. This is the root cause of the problems" (2001: 90).
The social context of the patient's digestive complaints is not rejected,
but in a hierarchy of priorities, the stomach comes first. One has to start
with the stomach and work "outward" from there. Ayurvedic remedies
should first "clean out" the patient's guts and restore strong digestion.
An improvement in the patient's mental state would occur immediately
upon improvement in the state of the belly, and even social relations
could only get better by improvements in digestion: "Achieving good
digestion would lead to better thinking capacity, self-control, a more
balanced emotional state, and self-confidence: all of which would result
in improved social relations in his household" (Nichter 2001: 92). For
Nichter, the Ayurvedic healer considers sociopolitical problems in his
diagnosis. However, therapeutic recommendations reveal, to Nichter,

that contemporary Ayurveda pursues a strategy of accommodation vis-à-vis the ills of modernity. Instead of going to the sociopolitical "root causes" of sickness, Ayurveda limits itself to more or less superficial cures of symptoms. Ayurveda acknowledges the ills of modernization, such as the overuse of chemical fertilizers to treat worn-out fields, and the overuse of allopathic drugs to treat worn-out bodies. But its critique did not become political. Instead, Ayurveda "co-opted" these ills to sell its own medications.

Nichter's findings from Karnataka hold true for Calcutta *kavirajs*, except that it is too strong to say that they "co-opt" defective modernization for commercial reasons. Instead, the Calcutta physicians claim that the kinds of medicines at their disposal cannot have effects on the mind without transforming a patient's digestion first.

Ayurvedic notions of *tridosha* and metabolism also made the Calcutta *kavirajs* distinguish between physically based mental health problems and unfounded whining. They veered back and forth between "true" physical reasons that could be tackled with medications and "mere" psychological suffering that was only amenable to talking and convincing. For example, when I asked one of the doctors, Dr. Sen, about the relations between Ayurveda and religious beliefs, he reflected on how he had first seen his father, a famous Bengali *kaviraj*, use placebos:

> Once there was a patient, he came with a stomach complaint. My father gave medicine. But I saw that it was not stomach medicine, so I asked him: "Why?" My father said: "He does not have a stomach problem! He's suffering from a mental problem." Then, fifteen days later, the patient said: "I'm alright." Mind and illness are very much related.

He went on to say that to spend time talking to patients and to recognize their difficulties was the best way to give them a "mental boost." They got "immediate relief" simply from seeing a doctor who knew them and understood them. When I asked if he also prescribed placebos for psychological problems, he said that he always aimed at improving overall health, and that meant giving medicines for a "fit and healthy liver." When a patient is feeling weak, he gives "hunger medicine" (*khider osudh*) to increase appetite. Whatever the medicine,

most important was that a medicine is prescribed at all: the comfort-
ing effect of being given a drug could not be replaced by any talking,
not least because patients expected to get medicated: "If you don't give
anything, they won't go away. So, you give something, and they feel they
are taking medicine for it, automatically the illness will go away." Dr.
Sen also advised his patients to perform their daily drug intake like a
religious ritual: "Take medicine, and salute God first. That helps. It's
psychological."

The *kavirajs* gave nearly identical answers to the question of how to
handle patients "psychologically." Many estimated that 10 or 20 percent of patients were "psychological" in the sense of suffering "without
any illness" and that Ayurvedic medicines could not help much with
this kind of hypochondria. Ayurvedic notions made them distinguish
between physically based mental health and unfounded whining. They
used the ambiguous notion of "hypochondria" that encapsulates the
shift of meaning that occurred in Europe during the nineteenth century. The term "hypochondria" is a composite of *hypo* (Greek "under")
and *khondros* ("breastbone"), meaning simply "the guts below the ribs."
In various formulations, from the Greeks up to the nineteenth century,
medical science held that the viscera of liver, gall bladder, and spleen
were the seat of melancholy (see Burton 2001 [1621]). It was only from
the late nineteenth century onward, when humoral medicine started to
be debunked, that "hypochondria" came to mean "unfounded belief"
in being ill and a persistent anxiety about one's health (*Shorter Oxford
English Dictionary* 2007: 1310).

Like the doctors interviewed by Nichter in Karnataka, Calcutta *kavirajs* also focus on belly and digestion. They recognize that there are
some forms of "psychological" suffering that cannot be clearly retraced
to a digestive disturbance, but beyond digestive aids, general immunity
boosters, and the placebo effect, they feel they had no drugs that could
remedy the problem:

> Out of ten [patients], one has psychological problems, everyday. They
> come and ask for medicines, without any illness. I understand their
> problems and I give placebos. I give them *amloki*, it's made of *amla*. I
> say: "This is a medicine for your problem." I don't say the name of the
> powder, I just give the powder. If he knew the name of the medicine, he

would not come to me. [. . .] Psychological problems we cannot cure. With the medicine we can control, but not cure. With digestion powders and tablets, you can keep it under control. The patient may say "I have this, that," but we know that there is no problem. (Dr. Barat)

The only way of dealing with "pure" psychological troubles was to go to the mind itself. Keeping one's mind "cool" was vital for good health. The proper routines of life could only be maintained if the mind was free of unresolved tensions and unfulfilled cravings. Dr. Sengupta's belief that his *moner jor* had allowed him to bounce back from his cancer is typical. Many of the Ayurvedic doctors pointed out the health benefits of doing Yogic exercises, both bodily postures (*yogashan*) and mental concentration (*moner yog*). One of the doctors (Dr. Nag) took an additional diploma course in Yoga cure, another doctor (Dr. Ghosal) kept a large image of his Yoga guru in his consultation room, and another (Dr. Barat) demonstrated a few Yogic postures to me during the interview. Thanks to Yoga, the sages of the mythical past could cleanse their minds and stomachs in ways that were unattainable to modern people: "They could see themselves, they could see what is going on inside. We have read so many stories of the sages: they take the stomach out of the body, wash it with the fresh water of the hill, and put it back inside. So many sages could do that. Really! They lived at least 500 years" (Dr. Nag).

As Caraka's compendium points out, the three pillars of good health are food, sleep, and a chaste life. True health can only come from a style of living that is mindful of the effects of every action and thought. Disrespect for these pillars brings disease. There are three modes of misuse: overuse, underuse, and abuse, and these misuses can occur in relation to time, to the senses, and to action (Wujastyk 1998: 67-69). Time, or "transformation," can lead to disease by giving too much or too little cold, heat, and rain. The five senses of sight, hearing, smell, taste, and touch can be mishandled. For example, it is an overuse of sight to look at bright objects for too long; an underuse to keep one's eyes closed for too long; an abuse to look at hideous and frightening objects. Actions of speech, mind, and body can also be misused. An abuse of speech, for example, includes "betrayal, lying, inappropriateness, quarreling, or words that are nasty, disconnected, impolite, or harsh." An abuse of the mind comes from "fear, grief, anger, greed, delusion, pride, envy, and holding false beliefs" (Wujastyk 1998: 69). These three sources of disease lead to three types of disease: "internal" are diseases of humoral imbalance; "invasive" diseases come from creatures, poison, wounds, and so on; and "mental" diseases are brought about "by not getting what one wants, or getting what one does not want" (Wujastyk 1998: 70).

The Sanskrit texts' emphasis on leading a life mindful of the proper use of one's senses, actions, and thoughts was echoed by all Calcutta *kavirajs*. Dr. Ghosal summed this up beautifully with the saying "*tumi er osudh acho*": "*You* are the medicine." "Stress" and "tension" should be avoided always, because they produce indigestion, blood sugar, thyroid, ulcers, and countless other troubles. The excessive heat generated by tension diminishes the body's youthful coolness and moisture, making it hot and dry (*tension dry kore dite pare*). To keep mind and body cool, one should not worry about what tomorrow will bring: "Don't think anything in advance. Don't think on Sunday about what you will do on Monday." One should keep oneself moderately busy and always find time for relaxation with friends and family. If trouble arises, one should take it easy: "If anything comes up, take it casual. Don't take it too serious. Only then will you be normal. For this there is no medicine. You *can* solve yourself! *You* are the medicine." Since no medication can truly keep the mind cool, many *kavirajs* thought it was wrong of allopaths to prescribe psychotropic drugs that only put people to sleep at the cost of heavy side effects: "What the doctors give for these things are just sleeping pills, it's just a drug that badly affects your body, with side effects and all. [. . .] There is no medicine for tension, this is all nonsense. You have to solve it yourself."

Sex and the Stomach

Until the 1980s, Ayurvedic manufacturers specialized in two types of products: digestives and aphrodisiacs (Bode 2008: 34). Since then, the manufacturers' product range has been greatly expanded, but Ayurvedic remedies remain popularly seen as dedicated to digestive and sexual troubles. This is no coincidence: sex and the stomach are closely related.

In the list of complaints that patients most often present to Calcutta's Ayurvedic physicians, issues around sex feature prominently: "Today, love problems, sex problems, are vital. [. . .] Suppressed desire has become the main cause of illness today," Dr. Sen explained. Some of them said that half of their patients came to them for help with sexual dysfunctions: "Fifty percent of patients are *sex-wallah*," according to Dr. Barat. Along with male "semen" problems, menstrual problems were a similarly common complaint.

As we have seen, Ayurveda sees an immediate relationship between semen and digestion. Semen is not just any other bodily substance produced from food, but it is the quintessence of the whole process, the "purest gold" (Ray 1937: 127). In turn, anxieties about the weakening effects of "semen loss" are a mainstay in ethnographies of Indian body concepts (e.g., Alter 1997, 1999; Bottéro 1991; Carstairs 1957; Parry 1989). Described as *dhat* (from *dhatu*) in the psychiatric literature, it is also South Asia's most discussed culture-bound syndrome (e.g., Jadhav 2007; Sumathipala, Siribaddana, and Bhugra 2004). For Calcutta's Ayurvedic doctors, semen is the most precious *dhatu* and, as such, was often equated to gold, or money:

> If you waste all your money in the bank, in the future you will face problems. Semen is like that. If you waste your semen, you will have problems. [. . .] If you waste it at an early stage, you'll have problems. If you really waste it, you will fall sick, your physical fitness will be less. That will affect health and brain. [. . .] Through proper food we can regain it. But after regaining, you have to hold on to it. (Dr. Datta)

All the Calcutta *kavirajs* I interviewed mentioned that semen is the most refined product of the digestive process. Ayurveda's expertise in this field gave it better remedies against sexual problems than those available in allopathy. Therapy consisted usually in a combination of dietary advice and Ayurvedic medications. In simple cases, digestive medicines were sufficient; in more complex cases, special sex remedies were advised:

> My treatment for sex problems: If patients ask me directly for a specific medicine, I give. If asked for advice, I first give stomach medicines, and see what happens. Only if they don't work, I give special sex medicine. Or I ask about complaints other than sex complaints. If there are absolutely no stomach or liver problems, then I might give sex medicine right away. (Dr. Kar)

Advertisements for tonics and tablets that promise to "remove tiredness" and to stimulate sexual powers thanks to "ancient Ayurvedic formulas" appear widely in daily newspapers. Across India, Ayurvedic
advertising talks of "vigor," but what is really meant is the distillation of
the most powerful *dhatu* (Bode 2008: 34). The squandering of semen,
digestion's finest product, causes a plethora of diseases. Since semen is
like the gold of the alchemists, gold is usually added to Ayurvedic sex
medicines, and "Gold" appears in many brand names for sex drugs. For
example, Vita Ex Gold is a best-selling product from Baidyanath Ltd.
(founded in Calcutta in 1917) that promises to "recharge, reactivate,
refresh your vitality and vigour" and to "increase your pleasure and
heighten your happiness for a longer time." For the same reasons, other
"potent" metals can be added, especially silver and mercury. In turn,
gold and other precious metals are used to "fortify" other health tonics, such as Himani Sona Chandi Chyawanprash, produced by Emami
Ltd. A disturbance of the digestive process is not the only link among
food, digestion, and semen. The model of the progressive metamorpho-
sis of food into semen is about the transformation of one "juice" into
another. Part of this model is the notion of *vayu* ("wind") as the principle of internal movement. The body is a container in which substances
are carried from one place to another. For movement, there must be
different degrees of "pressure" inside the body. The pressure exerted by
vayu is healthy and necessary as long as it occurs in moderation. If the
flow of substances in the body is out of balance, then too much pressure
builds up. The "gross" symptoms of this are burping, farting, and vomiting. A disturbance of internal pressures also has more subtle consequences, and one of them is semen loss. Anyone who suffers from *gas* is
at risk of losing precious semen, since too much pressure forces it out of
the body. This rule also applies to all other states of excessive pressure.
For example, constipation leads patients to strain themselves, and this
overexertion can cause semen loss:

> If your stool becomes hard, and you force yourself, give pressure, that
> will affect your body. There is *semen* in your body, if that comes out,
> that is very bad for health. *Automatically* that *semen* will come out with
> the pressure. So you will have a sexual problem, lots of problems. [. . .]

If *semen* becomes liquid, then all the power (*shakti*) comes out of your body. (Dr. Barat)

In his writings on sexuality in antiquity, Michel Foucault holds that Greco-Roman understandings of the body do not apply "moral" distinctions between "good" and "bad" behaviors, but embed sex in a nonmoral practice of bodily self-care (see Alter 1997). Ayurveda shares this view: the keeping or losing of semen is not a question of morality but a question of physiology. For example, Ayurvedic doctors in Calcutta commonly mentioned the dangers of masturbation, but always in relation to the health risks of losing semen, not in respect to morality. When I asked one of the physicians whether masturbation is "bad" (*kharap*), he questioned whether "bad" was the correct register of evaluation: "I wouldn't say 'good' or 'bad.' But you have to eat *sattvik* [cool, wholesome] food. You need to control yourself. Then twice in a month is not a factor. If a person does it many times, more than once a day, he will break and fall" (Dr. Datta).

For "modern" people, this kind of self-control was difficult or impossible to achieve. According to one *kaviraj*, bodily degradation through semen loss was a typical feature of modern times. Modern people got married much later in life than the earlier generations. If boys only married at the age of twenty-five or later, they "obviously" fell sick from masturbation. Bollywood movies, with all their hip-swinging action, perverted young people's minds and made it hard for them to keep their heads cool. He explained that an increasing number of his patients consisted of young boys who could not control themselves: "This is all because of these *TV-wallah* and *picture-wallah*, they make them mad" (Dr. Bhadari).

How to Diagnose "Maximum Complicated" Patients

To diagnose illness, classic Ayurveda draws evidence from different sources: direct perception of the patient with all bodily senses (sight, touch, smell, hearing, taste); logical inference; analogical reasoning; and recourse to authoritative texts. Calcutta physicians underlined three types of examination as standard: seeing (*darshana*), touching (*sparshana*), and questioning (*prashna*): "There are three types of things: looking at the patient, questioning, and then touching. Then we get the picture" (Dr. Bhadari). Among these three, seeing and questioning were the most straightforward techniques. Seeing the patient's face and body language was the initial step of any diagnosis. The most skilled physicians, especially those of the older generation, had such fine sensory skills that seeing a patient was sufficient for a proper diagnosis: "For the masters, seeing is diagnosis enough" (Dr. Nag).

But the *kavirajs* also agreed that the heyday of Ayurvedic diagnosing lay in the past. Due to changed diets and daily routines, people's *prakriti* (natural constitution, disposition) had changed. Earlier, Ayurvedic physicians could quickly determine which *dosha* was too dominant or too weak. Nowadays, however, it was hard to diagnose the *prakriti* properly: "We cannot diagnose in this way [anymore]. Because nowadays, the *prakriti* of patients is complicated. Single *prakriti* are not available nowadays. People are maximum complicated" (Dr. Nag).

This complicated, tense, and overmedicated patient is difficult to diagnose through Ayurveda's most emblematic method of examination: feeling the pulse (*nadi pariksha*). Patients usually expect the *kaviraj* to perform a pulse examination, since it is this technique that sets Ayurveda apart from other medical practices. By way of examining the pulse, the physician tries to determine both the patient's current sickness and her general constitution. Skillful physicians could even discern when and how a patient would die: "My grandfather could tell: 'You will die within three months'" (Dr. Bhattacharya). This magical strength of the Ayurvedic pulse exam to predict the future drives the narrative plot of a famous Bengali novel, *Arogyaniketan*, by Tarashankara Bandyopadhyaya (1998). The scope of the pulse diagnosis is much broader than a simple exam of pulse rate or blood pressure. *Nadi pariksha* was based on orally transmitted know-how and years of practical experience. The written sources on how to read the pulse tend to be cryptic, and are more *aide memoires* for the skilled practitioner than how-to manuals for the uninitiated. Here is, for example, an instruction from Sharngadhara's compendium (ca. 1300 CE): "When the wind is inflamed, the pulse produces the gait of a leech or snake. When choler is inflamed, the gait is that of a sparrow-hawk, crow, or frog. When phlegm is inflamed, the gait is that of a swan, or pigeon. When all the humors are inflamed, the gait is that of a bush quail, partridge, or bustard-quail" (Wujastyk 1998: 315). Today, the pulse examination is considered to be the quintessentially

"Ayurvedic" form of diagnosis and one of its most potent ways of creating "faith" in patients (Langford 1999: 39). Ironically, however, *nadi pariksha* is not mentioned in any of the canonical works by Sushruta, Caraka, or Vagbhata. Sanskritists speculate that the procedure was introduced from China after 1300 CE (Gutschow 1997: 3; Wujastyk 1998: 304).

All the Calcutta physicians I talked to were convinced of the astounding powers of the pulse examination, but most of them added that nowadays its uses were limited. All *kavirajs* practiced it, yet all said that they could not rely on it. There were many reasons for the decline of the pulse examination. Modern college education, which relied on textbook learning rather than on hands-on training through a senior *kaviraj*, gave little opportunity to practice *nadi pariksha*: "The main process is pulse-taking. [. . .] But to be very frank, we were not really taught that way in college" (Dr. Gangopadhyay). The pulse examination needed concentration and tranquility, but today's physicians were too restless and greedy to give sufficient time. This point was also underlined by Dr. Bhattacharya, who blamed the decline of the pulse examination on the doctors' "greed" for maximum money from a maximum number of patients: "If you don't have the concentration, conception, silence, tolerance, you can't do Ayurveda." Finally, the patients' *prakriti* was now often too complicated to feel through the pulse.

Ayurvedic diagnostics were now inseparably tied to allopathic diagnostics (see Nichter 2008: 99). One *kabiraj* even said there were no substantial differences in diagnostics anymore. What distinguished Ayurveda from biomedicine were solely the medicines prescribed, not the diagnostic techniques that led to the prescription:

> There is no difference in diagnosing the patients between us and them. Only the medicine is different. *Urine check, stool check,* everything is done in the *lab.* When we see that a patient is not in a good condition, we ask them to get more tests from the *lab.* The *lab* is all one (*sab eki*). We use it, allopathy uses it, others use it. (Dr. Datta)

The *kavirajs* pointed out that the use of laboratory reports had become an important part of their college education. While such educational "co-habitation" (Naraindas 2006: 2666) of Ayurveda and biomedicine created many epistemological confusions, in terms of diagnostics it was, according to Calcutta physicians, all positive. Today's difficulties of diagnosing patients by traditional means were offset by the advances of "scientific" testing. Dr. Datta's expression that "the *lab* is all one (*sab eki*)" resonates with Bengali notions of religious pluralism. When asked about differences between different religious creeds, Bengalis often refer to Ramakrishna, who said that "God is all one." Hindus may call God *bhagavan*, Muslims may call God "Allah," and Christians may refer to "the Lord," but they all referred to the same Supreme Being. Some of the doctors made this connection explicitly: "Ramakrishna Dev said: one goal, different paths. For each taste a different medical system" (Dr. Bhattacharya). All differences merely existed on the surface: "Everybody is under God's blessing. That's why I think that allopathy, homeopathy, Ayurveda, and all medicines are the same. Hindus talk about their gods, Christians about Jesus, Muslims about Allah, but human is one, and God is one. If you bring in artificial separations, you cannot develop anything" (Dr. Samanta).

There was more common ground among the different medical systems in the field of diagnostics than in any other field. Of course, the Ayurvedic doctors' appreciation of laboratory tests was also a matter of pragmatism. Since most chronic patients resort to allopathy first, then to homeopathy, and only thereafter to Ayurveda (if at all), *kavirajs* often do not need to send their patients away for laboratory testing: the patients have done all the tests when they enter the Ayurvedic practice. If the laboratories are available, if patients are willing to pay for them, and if many have already passed through a series of tests, then "why not make use of it?" (Dr. Chattopadhyay).

Moreover, patients had become so accustomed to allopathic diagnostics that they often demanded that they be performed to make sure that the full picture emerges: "Patients are not satisfied with pulse-taking only, not even in the villages. They demand pathological tests," explained Dr. Ghosal. Many of the doctors also mentioned a growing consumer consciousness among patients. In case of misdiagnosis (and wrong treatment resulting from it), patients might bring legal charges. With the Ayurvedic way of diagnosing patients, no "scientific" forms of documentation existed. With laboratory results, however, the doctor had written proof of the correctness of his treatments: "There's a consumer act. A patient may complain if he is treated in the wrong way. So doctors nowadays take the lab test. They say: 'This is the information, so I treat that way'" (Dr. Nag).

Even if the doctors believed that tests were useful, they also pointed out that they only sent patients to the labs when they deemed it necessary. The main objection against lab tests was that they were costly. The poor were often not sent to labs at all, but only examined by the *kaviraj* himself: "As much as I can, I do the diagnosis, I avoid the lab, because it is very expensive. They would run away from me! So I diagnose myself, and keep my patients" (Dr. Ghosal).

The most common criterion in support of diagnostic tests was, however, that they were "scientific," and transcended the boundaries of different medical systems. The doctors did not have a problem with the *lingua franca* of medical diagnostics being biomedical. I had expected to find orthodox proponents of Ayurveda who perceive allopathic tests as distorting in relation to their practice. Not one of the doctors I interviewed, however, raised any objections against the tests on the grounds that they belonged to a different scientific paradigm or were incompatible with their own tradition. I also asked them if there is some kind of "Ayurvedic" way of reading allopathic test results, for example, that white cell counts could also be interpreted in terms of *tridosha* or other Ayurvedic notions. This was not the case either.

How Ayurveda and allopathy can be translated into each other is a long-standing concern. During the twentieth century, a great number of Ayurvedic writers tried to build terminological bridges between Ayurveda and allopathy. Many argued that all differences between Ayurveda and biomedicine could be overcome through careful translation. A famous example is Dwarakanath's *Digestion and Metabolism in Ayurved*, published in Calcutta in 1963 (see Leslie 1992: 190-92; Zimmermann 1987: 162). Dwarakanath presents an intricate analysis of Ayurvedic theories of digestion, and translates Sanskrit terms into allopathic terms. For example, the various forms of *pitta* are translated as forms of "digestive enzymes," *pran vayu* becomes "oxygen," and so on. This postulate of commensurability also informs the branding of mass-manufactured drugs. For example, Himalaya Drug Company (2012) describes the action of the liver tonic Liv.52—one of India's best-selling medications across all products from allopathy, homeopathy, and Ayurveda—as follows: "Liv.52 restores the functional efficiency of the

liver by protecting the hepatic parenchyma and promoting hepatocel-
lular regeneration. The antiperoxidative activity of Liv.52 prevents the
loss of functional integrity of the cell membrane, maintains cytochrome
P-450." Here, Ayurvedic diagnostics are supplanted by a biomedical
language steeped in "molecularization" (Chadarevian and Kamminga
1998; Rose 2007).

Almost all the doctors supported "integrationism" against Sanskritic
"purism" (see Leslie 1992). Their argument in favor of integration was
the same as that in favor of diagnostic tests: even if there were different
paths, there is only "one goal." Scientists might use different languages
to express their findings, but science itself was universal: "It's a global
village. [. . .] Scientific language is *one* language. *Every* action in our
body is a chemical exchange, *only* a chemical exchange" (Dr. Samanta).
In any case, they said, Sanskrit texts were rarely drawn on by today's
kavirajs. Although many of my respondents were well-versed in Sanskrit and fluently quoted original *slokas*, several of them mentioned that
they only had a minimal knowledge of Sanskrit. Following the introduction of standardized, state-supervised curricula, first-hand knowledge of Sanskrit texts had been increasingly marginalized. In Calcutta,
there is no more confrontation between integrationists and purists in
the way that Leslie (1992) described it for earlier decades. Most practitioners now rely either on Bengali or on English translations of Sanskrit
texts, or on textbooks written by twentieth-century authors. These textbooks may not be as authentic as the Sanskrit texts, but they seem sufficient for daily practice. Even if the doctors learned a bit of Sanskrit in
college, there was "no profit" (Dr. Gangopadhyay) in it today. Patients
were not interested in Sanskrit diagnostics, but only in getting effective
treatment.

Defining Ayurvedic "Drugs"

If Ayurvedic and biomedical diagnostics have become so deeply
enmeshed with each other that they seem to be "all one" (*sab eki*), then
it could be expected that the decisive marker of difference would be the
prescribed treatments: "Only the medicine is different," as Dr. Datta suggested. The closer one looks at Ayurvedic medicines, however, the more
blurry become the boundaries between them and biomedical drugs.

Ayurvedic "drugs" are not drugs in the biomedical sense. Ayurvedic pharmacopoeias never underwent the kind of transformation that occurred in biomedicine between the eighteenth and nineteenth centuries, when new laboratory methods purged the materia medica of two-thirds of its previously used substances and when mass-produced compounds from the chemical industries came to dominate the market (Huwer 2008: 32-35). In the following, I want to disentangle the different meanings of "Ayurvedic medicines" and show why it is so difficult to define them.

Indian laws seeking to define what counts as an "Ayurvedic" remedy both reflect and extend the classificatory conundrum. First, the Indian government understands as Ayurvedic any medicine that is made by a physician who holds a bachelor's degree in Ayurvedic medicine and surgery (BAMS). Ayurvedic physicians in private practice are free to compound their own remedies in any way they see fit in accordance with their learning, and there is no state agency to control the quality, safety, or efficacy of these preparations. The Indian state only regulates remedies mass-produced by companies. There are three basic types of medications: classic formulations, over-the-counter remedies, and prescription-only drugs. However, as Maarten Bode (2008) argues, the decision about how a product is classified is not in the hands of Indian regulatory authorities but in the hands of Ayurvedic manufacturers. By comparing the product development and marketing of five Indian Ayurvedic and Yunani manufacturing houses, Bode shows that the "same" formula can be labeled as either a classic, a prescription-only, or an over-the-counter drug. Differences among these categories exist on the packaging labels but mean nothing in daily practice: for example, an estimated 75 percent of so-called prescription drugs are sold without prescriptions (Bode 2008: 63). The looseness of state regulations also allows products that no one believes to be "Ayurvedic" to be labeled as such. A notorious example is Vicks VapoRub, which Procter & Gamble India Ltd. calls an "Ayurvedic Proprietary Medicine" in order to profit from lower sales taxes levied on Ayurvedic products. Moreover, a product classified as a "Proprietary Medicine" does not have to be "medicine" in the biomedical sense of curing or alleviating disease symptoms. A large share of Ayurvedic products are meant to *enhance* health rather than to cure diseases, such as the countless liver tonics and aphrodisiacs. And most companies, among them industry leaders such as Dabur India Ltd. (founded in 1884 in Calcutta), make their biggest profits from hair oils, tooth powders, and food supplements that would not be classified as "medicinal" products outside of India.

The importance of digestion helps to explain why Ayurvedic notions of "drugs" are different from biomedical ones. In Ayurveda—as in other humoral traditions (Farquhar 2002: 47-77)—the notion that "food is medicine and medicine is food" (Bode 2008: 32) is central. As discussed earlier, dietary advice features in almost every Ayurvedic consultation. For the Calcutta *kavirajs*, one advantage of this is that many remedies are readily available to everyone, including poor people. For those patients who could not afford to spend money on medicines, food recommendations would often suffice: "Ayurveda is such a system, you can treat with costly medicine and with not so costly medicines. If the poor come, I stress food. Food is a must. Diet, it's vital. All the diseases come from it" (Dr. Sen). But this ready availability of medicines had the actual effect that treatment by professional *kavirajs* was not popular with poor people. The Calcutta physicians said that their patients came from the middle and upper classes, and only a few from the lower classes. Lower-class people had some Ayurvedic dietary know-how: "[Ayurveda] is in everybody's house. Like my maids, they use it in the house, but they don't use it in a medicine way, but in a diet way. So they don't fall sick too often, so they are happy" (Dr. Sen). Some of the physicians also suggested that Bengali home remedies (*totka*) were all "Ayurvedic" as well, and that looking at substances would seldom allow one to distinguish between "folk" and "Ayurvedic" remedies. However, popular knowledge about home remedies was declining and poor people found themselves ever more dependent on buying medicines from the shop: "If you don't practice, it's forgotten" (Dr. Barat). Moreover, people in rural areas were now less interested in Ayurveda because they could not avail themselves of either the herbs or the ready-made products.

All the *kaviraj* physicians who maintained a private chamber took pride in preparing their own medicines. Patients' demand for tailor-made remedies was one reason. It was also part of a standard consultation to dispense medicine directly so that patients did not need to get a written prescription filled at an outside shop, as is common in allopathy. There are two reasons for this: shops for Ayurveda are harder to find than those for allopathic medicine, and Ayurvedic practice downplays money transactions from patients to physicians. A tactful way of denying that a doctor gets rich from other people's suffering is to claim that payments are for the substantive medicines only, and not for the consultation.

An offshoot of medicine production is that the lines between "private chambers" and "medicine shops" are blurry in Ayurveda. It is common practice that a family of *kavirajs* runs a medicine shop where one or several family members see patients on the premises, and prescribe medicines that are bought from the shop. The same chamber/shop model is also used by Ayurvedic manufacturers, who employ a physician to sit in a shop and see patients "free of charge" but who only prescribe remedies that are to be bought straight from the shop. According to Mr. Mandal, a compounder employed at Dr. Burman's Ayurvedic Clinic, which is run by Dabur Ltd. (the company's name is a contraction of *Da*ktar *Bur*man), patients of all classes appreciated this model:

> All types of people come. Why? Because the doctor doesn't charge any fee. The doctor doesn't charge, but they have to buy medicine from here, about fifty rupees or sixty rupees. If they go to an allopath, he'll charge fifty rupees or one hundred rupees, just for the check-up. And he'll give you a prescription that you have to buy from outside, which is, of course, an expensive medicine.

Physicians working in such company-owned shops might not be consulted by customers, who can come and ask for a product directly. In those cases, the *kaviraj* would not insist on giving advice, but would wait to be asked. A *kaviraj* practicing in a company shop said that one of the advantages of not interfering was that patients could not expect to be cured by whatever they bought: "Many patients come and ask directly for a particular powder, without consulting me first. I don't question them. Later, when the medicine doesn't work, at least they cannot blame me for it not working!" (Dr. Samanta).

All the *kavirajs* who maintained a private chamber said that they wished to make medicines on their own premises. Being able to make one's own medicines was a distinctive difference between biomedical and Ayurvedic doctors: "In Ayurvedic medicine, we make it (*amra kori*)" (Dr. Sen). Making one's own medicines and testing them with patients was also seen as a way of becoming a true expert: "We *want* to practice Ayurveda, we *want* to see the results. Not just to make money or to run the house. We want to see: what are the effects of our medicines?" (Dr. Nag).

None of the Calcutta *kavirajs* complained about the availability of herbs and minerals, even if they could not source ingredients from their own gardens. Calcutta is one of India's busiest market cities, and among its tens of thousands of traders are enough to meet any request for materia medica. The *kavirajs* said that they received all roots, leaves, oils, and other materia medica from Burrabazaar, Calcutta's largest wholesale market.

Quantity of supplies was not the issue, but quality was. The *kavirajs* complained that some of the most potent herbs from high-altitude places in the Himalayas were difficult to get, and that herbs were more polluted by pesticides than in the past: "Earlier, all the medical substances came to us unpolluted, but now everything is polluted, so everything is much less effective" (Dr. Nag). The Calcutta doctors echoed Madhulika Banerjee's (2008: 203) claim that supplies of quality ingredients for those producing drugs on a small scale has deteriorated.

The problem with maintaining the traditional practice of dispensing one's own remedies was that it took so much effort to prepare them. The first requirement was lots of storage space: "You need a big space. But no one has that" (Dr. Kar). Good inventory control was needed so that none of the medicines would go to waste. Most needed were time and energy. A member of a *kaviraj* family that runs several shops in Calcutta complained about how making medicines is making life hard. To spend long hours preparing drugs was physically and mentally draining:

So many medicines I have to prepare, many types of tensions come with that. I have to concentrate very much in this work. Lots of irritation, tension. I have to work seventeen to eighteen hours daily. It's not like allopathy, where you just write down the medicine's name and that's it. (Dr. Chattopadhyay)

The more senior physicians relied on compounders to help them prepare medicines, but their salaries ranged from twenty-five hundred to four thousand rupees (forty-five to seventy-two dollars) per month, an expense that could only be recuperated if they saw lots of patients. Some doctors were pooling their efforts, or had agreements where one *kaviraj* supplied medicines from his workshop (*karkhana*) to another: "Dr. Mukherjee, he's like my older brother. He prepares, and we both use it. I am not preparing, because I don't have a center, and I don't have helping hands" (Dr. Datta). Owing to these supply difficulties, even physicians who preferred to make their own drugs were glad that mass-manufactured drugs were at hand. This way, they could fall back on market drugs if they did not have medicines ready: "We *have* to rely on factory medicine" (Dr. Datta).

Big companies had economies of scale to their advantage. Only they were able to produce enough medicines to meet the demand both in India and also internationally. In this way, profit-driven corporations could popularize Ayurveda far better than either individual physicians or the Ministry of Health's Department of AYUSH (Ayurveda, Yoga and Naturopathy, Unani, Siddha, Homoeopathy). Drug marketing helped to bring Ayurveda to all sections of society, from impoverished villagers to upper-class urbanites: "Advertising: they go to the innermost corner of our country, it's going to the upper echelons of society. [. . .] Herbal system is a craze today" (Dr. Chattopadhyay). After decades of decline, demand for Ayurveda was now growing, thanks to the ready availability of Ayurvedic products. In India and around the world, people's increasing awareness of allopathic drugs' damaging side effects was stimulating a new interest in Ayurveda as a soft, natural, "herbal" alternative. Many doctors held that individual practitioners had much to benefit from pharmaceutical companies growing the domestic and international markets: "Ayurveda has spread all over the world" (Dr. Datta).

Some of the Calcutta *kavirajs* said that Ayurveda was now beating biomedicine with its own weapons. Allopathy's hegemony had, at first, only negative effects on Ayurveda. Now, the benefits of this transformation were slowly emerging. With the tools and diagnostic procedures from biomedical pharmacology, Ayurveda was putting the efficacy of its drugs on a firm footing. The best preparations could be scientifically tested and normalized for global mass consumption (see Wahlberg 2008). The "scientific" approach to drug manufacturing was no longer an exclusive domain of biomedicine. The systematic work of standardization that manufacturers applied to the Ayurvedic pharmacopoeia was also seen as an advancement of the field as a whole. A few physicians projected that Ayurveda would eventually merge with biomedicine into a single super-science of healing that combined the best of both worlds. For example, there were "antibiotics" derived from Ayurvedic recipes that had all the power of allopathic drugs but none of the side effects; in turn, classic Ayurvedic formulas could be improved by identifying and eliminating risky or impure ingredients. Such "cocktail medicine," as Dr. Nag described it, had, on balance, more advantages than disadvantages.

The Consequences of Mass-Manufactured Medicines

One consistent criticism that Calcutta physicians voiced against relying on mass-manufactured drugs is that they do not have the full range of effects of medicines produced by hand from fresh plants. Manufacturers necessarily extracted specific alkaloids from the plants instead of using the entire plant; and they needed to dry up their juiciness for packaging and conservation. These reductions of the whole medical plant were unavoidable, but they diminished what Ayurveda could offer a patient: "They have standardized [drugs]. But by doing so, they are not 100 percent Ayurveda, because they take out the alkaloids. But there is no alternative. If you want to sell raw herbs, that's not possible" (Dr. Mistri).

None of the kavirajs felt that mass-manufactured medicines were a corruption of traditional Ayurveda as such. In his critique of modern Ayurveda as a "gentle purge," Francis Zimmermann (1992: 212) claims that factory-produced medications are eliminating the essential characteristic of Ayurvedic pharmacies, namely, their "wateriness, fluidity, oiliness." Previously, Ayurveda never used pharmaceutical cures in isolation from the whole range of therapeutic interventions, including "violent" purifying methods of vomiting, enemas, and blood-letting. The "managed violence" of Ayurveda is gradually erased by a repositioning as soft supplement to biomedicine. For Zimmermann, mass-produced pharmaceuticals are complicit with biomedical ideas of static anatomy, and they deprive patients of the intense sensory experience of fluid, oily treatments. As Halliburton (2009) highlights, Ayurveda's power to be sensually "pleasant" is an important reason for choosing it.

The Calcutta physicians also commented on the decline of "violent" forms of treatment, but none of them blamed Ayurvedic mass-produced drugs for it. Instead, they blamed the rise of biomedical drugs and the decline of people's health. Ayurveda had become "softer" than earlier *not* because of a Western misconception of Ayurveda as New Age flower power, but because modern Indian bodies had become frail. Rougher treatments of the body, such as the traditional *panchakarma*, could hardly be found in West Bengal because Bengalis could not endure these treatments anymore. All that patients wanted were the quick pharmaceutical fixes they were used to from allopathy: "Patients are so habituated to getting medicine. If they come and don't get medicine, they think: this doctor is no good" (Dr. Mistri). When purges were prescribed at all, they could only be applied with the lowest possible force: "In the *shastras*, it is indicated that *panchakarma* is only for those people who are healthy and strong. But nowadays we can only prescribe the lower dose. [. . .] They cannot concentrate. They cannot treat their body to gain extra power. [. . .] We are decaying day by day" (Dr. Kar). Although patients were weakened through the corrupting influence of modernity, their bodies were more in need of a thorough "clear-out" than ever before. The lingering side effects of biomedical drugs were particularly difficult to treat without a proper purge. Ayurvedic medicines worked well in a pure, "simple" body. But in the modern, complicated body, Ayurvedic treatment could not work as well as it should. Yet this very weakness also prevented a proper purification prior to the Ayurvedic cure: "Purifying the body is essential. Make him simple, *then* treat him. Then the medicine will work swiftly. If the system is cleared, the medicine will be absorbed" (Dr. Bhattacharya). In this modern age, such purification was difficult to attain, however.

A crucial question that Maarten Bode (2008) asks in his study of India's Ayurvedic (and Yunani) drug industry is whether the growth of the market for ready-made products also furthers the growth of Ayurvedic prescribers. On balance, Bode suggests that the rise of branded products has negative consequences for trained *kaviraj* prescribers. A vast number of prescriptions for Ayurvedic products are written not by *kavirajs* but by allopathic doctors, who frequently include an Ayurvedic liver tonic or a digestive aid in their poly-drug treatments to counter the toxic effects of their "chemical" drugs (Bode 2008: 157;

Greenhalgh 1987). Direct-to-consumer marketing tries to bypass all pre-scribers, including Ayurvedic ones. Ready-made drugs are dramatically narrowing the range of substances traditionally used. Taken together, these changes are gradually *deskilling* prescribers: "It seems that in spite of, or perhaps because of, the rise in the popularity of ayurvedic products the survival of Indian medicine is under threat" (Bode 2008: 71).

The Calcutta *kavirajs* I spoke to confirmed Bode's conclusions. For example, Dr. Sengupta complained that, because of factory medicines, doctors of the younger generation were increasingly unable to prepare their own medicines. Most Calcutta physicians, however, saw modern college education as the chief culprit, not the drug industry. Dr. Bhat-tacharya, for example, bemoaned that today's Ayurveda college gradu-ates "don't even know more than ten herbs" because college education was too focused on "dry" book knowledge and the students were not given enough time to learn "from nature." Most colleges did not even have a herbarium, he scowled.

All the older *kavirajs* also complained that the state was not active enough against doctors who only pretended to be knowledgeable in Ayurveda. They concocted their own spurious remedies by grinding up a few well-known herbs, such as *neem* leaves. Or they bought brand medicines from pharmaceutical companies and sold them as their own "family recipe": "They remove the labels from the patent medicine and use it as their own" (Dr. Bhadari). There were many practitioners who had no qualifications in Ayurveda, yet no one intervened. Such quack-ery was not at all confined to low-end doctors in the bazaars but had also infected the highest ranks of the profession. One *kaviraj*, Dr. Nag, alleged that several of the professors at Calcutta's main Ayurveda college were "absolutely bogus." Speaking about one of the professors (whom I did not have the chance to interview myself), he said that he never treated patients because he knows that he cannot do it: "He's only lectur-ing. He's a professor. He compiles notes from the *shastras* and lectures on it. But he doesn't understand anything." Even the principal of the college was not qualified to teach or practice Ayurveda: "He doesn't even have a bachelor's degree! The principal! He has no doctorate, no diploma, nothing." He only came to occupy this position because he had the right political connections and money for large bribes. When a principal was unqualified, he could not intervene in even the most egregious instances of malpractice without running the risk of getting denounced himself. Across the board, teachers were not as competent as they used to be, and there were very few outstanding *kavirajs* to whom the younger generation could look up: "There is a dearth of eminent people," as Dr. Nag put it. In turn, the quality of the students coming into Ayurveda was far lower than that of students in biomedicine. Pupils with the highest grades aspired to become allopaths, and only those who failed to secure a seat in an allopathic college turned to Ayurveda.

Where modern Ayurvedic education also failed was in forcing graduates to prescribe *allopathic* drugs during their one-year internships. These internships are more commonly available in allopathic wards than in Ayurvedic ones, and so the interns get habituated to allopathic prescribing. In turn, those who did their internships in Ayurvedic wards often found that the needed drugs were not available. In turn, closing down wards and turning away patients gave government-funded Ayurveda a bad name:

> In some places, they have only the chamber but no medicines, because the government is not supplying the medicines. People come for medicine, but we can't give them, because there is no medicine in the hospital medicine shops. In this case, we close the shops. In most of the places, people are complaining that the shops get closed, that chambers get closed. They go to the director's level [at Writers Building] to complain, and the director catches us: "What happened to you people, not opening your chambers?" We say: "If the medicine is not there, we cannot help patients." (Dr. Ghosal)

Moreover, BAMS graduates working in allopathic hospitals were told that, to be proper "doctors," to keep patients happy, and to earn good money, they should use allopathic drugs.

Surprisingly, however, many of the *kavirajs* said that the gravest danger to their reputation did not come from those who gave herbal medicines under false pretense. Instead, the worst Ayurvedic quacks were those who mixed up Ayurvedic and allopathic medicines and declared them as "purely herbal." They were administering medicines fabricated from a few herbs and high-potency biomedical drugs. Steroids were commonly used in this way. Usually, at first, a patient felt better, but in time, great damage ensued. On the bright side, however, such blatant malpractice was less common today than in earlier years, and now prevailed only in rural areas and in the bazaars of central Calcutta. Patients had become more aware of scams and had learned to distinguish more accurately between trained prescribers and imposters. To this extent, state-accredited teaching colleges and professional certificates had made a positive difference. From this perspective, the increasing use of mass-manufactured Ayurvedic drugs was by far the lesser evil.

3

Homeopathy

Immaterial Medicines

An Indian System of Medicine

In Calcutta, as in most of northern India, homeopathy is the second most popular system of medicine after allopathy. Among homeopaths, Calcutta is known as the "world capital of homeopathy." The first homeopathic college in Asia was the Calcutta Homoeopathic Medical College, which opened in 1881. The National Institute of Homeopathy was established in 1975 to rival the flagship national institutes of other medical systems that had been set up in other Indian cities. Founded in Calcutta, the Homoeopathic Medical Association of India (HMAI) is probably the world's largest homeopathic professional association. There were more than eight thousand registered homeopaths in Calcutta in 2007, according to market data used by homeopathic drug manufacturers. A survey by the Indian Ministry of Health and Family Welfare (2007) counted 39,547 registered homeopaths in West Bengal state, out of a total of 217,860 across India. That means that every sixth Indian homeopath practices in West Bengal.

The regional strength of homeopathy becomes even clearer if the numbers are compared to those of Ayurveda, its main competitor across India. Among a total of 453,661 Ayurveda practitioners in India, only 3,234 (i.e., 0.7 percent) are based in West Bengal. In India at large, there are around twice as many Ayurveda doctors as homeopaths. By contrast, there are twelve times more practitioners of homeopathy than of Ayurveda in West Bengal. One of the doctors summarized these statistics vividly: "In this country, if you throw a stone, it will hit a homeopath" (Dr. Bannerjee).

Invented by the German physician Samuel Hahnemann (1755-1843), homeopathy has been practiced in India since the early nineteenth century. The first people to bring homeopathy to India were a cosmopolitan mixture of explorers, physicians, and traders from Europe and beyond (one of the cofounders of the Calcutta Homoeopathic Medical College was W. Younan from Syria). Hahnemann had left Germany in 1835 and lived the last years of his life in Paris, which helped to further internationalize homeopathy. A Transylvanian Saxon, Johann Martin Honigberger (1795-1869), is seen as the "father of Indian homeopathy." Honigberger had become court physician of the Punjabi Sikh ruler Ranjit Singh when, on a European sojourn, he met Hahnemann in Paris in 1835. Impressed by Hahnemann's therapeutic success, he bought a stockpile of homeopathic remedies from Hahnemann's German pharmacist in Köthen and took them back to India in 1839 (Honigberger 1853). Homeopathy had spread haphazardly along trading routes and colonial port cities, but Calcutta, then the capital of British India, became the center of Indian homeopathy from the mid-nineteenth century onward (Bhardwaj 1980; Jütte 1996b; Warren 1991).

Its most influential proponent was Mahendralal Sarkar (1833-1904). Born near Calcutta, Sarkar was one of the first Indians to graduate from Calcutta Medical College, then the subcontinent's prime bastion of allopathic medicine. His "conversion" to homeopathy in the 1860s scandalized the colonial medical establishment (Biswas 2000). For its biomedical critics then (as today), homeopathy was irrational quackery that was as wrong in India as it was wrong in Europe. Yet its difference from allopathy gained it enthusiastic support from leading Bengali intellectuals (even Ramakrishna sought its treatment). The adoption of homeopathy by Sarkar, a leading scientist of his time and first director of the Indian Association for the Cultivation of Science (IACS), firmly anchored it as the most "rational" and "scientific" form of healing in Bengal and beyond (Gose 1935). Many members of the educated elite took up homeopathy—also called "German medicine"—as an alternative to "English" allopathic medicine (Arnold and Sarkar 2000). One irony of such anti-English sentiments is that, since the late 1820s, the

British royal family and the upper classes were loyal supporters of homeopathy as well (Porter 1997: 391).

Under Indira Gandhi, in 1973 the Indian Parliament recognized homeopathy as one of seven "national systems of medicine." Today homeopathy is supervised alongside other forms of Indian medicine in a department of the Ministry of Health and Family Welfare called AYUSH (Ayurveda, Yoga and Naturopathy, Unani, Siddha, Homoeopathy). Indian homeopaths have no doubts that homeopathy is every bit as "Indian" as other medical systems: "Even being a *foreign* system of medicine it found very fertile ground for being rooted firmly in the very heart of even the remotest corner of the country . . . *as if* it is the *traditional* way of treating with it" (Homoeopathic Medical Association of India 1999: 42; my emphasis). K. G. Saxena, one of Indian homeopathy's most prominent promoters (see Jütte 1996b: 361-62), considers homeopathy's prodigious success in India to be the harbinger of its future success on a global scale: "I foresee in the years to come India will be the nucleus and citadel of Homoeopathy in the world and the cult of Homoeopathy will spread out like Buddhism in the developing countries of the world" (Saxena 1992: preface).

Surprising evidence for homeopathy's deep roots in India is that the term "allopathy" is established on the subcontinent as the common name for biomedicine—but the word "allopathy" was coined as a derisive characterization of "old medicine" by Hahnemann (1994 [1833]: 1). Far from being the "rational medicine" that its proponents see it as being, allopathy is, according to Hahnemann, thoroughly irrational, crude, and harmful. Throughout the nineteenth century, the scornful connotations of allopathy were still understood, and proponents of conventional medicine resisted being called by this name (Jütte 1996a: 23-27). In contemporary India, as elsewhere, the word "allopathy" has lost all traces of this mocking undertone. The irony remains, however, that the hegemonic system of medicine received its name from its less powerful competitor (Arnold and Sarkar 2000: 45).

Despite homeopathy's huge popularity in India, it has hardly attracted any interest from medical anthropologists. In his survey of medical pluralism in India, Charles Leslie (1976: 359) mentions homeopathy as one among nine prevalent medical systems. He claims that the practice of homeopathy in India "assimilates elements from Ayurveda and Yunani traditions to form a distinctive popular-culture medicine" (1976: 359; diacritics omitted). In Leslie's classification, "popular-culture medicine" is defined as "an amalgam of concepts and practices" (1976: 359), a *masala* mixture of traditional and modern elements. Leslie does not, however, present evidence for his claims. Jeffery (1988: 43) also mentions homeopathy briefly as one of the most popular systems of medicine after Ayurveda and Yunani, yet again without presenting further details. Apart from Borghardt's (1990) study on Indian homeopaths' professional biographies and Schumann's (1993) insights into homeopathy as practiced in private chambers, no anthropological research exists on Indian homeopathy. Historiographic engagements are also rare: Jütte (1996b) presents a compact history of India as a "late superpower" of homeopathy, but only includes a few data about the current situation. Hausman (2002) describes how homeopathy became popular in colonial Madras (now Chennai). Most writings on the history of homeopathy in colonial India reiterate a few standard facts but contribute little that is new. Hence Indian homeopathy remained firmly lodged "on the margins of everything" (Degele 2005).

That Indian homeopathy failed to fascinate Western scholars is revealing of their own prejudices. Anthropological inquiries continue to be motivated by binary dichotomies (Frank and Ecks 2004). The question of what happens "when a great tradition modernizes" (Singer 1972) might have been answered in new and subtle ways in the postcolonial literature, but the question itself has never been discarded. Homeopathy complicates attempts to understand it in binary classifications of "traditional/modern" and "Indian/Western," and this is why it has received far less interest than any other system grouped under the AYUSH banner.

Originating in Germany, it is clearly not "indigenous" to India. Nor is it judged to be "Western" medicine, since the "West" is identified with the hegemony of allopathy (Khan 2006). For its European founders, homeopathy was not meant as a counteralternative to "Western modernity" but as a "truly modern" medicine that should be of benefit to all humankind. Its Bengali supporters see homeopathy as a kind of *hyper*modern medicine: *more* scientific than allopathy and free from the colonial baggage of "English" medicine (as discussed in chapter 1). An ideology of enlightened rationalism is at the heart of homeopathic self-descriptions. The logo of the HMAI is a torch of fire with two coiled snakes. The torch stands for the light of knowledge that illuminates the path for humanity; the double snake symbolizes the homeopathic principle that "like shall cure like" ("*similia similibus curantur*" in Latin; "*eki jinis ekibhabe kaj kare*" in Bengali).

The claim to be more modern than allopathic medicine can be traced to the beginnings of homeopathy in the late eighteenth century. A fierce critique of "allopathy"—as it was practiced in that era—provided the basis for homeopathy's self-definition. Hahnemann charged that allopathic medicine was an "old" and "irrational" system that did more harm than good. The "old school" of medicine that Hahnemann attacked was, of course, the humoral allopathy of his era (which is probably closer to today's Ayurveda than to today's biomedicine). Hahnemann's homeopathy warned against the fashionable therapeutics of the time: violent bleedings, emetics, and laxatives aiming to reduce an excess of blood and other humors (1994: ix). Hahnemann's homeopathy was a reaction against the "golden age of quackery" (Britten 2008: 7), when ineffective and dangerous potions were on sale everywhere. Homeopathy promoted an enlightened path to pharmaceuticals. Hahnemann scolded allopaths for prescribing too many powerful drugs:

[Allopathy] assails the body with large doses of powerful medicines, often repeated in rapid succession for a long time, whose long-enduring, not infrequently frightful effects it knows not, and which it, purposely it would almost seem, makes unrecognisable by the commingling of several such unknown substances in one prescription, and by their long-continued employment it develops in the body new and often ineradicable medicinal diseases. Whenever it can, it employs, in order to keep in favour with its patient, remedies that immediately suppress and hide the morbid symptoms by opposition (*contraria contrariis*) for a short time (palliatives), but that leave the disposition to these symptoms (the disease itself) strengthened and aggravated. (Hahnemann 1994: ix)

This excerpt from the founding text of homeopathy, Hahnemann's *Organon* (first published in 1810), encapsulates most of what was—and continues to be—hazardous about "allopathic" effects in the sense of going counter (*allo-*) to the suffering (*-pathy*). They "assail" the body and risk producing iatrogenic diseases. Allopathic effects temporarily "suppress" outward symptoms without giving a permanent cure by reaching the roots of the disease. This suppression creates the risk that the disease will return after the allopathic treatment has stopped. Treatments are given in doses that are too high to tolerate. They are given too often and for too long. Biomedicine administers drugs without fully knowing their long-term effects. Allopathy considers too little how drugs interact with each other when ingested at the same time. The homeopathic model of drug effects inverts all principles of allopathy: no drug should have iatrogenic side effects; they should go to the root of the disease instead of symptom suppression; doses must be minute; preferably, a medicine should only be administered once; the long-term effects of drugs are to be studied thoroughly; and to avoid unwanted drug-drug interactions, they should be given as single remedies.

Hahnemann's radical revision of drug effects set the standards that Bengali homeopaths are still aspiring to—and struggling with—in daily practice. Hahnemann's remark on *patients'* demand for quick relief ("to keep in favour with its patient") makes clear that the blame for the misuse of allopathic medicines is not solely the fault of allopathic doctors but also of patients' exaggerated expectations of getting healthy quickly. Can Calcutta homeopaths maintain Hahnemann's radical paradigm when treating the bodies and minds of patients who are excessively habituated to biomedical drugs?

Homeopathic Dispensing and Prescribing

The tradition of the self-taught homeopath (as discussed in chapter 1) blurs the boundaries between amateurs and professionals. There are "doctors" who have no training apart from evening classes, who see patients from the neighborhood or their family like a "regular" doctor. Better-trained homeopaths hold the degree of Bachelor of Homeopathic Medicine and Surgery (BHMS), a five-and-a-half-year qualification offered by colleges accredited by the government of India's Central Council of Homoeopathy (CCH). The BHMS degree includes an internship at a government homeopathic hospital or at a general hospital where homeopathy is practiced side by side with allopathy. At the lowest end, BHMS graduates practice in their own houses. Local youth clubs and welfare associations also provide rooms for homeopaths who charge only nominal fees. Small-time homeopaths earn no more than twenty to thirty rupees per consultation, and they struggle to keep at least a lower-middle-class standing.

To illustrate how low many homeopaths' earnings are, I will recount my participation in a members' meeting of the Homoeopathic Association of India (HMAI). A homeopath close to where I lived said that he was going there and invited me to join him. On the drive there, no less than seven homeopaths and I squeezed into a sedan taxi. About fifty people gathered in a dingy room on the campus of Calcutta University. Everyone sat on mats on the floor because there were no chairs or tables. The meeting lasted from morning until the middle of the afternoon. A number of issues were addressed, but the longest and most heated discussion revolved around the chairman's motion to increase annual membership fees from one hundred rupees ($1.80) to two hundred rupees ($3.60). At the end of the debate, the majority of members present voted against the increase, on the grounds that regular homeopaths could hardly afford to spend so much money.

The next step up the professional ladder is to sit in a shop for a couple of hours per day. Shops invite homeopaths to sit on their premises to attract more customers. The doctors earn a consultation fee from the patient, and the shop sells the medicine. Shops give younger homeopaths an opportunity to establish themselves, but they are also used by senior doctors who want to extend their geographical reach across the city. Less well-known doctors can be charged a maintenance fee for using a consultation room in a shop, especially if there are added running costs for air conditioning or similar luxuries. These charges are dropped when the doctor sees many patients and gives enough business to the retailer. The prestige of the shops and the prestige of the doctors go hand in hand: "good" shops will invite "good" doctors, and good doctors will only sit in good shops. Allopathic shops usually do not invite homeopaths to sit on their premises. The licenses required for homeopathic and allopathic remedies are separate. Whereas allopathic shops can sell "Ayurvedic" products (mostly cosmetics), they do not sell homeopathic remedies. When the shops do not stock homeopathy, there is no gain in inviting homeopaths.

Top homeopaths look like well-off allopathic physicians: they wear suits and ties, speak fluent English, and are chauffeured around the city in their own cars. They practice in their own private chambers, inclusive of air conditioning and soothing background music. Many of them proudly continue a family tradition. Some of them are able to trace their genealogies back to the beginnings of homeopathy in colonial Bengal. The highest possible credential was to have links to foreign countries that go back generations. Dr. Bannerjee exemplifies this select group: "My great-great-grandfather was a homeopath. He practiced for forty-two years. And then my grandfather was a homeopath, who studied miasms with Dr. John Henry Allen back in the U.S." Elite homeopaths can see up to 150 patients a day and charge anything between one hundred and eight hundred rupees per consultation. According to homeopathic manufacturers, a top doctor is someone who generates drug prescriptions worth twenty thousand rupees ($360) per month. Only a few Calcutta homeopaths would be part of this group. Prescriptions worth ten thousand rupees ($180) would reflect a good performance. In terms of personal income, elite doctors can make up to six hundred thousand rupees ($10,780) per month. Given that a regular white-collar job earns around fifteen to twenty-five thousand rupees per month, homeopathy can be a lucrative line of business.

Among the top doctors are also a handful who focus on publishing rather than prescribing. For example, Prof. Thakur had his main chamber in an old house in North Calcutta. The first floor of the house was dedicated to homeopathy, the second floor to his private household. The first floor comprised two large rooms. One was devoted to publishing. Seven writing tables were crammed into it for research assistants. Books and documents—in various stages of decay because of the heat and humidity—were piled up high inside and on top of steel cabinets. One of the cabinets was stacked with homeopathic tinctures. While I was sitting on a wooden bench for visitors one day, I saw how one of his assistants accessed the medicine cabinet every ten minutes to prepare vials of remedies. In the second room, Prof. Thakur worked on his writings, saw patients, and received junior doctors who came to him for advice. Along the walls were more piles of books and papers. In the middle of the room stood a flat bench with a mattress and cushions. Whereas Prof. Thakur wore suit and tie outside his house, in his own hub he donned white *kurta pajama*, giving him an air of a traditional pundit.

Professional homeopaths have different methods of transacting remedies to patients. Continuous with the "homeo chest" tradition, doctors can keep their own stock of remedies and give them to patients during consultations. It is common to give patients the first dose of a remedy by hand, and the rest of it in a vial. When I once said hello to one of the homeopaths in a local shop and mentioned that I had not been sleeping well lately, he immediately pulled out a few globules of homeopathic arsenic, asked me to open my mouth, and put them right down my throat. Another option is to write down a remedy for patients to buy at a medicine shop. If the doctor practices in a shop, the expectation is that the medicine is bought there, but patients can take the prescription elsewhere. Homeopaths can switch between prescribing and dispensing according to circumstances. Many homeopaths dispense remedies from their own stock while they are in their chambers, and write prescriptions when they are in polyclinics. When they dispense themselves, they can either charge one combined fee for consultation and medicine or charge for each separately.

Self-dispensing was sometimes regarded as less "ethical" than prescribing, because the patient did not learn what remedy he or she received. "Empowering patients" has become more important over the past decade, not least because of the strengthening of consumer rights:

> We always write a prescription. One advantage is that the patient is free to consult any other doctor. And besides, his consumer rights are protected. I make a mistake in diagnostics, I make a mistake in prescription, I overcharge him in medicine or in fee—if I give a prescription, he can consult any doctor and can find out what I have been doing. The patient is entitled to know what I think, entitled to know what I am doing. (Prof. Thakur)

Homeopathic prescriptions can "float" within homeopathy, as biomedical ones do within allopathy. It also happens that biomedical prescriptions "float" into homeopathy via the files that patients bring to them. One homeopath retold how adopting a floating prescription from an allopath backfired on him. A few years earlier, a man came to his chamber and asked for a remedy against "schizophrenia." He said that his wife was suffering from "schizophrenia" and described her symptoms to the doctor. The woman herself was not present because, as the man explained, she was too ill to leave the house. That the woman was schizophrenic was seemingly evidenced by a prescription from an allopathic doctor that the husband showed to the homeopath. When writing his own remedy, the homeopath also wrote down "schizophrenia." More than a year later it transpired that the husband was trying to get a divorce from his wife, and wanted to support his legal case by getting several doctors to declare her mentally insane: "This man has only brought everything on paper. [But he] had never given a drug to her. She did not have any problem." When the husband submitted the "schizophrenia" prescriptions to a court, the judge asked the homeopath to appear and to testify to the accuracy of his diagnosis. In court, the homeopath had to own up to never diagnosing "schizophrenia" himself, and admitted that he only copied the term from allopathic prescriptions.

A homeopath's choice between dispensing and prescribing is also related to geography, patient turnover, and access to shops. Homeopaths and retailers estimate that 20-40 percent of urban practitioners dispense and 60-80 percent prescribe, whereas only 10-20 percent of rural practitioners prescribe. Least likely to dispense are "big" Calcutta-based practitioners who make enough from consultation fees that they need not bother with dispensing. The doctors most likely to dispense are peri-urban and rural practitioners who do not have a homeopathy shop nearby or who rely on the double income from consulting and dispensing. It was debated, however, whether self-dispensing generated more net income than prescribing. Some homeopaths suggested that one could earn more by working with shops instead of dispensing oneself, because many gave cash kickbacks. On the other hand, dispensing was cheaper for the patient because it cut out the retailers.

"Good-Quality Remedies" in Homeopathy

The first principle of homeopathy is that "like cures like." The second principle is that the patient should never be assailed by high dosages. Hahnemann developed the practice of "potentizing," whereby an active ingredient is serially diluted and forcefully shaken ten times at each stage ("succussion"). Through this process, the remedies get so diluted that none of the original substance remains. Progressive dilution has been the target of biomedical scorn since Hahnemann's era. The charge is that homeopathy must be bogus because the remedies contain no active ingredient. Detractors illustrate the absurd immensity of homeopathic dilutions by comparing the dosage to a pinch of salt in the Atlantic Ocean or to a single molecule in the space between the sun and the earth. That there is no "active ingredient" that can measured by standard biochemical tests raises many tricky questions. One of them is, how can one distinguish between homeopathic drugs of "good" or "bad" quality? Probed on this issue, no homeopath I interviewed ever claimed that there were clear-cut criteria for quality. Prof. Thakur, a member of the Central Council of Homoeopathy (CCH), told me that "it is such a funny thing that there is no measure in homeopathy by which you judge that this medicine is genuine or not." At the same time, the doctors held strong opinions about "good" or "bad" homeopathic remedies. In this section, I analyze how Calcutta homeopaths make sense of drug quality where there are no laboratory standards for what should count as drug quality.

The first criterion for a "good" drug is whether it is prepared according to the principles of homeopathic pharmacy. Rule 2(dd) of the Drugs and Cosmetics Rules defines homeopathic medicines as "any drug which is recorded in homoeopathic provings of therapeutic efficacy of which has been established through long clinical experience" (cited in Banerjee 2006: 540). This required the development of a comprehensive pharmacopeia that lists ingredients and standardizes how they should be handled. The first Indian homeopathic pharmacopeia, the *Pharmaceutics Manual*, was published in Calcutta by the pharmacy M. Bhattacharya & Co. in the late nineteenth century. It remained the unofficial Indian pharmacopeia until the Ministry of Health and Family Welfare started to bring out a multivolume pharmacopeia from 1971 onward (Banerjee 2006: 7-8). Given that much of the foundational drug proving (*Prüfung* in German) was done with ingredients available in Europe and North America, one aim of the Indian pharmacopeia is to describe plant and animal substances that are native and common to the subcontinent.

M. Bhattacharya & Co. was not only the first Indian publisher of a pharmacopeia but also the first Calcutta-based manufacturer of homeopathic medicines, an operation founded in 1892. Up to that point, most remedies were imported from abroad and sold at foreign-owned shops such as C. Ringer & Co. in Calcutta's Lal Bazaar. Since the late nineteenth century, the number of homeopathic manufacturers has grown significantly. There are now around five hundred private manufacturers with an estimated annual turnover of $125 million (Bode 2008: 74-75). These figures are rough estimates only—the exact number of *allopathic* drug manufacturers in India is also just guesswork—but it is safe to say that India is one of the world's largest homeopathic drug producers, certainly as measured by the number of companies in business. Global biomedical corporations have started to shift production facilities to India, and on a much smaller level, a similar process can be observed in India. For example, the German company Dr. Willmar Schwabe opened a production plant near New Delhi in 1997. It remains standard, however, that manufacturers obtain raw materials from domestic and international markets and do not prepare their own plant, animal, and metallic extracts. Only about ten manufacturers market their products across India, among them Dr. Willmar Schwabe (part imported, part India-made), Dr. Reckeweg & Co. (all imported from Germany), and SBL (all India-made).

Many companies are based in Calcutta. There are around twenty-five smaller and twenty larger companies, among them Hahnemann Laboratories Ltd., National Homoeo Laboratory, Economic Homoeo Pharmacy, Homoeopathic Research Institute, International Homoeo Research, Hahnemann Pharmaceutical Laboratory, King & Co., P. Banrjee, N. P. Dutta & Sons, and Lord Hahnemann Laboratory. Probably the best-known company from Calcutta is Hahnemann Publishing Company (HAPCO). It was founded in 1917 as a publishing enterprise, with a mission to spread homeopathic knowledge among the general population by translating homeopathic texts into Bengali. In 1922 a manufacturing arm was added. Most of the homeopaths I talked to mentioned HAPCO as one of the most trustworthy companies because it loyally follows Hahnemann.

While doctors stress allegiance to Hahnemann's principles as a marker of quality, companies themselves are increasingly defining "quality" through adherence to global quality standards, above all to Good Manufacturing Practice (GMP). A promotional video on SBL

(Sarda Boiron Laboratories) opens with a motto from Hahnemann ("A dedicated physician can only be sure about the healing properties of a drug when it is made as pure and as perfect as possible."), but never mentions the founder afterward. Instead, the film is all about how SBL's manufacturing facilities stick to the highest-level quality parameters. All stages of the drug production process are fully automated, so that there is "no touch of a human hand" until the remedies are sealed and ready to ship. SBL claims to be the only company in India that prepares all its dilutions through "electronic potentizers" instead of manual succussion. Technical jargon, such as "gas-liquid chromatography," pervades the presentation. The film shows workers in white coats and clinical face masks, speckless production floors, stainless steel containers, and hydraulic presses for optimal extraction of tinctures from "organically grown herbs sourced at the prime time of their bioavailability." SBL also highlights that it is a global player. The company's motto is "SBL—World Class Homoeopathy," and the film points out that SBL was launched in collaboration with the French company Laboratoires Boiron, and that SBL is not only the leading brand in India but also exports to "developed nations" such as France and the United States. Extracts from plants were all made by SBL in India, but other ingredients that could not be supplied at global standards from Indian sources were imported: "We use HMS lactose from Holland, instead of locally available, low-grade sucrose." It is also claimed that SBL remedies are subjected to "stringent clinical trials at renowned Indian institutions," and two doctors are presented who speak to the good clinical results achieved with SBL products. Yet the focus of the film is almost exclusively on standardized, quality-controlled production methods. The question of how remedies could be proven to be any better than those of other producers is evaded with a list of all the quality-control steps taken.

Since the mid-2000s, GMP requirements for homeopathic drugs are no longer a voluntary measure, but are now mandatory under Schedule M-I, Rule 85-E(2). GMP compliance is a double-edged sword for manufacturers. It gives companies like SBL greater credibility with doctors and, increasingly, with patients. However, it is expensive to implement, and only large companies are able to pay for it. By the late 2000s, the full effects of implementing GMP requirements were not yet foreseeable,

and the precise conditions were still negotiated. Mr. De, the marketing director for Hahnemann Laboratories, a Calcutta-based company,
was not too pessimistic. He said that GMP posed a problem because
it needed great investments in new machinery, new production floors,
and new air conditioning. The company was planning to take the necessary steps, but not within the time scale stipulated by the Indian government; there was room for negotiation on the deadlines for full GMP
compliance. In turn, well-financed companies seem sure that GMP will
strengthen their market position. A sales director for Schwabe, Mr.
Biswas, predicted that "99 percent" of all Indian homeopathic manufacturers would close down in the coming years because they were unable,
or unwilling, to introduce GMP standards: "GMP is good for the good
companies, and bad for the bad ones." Mr. Biswas was looking forward
to times when Bengali homeopaths could only prescribe GMP-standard
remedies instead of cheap local products: "Doctors here often don't go
for quality. They want to profit only."

Homeopathic drug distribution is modeled after biomedicine. From
manufacturers, products are shipped by Carrying and Forwarding
Agents (CFAs) to licensed dealers and wholesalers, who then supply
retailers. Large shops can act like wholesalers to smaller shops for specific companies. For example, a shop specializing in SBL remedies can
resell a few products to smaller shops whose turnover does not require a
direct relation with a dealer. As in the allopathic drugs business, manufacturers can outdo competitors by spending money on advertising, on
larger sales forces, or on discounts for bulk orders. In the late 2000s, the
market for homeopathic remedies was too small to be covered by market research companies. In the absence of independent market surveys,
manufacturers' sales representatives conduct their own retail audits.
For example, Schwabe India employs around 180 sales representatives
across India. Each so-called field sales executive (FSE) looks after two
hundred doctors and one hundred shops, visiting around eight doctors
and four shops per day. In the Bengal region, all FSEs, including the
regional manager, previously worked for allopathic companies, so they
are well acquainted with the methods used there. Mr. Das, a retailer in
a small medicine shop, confirmed that Schwabe representatives come
to visit every ten to twelve days to ask about how sales were going, if
stocks needed refilling, and how competitors were doing.

For manufacturers—who rely on shops to prepare remedies properly—not all shops are "good" shops. There is much room for cheating: single remedies are supplied to shops as sealed files of liquids of
various sizes (e.g., 100ml or 450ml). Taking one drop and mixing it with
ninety-nine drops of alcohol produces a remedy of one power; from
this, one drop mixed with ninety-nine drops of alcohol produces two
power, and so on. These dilutions are prepared by compounders in the
shops. Compounders can refill empty files from brand manufacturers
with tinctures from cheaper companies yet still charge the premium
price. Indeed, under government regulations, shops are not required to
maintain sales records. According to Rule 67-G of the Drugs and Cosmetics Rules, "no records of sale in respect of homoeopathic potentised
preparation in containers of 30ml. or lower capacity and in respect of
mother tincture made up in quantities up to 60ml. need be maintained"
(cited in Banerjee 2006: 541). Even without fraudulent intent, shops are
a weak link in the chain because they employ many untrained people
as compounders. For these reasons, it was much more important to go
to a trustworthy shop in homeopathy than in allopathy. Mr. Biswas, the
Schwabe sales manager, estimated that out of four hundred shops in
Calcutta, merely ten were "good." The risk of cheating was smaller with
"patent" medicines, that is, companies' prepackaged combinations of
several remedies.

These quality concerns were redefined in the latest development in
commercial homeopathy: the emergence of franchise chains that inte-
grate manufacturing, compounding, and prescribing. The largest of
these businesses is Dr. Batra's Positive Health Clinic Pvt. Ltd., which was
founded in Bombay in 1982. In 2012, Dr. Batra's ran ninety-nine centers across forty-two cities in India, Dubai, and the United Kingdom,
with a few hundred homeopaths on the payroll. For the opening of the
first Dr. Batra clinic in Calcutta in 2000, the company ran a marketing
campaign that celebrated "treatment @ the speed of thought!" in "the
world's first chain of ISO 9002 certified homeopathic clinics." Dr. Batra
mimics private allopathic chains down to "corporate social responsibility" pronouncements. Similar to manufacturers, Dr. Batra highlights its
ISO certification and the "cutting-edge" technology used in its clinics.
Remedies used in the branch clinics partly come from Indian companies, partly from Dr. Batra's own manufacturing unit. But independent

homeopaths saw the rhetoric of ISO certificates as trickery. Dr. Batra's promise to remedy hair loss and suggestions that even cancer could be treated were seen as fraudulent. According to one of the homeopaths I interviewed, the only reason why Dr. Batra had not yet been sued was that the Indian legal system could not be trusted to deliver justice.

Calcuttan homeopaths were ambivalent about manufacturers' claims to reliable quality. Claims to quality were a standard marketing rhetoric that could not be backed up with proof of "real" differences. Companies that could afford television and newspaper advertisements were seen as having better-quality products even if there was no proof for this. Anyone who knew how homeopathic remedies were prepared also knew that they could never be expensive to make. As Prof. Thakur underlined, "homeopathy medicines *cannot* be costly" because of their ingredients. Price differences only came from companies exploiting brand reputation. On the other hand, there was also a sense that prescribing products from "good" companies and urging patients to go to "good" shops made a difference for clinical success. A shop owner and practitioner, Dr. Nandy, said that experience showed that remedies from "good" companies made satisfied patients, and remedies from bad ones led to disappointments: "By using medicines like Nux Vomica [strychine tree] from that company, you find it works. But using from other companies, patients come back, and you find that there is no change in symptoms."

The "Vital Force"

Homeopathy needed a different foundation than "old" humoral pathology. For this, Hahnemann adopted a concept that was fashionable in European medical theory at the time: the "vital force" (*Autocratie* or *Lebenskraft* in German). The most famous proponent of *Lebenskraft* therapeutics was C. M. Hufeland (1762-1836), who developed the macrobiotic diet. *Geist*, spirituality, and immaterial energy were important in the philosophical and literary discourse of the era, far beyond medicine (Safranski 2007). While *Lebenskraft* disappeared from biomedical thought from the middle of the nineteenth century onward (Bergdolt 2008), the vital force retained its central place in homeopathic thought.

Hahnemann defines the vital force as "life itself": when in order, the vital force guarantees health; when "morbidly affected," it produces

illness symptoms. Drawing a line between "old medicine" and homeopathy, Hahnemann insists that the allopathic quest for the causes of
diseases is both unnecessary and futile. Disease etiology is irrelevant to
the medical practitioner: "*How* the vital force causes the organism to
display morbid phenomena, that is, *how* it produces disease, it would be
of no practical utility to the physician to know" (Hahnemann 1994: §12,
fn. 1).

Today, Indian homeopaths firmly hold onto the concept of the vital
force. Indian textbooks on homeopathy all mention the vital force and
argue that the source of sickness must *not* be attributed to a particular
region of the body. Neither the stomach, nor the heart, nor any other
part should be designated as the "root" of health problems. Instead,
homeopathy "treats the patient as a whole and not disease alone. [. . .]
Homoeopathic medicines act on a dynamic plane to heal the deranged
vital force" (Banerjee 2006: 4, 5). In biomedicine, there need not be
any response from the human organism to the drug taken, as long as
the drug interacts specifically with the pathogen. Allopathic antibiotics destroy bacteria without interacting with the host organism. The
less interaction there is, the more "magic" these "bullets" are. By contrast, homeopathic remedies never go against the origins of the disease. Instead, they induce a response in the organism that reinvigorates
the vital force. A homeopathic remedy does not target the disease in
a "host" but sparks a response from the whole organism. Hence the
vital force is an irreplaceable corollary to the "like cures like" principle.
"Potency" through progressive dilution of remedies only makes sense if
the notion of vital force is maintained.

To illustrate how the vital force is related to drug effects, Dr. Bannerjee told me the following allegory: the vital force and the disease
force are similar to two high-speed trains, "like the French TGV." When
the disease force gets out of control, it must be stopped. There are two
approaches to stopping the train. One is through a full-on collision
with another train, which is the method of allopathy; that way the train
will be stopped quickly, but there will also be great collateral damage.
The other method is to send a train on a parallel track that is even faster
than the first train, to link the two trains together and then to slowly
halt the dangerous train. In this manner, the disease force is extin-
guished without any damage. This second method is the homeopathic

method, effecting an alteration of the vital force that gradually extinguishes the disease force:

> [The faster train] comes near to [the slower train] and it is running the two together. You anchor it and then you can control it. And this is the homeopathic medicine. [. . .] So I believe that when you give a homeopathic medicine and by virtue of potency and dose, you can control that power, which is mentioned by Hahnemann in his Organon: "A weaker dynamic affection is permanently extinguished by a stronger one." (Dr. Bannerjee)

When asked about the place of Hahnemann's vital force in daily practice, all Calcutta homeopaths maintained that they could not practice without it: "Vital force is the main thing in homeopathy. When collecting the totality of the symptoms, I particularly have the vital force in mind and then I select the medicine" (Dr. Raut). Without the vital force, it was impossible to understand how homeopathy's minute doses could work.

Homeopathy's approach is to enliven the patient's vital force irrespective of the causes of illness. Stretching this theory to the extreme, some homeopaths said that not even nauseating food or dirty water will cause illness symptoms if the force is strong: "At first, our vitality is lost, vital force is the basic factor. Secondary is the germs. And this is the homeopathic theory. So always we insist on the increase of the strength of the vital force. Then there will be no germs, no infection" (Dr. Shah). Since disease etiologies are explicitly not of interest to homeopathy, even health problems for which allopathy has no good remedies can be treated. Based on the principle that "like cures like," homeopathy focuses on the symptoms and treats with drugs that produce these symptoms if administered in a high dose. For example, asthma related to air pollution can be treated by remedies that produce asthmatic symptoms if given in gross form. Hence all the homeopaths I interviewed claimed to be able to treat illnesses that are caused by hectic city life and environmental pollution, not by targeting causes but by boosting the vital force: "Some people are hypersensitive to pollution. Of course, you can take care of that" (Dr. Bannerjee). Prof. Thakur was particularly fond of pointing out the therapeutic superiority of homeopathy in the modern industrial age. From among "forty-six types of industrial pollution," homeopathy was able to treat "forty-three," he claimed: "Industrial toxicity, overpopulation, the impact of noise: homeopathy has specific medicines for that. We have medicines for the bad effect of sound, of noise, for industrial poisoning, for toxic effects of metals, all these drugs are described in our books."

Against the "old" humoral paradigm, Hahnemann stressed that homeopathic remedies are so subtle that they do not have to be "digested." Instead of "assailing the body with large doses of powerful medicine," which inevitably strains the digestive organs and the whole body, homeopathic medicine bypasses digestion altogether. Tongue, stomach, and guts all but lose their privileged role in the assimilation of medicine: "Besides the stomach, the tongue and the mouth are the parts most susceptible to the medicinal influences; but the interior of the nose is more especially so, and the rectum, the genitals, as also all particularly sensitive parts of our body are almost equally capable of receiving the medicinal action" (Hahnemann 1994: §290). Other than "grossly" material medicines, which the body needs to assimilate, homeopathic remedies can pervade the entire body at once and affect the vital force directly.

Calcutta homeopaths had their own explanations for how their hypersubtle drugs could work. To attain the "magical relief from olfaction treatment" (Dr. Shah), one had to take a single globule, dissolve it in three drops of water, and make the patient smell it. A notion of "nerves" was often mentioned in this regard: "The action [of the medicine] comes through the nerves. You put it to the mouth. Or you rub it, by rubbing it, it goes to the nerves. If it is not possible, you give by olfaction" (Dr. Shah). Once the "nerves" are reached, the "vital force" could be guided into a new direction. One of the great advantages was that drugs could be delivered even from a distance, and even to patients without consciousness: "It guides the entire system, the entire vital force, entire body and mind. [...] If you smell it from a distance, it will work. Once I had a coma patient, I gave medicine to inhale, and the senses came back" (Dr. Choudhuri). What homeopathic remedies proved was that there is no firm boundary between the individual human body and the rest of the universe; the vital force pervades the body and is affected by the universe at all times: "Our body comprises some holes and some gaps, so these orifices are having contact with the rest of the universe" (Dr. Santra). In Hindu *puja*, the deity can ingest food offerings simply by smelling it. Parry notes that, for Hindus, "smelling is a kind of consumption equivalent to eating" (1985: 629, fn.10). Both homeopathy and Hindu *puja* (as discussed in chapter 1) assume the reality of immaterial ingestion.

Calcutta homeopaths were entirely unfazed by criticisms that hypersubtle remedies cannot work (Frank 2004: 145). They argued two points. On the one hand, homeopathy is scientifically too advanced for the crude instruments that mainstream science has at its disposal at the moment: "It does not worry me how the medicine works. This is a problem that will be solved in thirty, forty years" (Prof. Thakur). On the other hand, homeopathy transcends the methods of the positivistic sciences altogether. Just as the mind is both immaterial and yet supremely powerful, so is the vital force:

> If we think about the mind, and mind is not material, it is dynamic and body is material. And we think that mind controls the body. So we think that immaterial power is also necessary to the body. [. . .] In a chemical laboratory, homeopathic power cannot be established. So, in homeopathy, there is some power above the material body. (Dr. Shah)

Many Calcutta homeopaths saw a deep affinity between Bengali notions of *mon* and the vital force. Like Hahnemann, Bengalis put mind over matter. Aiming to transcend the gross materialism of the modern world, Bengalis discovered homeopathy as their favorite system of healing. Asked why homeopathy is so successful in Bengal, one homeopath replied, "Because people have belief in God. You see, God is invisible, and so is homeopathy! [*laughs*] [. . .] Where everything is more mechanical, where there is more materialistic thinking, there homeopathy has trouble" (Dr. Gose).

Subtle drugs effects and direct action on the "nerves" also singled out homeopathy as the best medicine for psychiatric problems. Given the centrality of the vital force, treating mental illness was part of homeopathy from the start. Accordingly, in a textbook on homeopathic materia medica, the author advocates a more prominent role of homeopathy in the treatment of psychiatric patients. Homeopathy was better suited to today's mental diseases than allopathy, and it was high time that homeopathic psychiatric hospitals were founded: "I do not understand why in India we do not have any mental hospital under homoeopathy. Many persons would have not become criminals, had homoeopathy taken care of their tendencies in their childhood" (Singh 2003: 12). Several Calcutta homeopaths extended this claim about their medicine's superiority in dealing with mental problems into an all-encompassing homeopathic biopolitics. Reminiscent of Freudian theories, Prof. Thakur equated children with neurotics and defined both as being in need of homeopathic intervention:

> The great advantage is that [homeopathy] can cure susceptibility. Also character traits: tendency to lie, tendency to cry, tendency to forget, inability to concentrate, the child not performing up to the mark, not getting good results. Homeopathy has medicines which bring about a basic change of character. It can make you more concentrated, it can make a dull child an intelligent one, it can cure a timid person, it can cure a person who is too religious, too fanatic. There are medicines for curing these aberrations. That is why most guardians bring their children to homeopathy.

One of Prof. Thakur's favorite remedies was *Sepia officinalis*, ink extracted from cuttlefish, which was useful for all kinds of mood disorders. Through the concept of the vital force and through a strict attention to symptoms over etiology, homeopaths were not afraid to claim that their remedies could alleviate all the ills of modernity: mental stress, hyperactive children, environmental pollution, and even religious fanaticism.

Sour, Sweet, Salty, or Spicy? Diagnosing through Tastes

Hahnemann marked homeopathy's radical departure from "old" therapy by stating that there was "no practical utility" in knowing how diseases are caused. By foregrounding the vital force and by dismissing disease etiology as useless, Hahnemann also dismissed the methods of humoral medicine, which had to be completely abandoned: "Homoeopathy sheds not a drop of blood, administers no emetics, purgatives, laxatives or diaphoretics, drives off no external affection by external means" (Hahnemann 1994: xi). The vital force pervades the whole organism and is not tied to an anatomical location or an internal process. Along with emetics and laxatives, Hahnemann tossed aside the idea that good digestion is the main pillar of health.

Hahnemann's radical departure from "old" medicine puts Indian homeopaths in a tense relation to patients' humoralist notions. On the one hand, the homeopaths I spoke to never opposed the commonsense notion that food, digestion, and a balanced daily routine helped to maintain good health, and most of them felt that good nutrition has a place in their therapeutics. Dietary recommendations were a common element in consultations: "I give food advice, because there is a very good relation of food and homeopathy" (Dr. Niyogi). Even if they did not advocate purges and other "clear-outs," homeopaths do not doubt that bad food and environmental pollution affect people's health. Most of the homeopaths agreed that the digestive health of Bengalis is frail, that "rich foods, spicy foods" (Dr. Patel) and contaminated water and urban living depressed the vital force. Their advice on what food to take and what to avoid followed common Bengali ideas about nutrition.

But their emphasis on food while talking to patients was not matched by a conceptual notion that bad digestion was the *primary* cause of bad health. When I asked directly whether digestion is central to health, only one homeopath answered positively that "bowels is the main thing" (Dr. Khan). All others stressed that homeopathic and popular Bengali ideas are fundamentally opposed to each other: "What are *they* telling, what are *you* going to do? Tell me! Whether their ideas are true or not is immaterial. Why give importance to stomach? To heart? To lungs? If you go in that way, there is no solution. Taking only the part into consideration will lead you nowhere. Take the man as a whole!" (Dr. Chodhuri).

Only through consideration of the vital force and the totality of symptoms could the right drug be chosen. Any organ-specific approach was principally wrong. Allopathy treats a patient after a heart attack and then he dies of a brain tumor; it suppresses the symptoms of tuberculosis only to see a patient develop cancer. A weakened vital force will make itself felt, no matter how hard the symptoms are attacked.

As much as the homeopaths might uphold Hahnemann's "vital force" and reject popular Bengali notions of disease etiology, they still have to reckon with digestion-focused ideas in patient consultations. Instead of confronting patients about "false" beliefs and trying to educate them in the theories of homeopathy, they rather turn it into an advantage that patients are "cued into" food and digestion (as discussed in chapter 0). The following observations on homeopathic consultations were made in a charitable "slum clinic" in central Calcutta. They exemplify how Calcutta homeopaths work *with*, rather than against, their Bengali patients' expectations.

Dr. Bannerjee set up his slum clinic in close proximity to the Calcutta Medical College in order to "beat allopathy in its own terrain" (Dr. Bannerjee). He published several books, lectured and practiced in Europe and North America, won gold medals from Calcutta University, and is a fellow of homeopathic associations in Australia, Germany, the United Kingdom, and the United States. At the time of our meetings, Dr. Bannerjee practiced mostly in two private chambers, one in central Calcutta and one in South Calcutta. He also maintained close links to the United Kingdom, spending a couple of months every year at a teaching college in England. Emulating charitable works of allopathic doctors, he used the premises of a *bustee* (slum) youth club to treat patients free of cost, twice a week, for two hours. Before I met Dr. Bannerjee in the clinic, he characterized the slum clientele as "poor but happy": "They have taken everything from them, but not the smile" (Dr. Bannerjee). He enjoyed prescribing homeopathy to slum dwellers: their symptoms were easy to read and their bodies responsive to homeopathic remedies: "You give the medicine and in two days: fine! Even with much more advanced pathology. [. . .] Although they live in a very unhygienic condition, poor sanitation, but still, their vitality is stronger" (Dr. Bannerjee). Dr. Bannerjee saw around fifty patients within two hours. Since there was only a minimum amount of time available for each patient, he reduced his questions and recommendations to the bare basics. The minimalist diagnostics bore no resemblance to the extensive history taking that is a trademark of homeopathy. Ideally, patients are asked a wide range of questions to capture the "totality of symptoms." Depending on a doctor's experience, history taking, or *anamnesis* (Greek for "remembrance"), takes up to two hours. Most Calcutta homeopaths claim to spend between thirty and forty-five minutes per first anamnesis, but from my observations of daily practice, this varies considerably according to different treatment styles. Busy doctors who grapple with a large number of patients depend on questionnaires that assistants fill in with patients: "I have two assistants working for me, so they go through the booklet. [. . .] A case well taken is half cured" (Dr. Bannerjee). He admitted that he hardly gave more than ten minutes of his own time for an anamnesis, even for premium-fee patients. In the slum clinic, where patients got one or two minutes, Dr. Bannerjee did not do any extensive history taking. Instead, he went straight to the center: digestion and food preferences.

Verbal questioning of patients was the focus of every consultation. Dr. Bannerjee usually remained seated behind his desk, and only occasionally got up from his chair to touch patients (no diagnostic instruments were available). Within the few minutes given to each patient, he would start with a quick question about the patient's main complaints and the duration of the problem. To make a diagnosis, he commonly asked the following questions: What food do you like, sour, sweet, salty, or spicy? What food do you like: fish, meat, or egg? How are your motions? What time do you have your meals? Do you have a good appetite? What affects you most, hot or cold? "Hot" and "cold" included the temperature of food, of bath water, or of the seasons. To be sure, questions about food preferences are part of the orthodox Hahnemannian repertoire. Yet Dr. Bannerjee focused entirely on these questions, irrespective of the patient's complaints. Even patients with pain in the legs, eye problems, or skin diseases were asked about digestion. For example, one male patient (about fifty years old) came on a return visit regarding a number of illnesses, among them a dry gangrene of the leg, from which he had been suffering for fifteen years. Dr. Bannerjee commented that allopathy would have been unable to deal with the problem. Even if his medicine was not able to cure the gangrene, at least it saved the patient from an amputation. All other problems mentioned by the patient were sidelined because of the time pressure:

DOCTOR: How are you?

PATIENT: My health is not good.

DOCTOR: How is your leg? Show me your leg. [*Examines the leg for about thirty seconds*]

PATIENT: Sir, the cold is not going.

DOCTOR: Anything else?

PATIENT: I won't show to another doctor. I will come to you only. It doesn't matter if I die.

DOCTOR: Do you feel hungry?

PATIENT: No, it's not good. But I eat at home. I eat all, fish, rice, meat and all. But I don't feel the taste. This is the main problem. And I have problems going to the toilet [constipation]. When I walk, my leg pains very much.

DOCTOR: Buy medicine from a good shop!

PATIENT: Fine . . . I have this taste problem for the last one year.

DOCTOR (turns head): Next!

Dr. Bannerjee commonly asked patients if they had seen other doctors, if they had followed his prescriptions faithfully, and if their health had improved. Dr. Bannerjee usually formulated queries about improvement in a leading way, such as, "How many percent betterment? Eighty percent? Ninety percent?" After his diagnosis, Dr. Bannerjee wrote a prescription. While handing over the paper, he commonly urged patients to go to "good shops," suggesting that many homeopathic pharmacies sold substandard products.

He gave simple dietary advice to many of his patients, such as, "Take food in time" or "Don't take *masala*, OK? No *masala*!" On one occasion, a middle-aged lady who suffered from chronic diarrhea also complained that her hair was not growing as strongly as it used to. After she had left, Dr. Bannerjee turned toward me and said in a hushed tone, "All they want is magic! . . . The main thing is plenty of fruit and vegetables. Too much of rice! Rice and *dal*, rice and *dal*, rice and *dal*. The food concept is very poor in this country."

Dr. Bannerjee and most other Calcutta homeopaths were tapping into their patients' focus on eating, tastes, and bowel movements. For their Bengali patients, this creates a semblance of agreement between their own ideas and those of the doctors. A patient seen by Dr. Bannerjee would hardly be able to tell the difference between homeopathy and other medical specialties. Behind this facade, the Calcutta homeopaths hide another rift between homeopathic and popular notions of pharmacy: the antidotes to medicine.

"No Toothpaste Allowed": Antidotes to Medicine

Calcutta homeopaths hold that their remedies' immaterial subtlety enables them to "go deep" into the patient's system and to redirect the vital force toward health. But this subtleness raises the question of how vulnerable they are to influences from other ingested substances, or indeed any event affecting the "nerves." To see food as a potential anti-dote to medicine rather than a potential source of health is characteristic of homeopathy. Hahnemann formulated this as follows:

> Considering the minuteness of the doses necessary and proper in homoeopathic treatment, we can easily understand that during the treatment everything must be removed from the *diet and regimen* which can have any medicinal action, in order that the small dose may not be overwhelmed and extinguished or disturbed by any foreign medicinal irritant. (Hahnemann 1994: §259; italics in original)

In the *Organon*, Hahnemann devotes several paragraphs to the discussion of the problem (§259-63), with most of the specific recommendations in a long footnote rather than in the main text (§260, fn. 2). The list of items to avoid reads like a humoral almanac for the everyday care of the self. Like the recommendations for daily regimen given by humoral medicine, food, exercise, hygiene, sexuality, and morality are all taken into consideration. In order for homeopathic medicine to work, the following "noxious influences" must be avoided:

> tooth powders and essences and perfumed sachets compounded of drugs; highly spiced dishes and sauces; spiced cakes and ices; crude medicinal vegetables for soups; dishes of herbs, roots and stalks of plants possessing medicinal qualities; [. . .] heated rooms, [. . .] a sedentary life in closed apartments, or the frequent indulgence in mere passive exercise, [. . .] taking a long siesta in a recumbent posture (in bed), sitting up long at night, uncleanliness, unnatural debauchery, enervation by reading obscene books, subjects of anger, grief, or vexation, a passion for play, over-exertion of mind and body, dwelling in marshy districts, damp rooms, penurious living, &c. [. . .] (Hahnemann 1994: §260, fn. 2)

Distinguishing between acute and chronic conditions, strict dietary rules only apply to patients who suffer from chronic diseases (Hahnemann 1994: §260). In case of acute diseases, the patient's cravings and desires are to be given free rein: "put no obstacles in the way of this voice of nature by refusing anything the patient urgently desires" (1994: §262).

When Calcuttan homeopaths talked about dietary recommenda-tions, the risk of antidoting was a contested issue. Calcutta homeopaths portray themselves as faithful followers of every word of Hahnemann. Homeopaths uttered solemn pledges of allegiance, describing them-selves as "strict practitioners" and "lovers of homeopathy" who treated Hahnemann like a "god." Yet for antidotes to medicines, Hahnemann's rules were rarely followed. Attitudes ranged from the extremely relaxed to the extremely restrictive. For example, Dr. Bannerjee told me an anecdote about a female migraine patient who was addicted to *pan* (betel nut with condiments). The doctor advised her to stop chewing *pan* so that the medicine would not be antidoted. One year later, the woman returned for a different ailment. Asked about the migraine, she replied, "'Oh, that was good. You gave me that dose and it was fine. But you told me not to chew betel-leaf when I take my first dose. But I couldn't do that. I put my medicine on top of the betel-leaf and *mmmmh*'" (Dr. Bannerjee). Startled by this experience, Dr. Bannerjee concluded that homeopathic medicine, however subtle it may be, was not easily antidoted, not even by pernicious substances such as betel nuts, spicy Indian food, or exhaust fumes from cars:

> In this country, you get the betel leaf with strong tobacco, and since then I decided, homeopathy is not that fragile. If it is the right medicine, it will act. [. . .] In this country, the typical Indian food, so much of spice and aroma, and India is the best country where homeopathy acts superb. You go to a bus and contract smoke—"everything will be antidoted"? I think that's a rubbish thought! I'm sorry, I get excited about it. I have a passion for this great science and I love it! And I don't want to say that homeopathy is that fragile. (Dr. Bannerjee)

On the opposite end of the spectrum, other homeopaths strictly applied Hahnemann's warnings about antidotes in food and a whole range of daily activities, including brushing teeth with toothpaste. One homeopath, son of one of Bengal's most well-known homeopaths, pointed out how he always had to argue with patients who were unable to follow his rigorous approach. He told patients that they had to make profound changes to their lifestyles: "I tell them not to use toothpaste: 'No toothpaste allowed!' [. . .] If you use toothpaste, it antidotes the action of the medicine. There's a lot of interaction. It will not allow the medicine to work" (Dr. Chodhuri). When I asked him how he deals with patients who are unwilling to make these changes, he said that his pure Hahnemannian style would never be compromised: "If I find that this man will not adjust to my diet, I simply turn him out. I say: 'Go to another doctor! I won't treat you!'" (Dr. Chodhuri). But such an exacting attitude did not go down well either with patients or within the homeopathic fraternity. I visited him again a few years after our first interview, and heard that meanwhile he had been ousted from a lectureship position at a homeopathic college, that his chamber had not been going well, and that it was now impossible to find a true Hahnemannian prescriber in all of Calcutta except himself.

These two doctors held extreme positions. Most homeopaths expressed opinions that lay somewhere in between. Those who restricted their patients' diet and regimen, as opposed to those who had a relaxed attitude, were clearly more numerous. Since there is an open debate about the effects of antidotes, homeopaths can use their recommendations flexibly: be strict to patients who *demand* a strict regimen, and be accommodating to patients who do not want to change their daily habits. In all cases, however, the recipe for success in private homeopathic practice is not to alienate patients by sticking to every letter of Hahnemann's *Organon*.

Disease in the "Modern World of Suppression"

It is widely believed in Calcutta that homeopathic remedies are able to achieve a permanent cure from illness. Instead of only giving a "quick fix," homeopathic remedies are said to take the illness out by its "root." Popular explanatory models commonly see wrong eating habits and a disturbed digestion as this root of illness. Since homeopaths ask their patients many questions about food and digestion, since most of them also give dietary advice, and since the medicines they prescribe are "subtle" enough not to produce digestive side effects, no clash between popular and homeopathic explanatory models arises. It may *seem* to patients that homeopathy also sees digestion as the root of disease.

Yet homeopathy contradicts popular ideas by highlighting that if there is a root of disease, it would have to be one of three chronic "miasms": syphilis, sycosis, or psora (Hahnemann 1994: §204). Hahnemann's use of the term "miasm" seems to suggest an affinity for humoral etiologies common in European medicine from antiquity up to the nineteenth century (Cipolla 1992; Latour 1988; Parker 1996; Vigarello 1988). In humoral medicine, "miasma" stands for any kind of "putrefaction" of the air, "vapors" from stagnant water, rotting corpses, or decaying vegetable matter (Hannaway 1993: 295). Hahnemann's "miasm" retains an idea of "noxious influence," but locates miasm not in the environment, but *inside* the human organism. Miasm is the reason behind all "true natural *chronic* diseases" (Hahnemann 1994: §78). It is a kind of hereditary condition, being transmitted from one generation to the next, afflicting mankind "for hundreds and thousands of years" (1994: §204). Among all medicines available, only homeopathy has a cure against miasm. If treated superficially, as in allopathy, the symptoms are only "suppressed," and are bound to reemerge even more lethally than before.

The usual metaphors used to describe miasms are either that of the "root" of a dangerous plant or that of the "soil" in which dangerous plants can thrive. This is how a homeopathic author analyzes Hahnemann's notion of psora for a contemporary audience:

Hahnemann explained Psora as a diseased condition or disposition to disease transferring from generation to generation for thousands of years behaving as a fostering soil for almost every possible diseased condition. Seed, being sown in the soil produces plant. But without extermination of the root, in spite of cutting off plant from the soil, the plant tends to grow again and again from the remaining root. Though the plant originated from a seed primarily now the remnant serves the cause of further growth of the plant. (Ghosh in HMAI 1999: 90)

Allopathy only cuts off the visible part of the plant, but leaves the root in the soil. Eventually, the disease will break forth again, with even greater danger to the organism than before. Skin disorders are among the most common manifestations of the miasmatic "soil" and "root." Allopathy's "quick fix" approach to disease risks aggravating the condition beyond a point of no return: "Some eminent modern dermatologists' perspicacious observation reveals that suppression of some kind of skin diseases results in virulent internal disorder and occasional death ultimately" (Ghosh in HMAI 1999: 92; see Hahnemann 1994: §203-6).

Calcutta homeopaths see miasm as essential for practice. Along with the vital force, miasm is said to be "very important" (Dr. Panja), "very very very important" (Dr. Khan), or "fundamental, fundamental" (Dr. Maitra). Miasm "should be considered first" (Dr. Patel), and "without miasm, you cannot practice" (Dr. Chodhuri). Especially for chronic diseases, diagnosis of the patient's miasmic constitution is the basis of treatment. Properly applied, an antimiasmatic remedy exercised a kind of "centrifugal" action. The concept of miasm is closely related to that of "suppression" of symptoms. In the *Organon*, suppression signifies allopathy's vain and perilous attempts to cure disease by removing superficial symptoms. Among contemporary homeopaths in Calcutta, "suppression" and "miasm" are always used in connection with each other. Only through targeting miasms was it possible to rectify diseases that had been passed down through the generations but that had only been "suppressed" with old-school remedies: "while you are treating present complaints, you can also rectify mistakes of the past. With suppressions, whether emotional or physical or traumatic suppression or drug suppression" (Prof. Thakur). Dr. Bannerjee explained that miasm was his "main concept," and had been the main concept of his father and grandfather as well, because it "goes deep into the system and brings suppressed symptoms to the surface." Such a deep-down therapy was mandatory "in the modern world of suppression," where patients have been maltreated by allopaths for generations and where symptom presentations are muddled up beyond recognition. The similarity of miasm and suppression makes "plant" and "soil" comparisons obvious: even if the visible manifestations of disease are eliminated and its "branches" cut off, the "root" lingers on.

Although Hahnemann does not blame the occurrence of miasm on allopathy, Calcutta homeopaths often ascribe the origin to it. Miasm, suppression, the side effects of allopathic drugs, and modern lifestyles become almost indistinguishable. In this homeopath's statement, the "foreign bodies" of allopathic drugs lead to miasmatic changes in the

body; these, in turn, lead to "genetic defects": "Modernization, development of mental conditions, psychosomatic, and also the vaccinations
and inoculations: foreign bodies are being introduced. [. . .] Today's
genetic defects: the background is miasm" (Dr. Maitra). Hahnemann
stated that the three miasms have become "intermingled" in the modern patient's constitution. The confusing mixture of internal and external makes homeopathic cure very difficult: "Mixed miasms are very
complicated" (Dr. Khan).

When Calcutta homeopaths speak about their patients, "suppression" also comes to stand for any kind of "complicated" personality.
This analysis of "complicated" patients is commonly mapped onto the
socioeconomic hierarchy. "Small" people are simple, "big" people are
complicated. The higher patients' socioeconomic standing, the more
likely they are to have undergone endless allopathic treatments that
"suppressed" their symptoms and their vital force: "Upper-class patients
consult too many specialists, so they come with very big files from
the allopaths, having all the information. The rich class suffers more,
because of suppression. Recently, it has become a status symbol: 'Just to
prove how rich I am and how big I am, I have consulted all these doctors!'" (Prof. Thakur).

"Big" people are better educated, and education results in a tendency
to dissociate the mind from the body, hence leading to a "suppression"
of immediate, unadulterated symptom expression. This model disputes
two conventional truths of (biomedical) public health, namely, that
"wealth is health" (people can afford to get medical treatment), and that
better education translates into better health (people know better what
is good and what is bad for them). Since higher incomes and higher
educational levels are seen as elements of modernization, homeopaths
think that modernization is bad for health. Given that homeopaths
equate modernization with Western lifestyles, a further conclusion is
inevitable to them, namely, that the constitution of the Indian patient is
healthier than the constitution of the Western patient, but that further
modernization will soon make the Indian patient as complicated as the
Western patient. Dr. Bannerjee, drawing comparisons between patients
encountered in three different settings (the slum clinic, the South Calcutta chamber for well-off Indians, and his chamber in the southeast
of England), concluded that the poor/simple/non-Westernized slum

dwellers may be poor, but the relative lack of suppression makes them healthier than the rich/difficult/Westernized Indian patients:

> When [the poor] come up with any problem, they will give you the words of the *Materia Medica*. The symptoms are so open: no suppression. [. . .] In the south [Calcuttan] clinic and in my clinic in England, they are almost the same, because in both these two clinics, there is suppression. And I think, in England it is more emotional suppression perhaps, and in the south clinic, there is more iatrogenic, like, if their child sneezes one time, they will take it down to the pediatrician. (Dr. Bannerjee)

The more patients are "modernized," the more they suppress. The more they suppress, the more they suffer: "They are really having some explosion of the mind" (Dr. Ali). The more they suppress, the more difficult it becomes to diagnose them; the harder they are to diagnose, the harder they are to treat. Poor people, "they enjoy life, they do not bother about their fever—and that is very good for them" (Prof. Thakur). Rich people, on the other hand, tend to worry about even the smallest ailment and overmedicate themselves and their families with biomedical drugs.

How to Medicate Overmedicated Patients

Hahnemann blamed not only allopathic doctors for prescribing quick-fix medicine but also the patients for *demanding* quick relief. This demand does not, of course, stop at the door of the homeopathic practice. Calcutta homeopaths feel pressured to deliver good health as quickly as allopaths. The need for economic survival makes homeopaths think hard about how to speed up diagnosis and therapy.

Problems with patients' expectations can begin with the diagnostic process. If a patient comes to a homeopath for the first time, the doctor needs to ask a broad range of questions in order to capture the totality of symptoms (on follow-up visits, much less time is needed). Three factors influence how much time a homeopath takes per patient: the number of patients seen during the day, the level of fees paid, and the patients' expectations. These factors are only loosely correlated with each other: many of the elite homeopaths see many patients *and* charge high fees, low-ranking homeopaths may charge low fees but still spend lots of time per patient, or elite homeopaths can spend a long time with elite patients who expect elite treatment.

Conflicts with patients arise about the duration and the content of history taking. In terms of duration, it could be expected that patients are happier when they are given more time by the doctor, but the opposite is the case: homeopaths complained that patients get easily bored or annoyed, especially the "modern" patients, those who lead a "fast life" and are used to the speed of allopathic consultations: "Some of the people who live a very fast life and who are accustomed to going to a doctor and telling them, 'Oh, I got a fever,' and immediately the doctor writes the medicine. [. . .] They don't understand why it is important to ask so many questions" (Prof. Thakur).

In terms of content, patients often do not understand why the doctor asks them about symptoms that seem unrelated to the health problem at hand, such as dreams, sexual desires, or attitudes to other people. Questions such as "Are you addicted to masturbation?" or "Do you lie to other people?" (which appear in this or a similar formulation in many questionnaires) may seem either too ridiculous or too intimate to be answered. But for some patients, even questions relating to food preferences and digestion, which otherwise build on a strong cultural consensus, may sometimes seem too onerous: "If it is a new patient who has come to try homeopathy, they do wonder: 'I have come with pain in my leg. Why are you asking how am I passing my bowels and about my sleep?'" (Dr. Gose).

Further problems arise in relation to patients' ability to articulate their symptoms. All the homeopaths agreed that the body language of "simple" patients is much easier to read than that of educated patients, because they suffered from less suppression than the more educated patients: "In case of lower-class patients, I take the help from the body language. There we are going to see the exact thing. The more sophisticated, the more intellectual, the more the body language is controlled by the emotion, and it is very difficult to take the case in the upper class in this way" (Prof. Thakur).

Poorer patients were said to be unable to answer *verbal* questions properly. "They are illiterate" was a stock description of lower-class patients:

"They cannot say anything. There is a problem here" (Dr. Patel). If they complained about pain and the doctor asked how the pain felt, they could only answer that "pain is there" (*byaetha lagche*) and nothing else beyond this. On the other hand, literate patients were also difficult to diagnose, partly because they did not want to spend time and partly because they had learned enough to challenge the doctor. Patients who came with "big files" from prior consultations with allopaths or other homeopaths tended to be the most obstinate: "Maybe the patient has taken this medicine before without success. So he may know the name of the medicine" (Dr. Shah). Patients who "know too much" had risen considerably over the years, not least with the rise of the internet. The doctors often tried to resolve such conflicts by professional authority rather than by explaining and convincing: "Sometimes they give me a look and I am saying: 'You might have had Nux Vomica, but you haven't had *my* Nux Vomica.' I have to say, they know the ins and outs" (Dr. Bannerjee).

Mismatched expectations about *remedies* are the greatest source of conflicts between homeopaths and patients. According to Hahnemannian orthodoxy, the best treatment is to admininster a single remedy, given in one dose at one time, and then to wait for several weeks or even months for it to produce results: "In no case under treatment is it necessary and *therefore not permissible* to administer to a patient more than *one single, simple medicinal* substance at a time. [. . .] It is absolutely not allowed in homeopathy, the one true, simple and natural art of healing, to give the patient *at one time* two different medicinal substances" (Hahnemann 1994: §273; emphasis in original). This is restated in most homeopathic publications. The HMAI, for example, upholds the principle of single dose as the second of three fundamentals of homeopathy, along with the law of similia and the principle of minimum dose (HMAI 1999: 13). In his book *Pleasure of Prescribing*, the director of the National Institute of Homeopathy also highlighted Hahnemann's dictum of single dose and remedy as the "golden rule" (Khan 2003: 41). In homeopathy, one remedy should be identified that precisely fits the patient's totality of symptoms. Once this remedy is found, it should not be given repeatedly because it acts so subtly on the vital force that two or more doses might antidote each other.

Yet to practice by this rule was not easy. Varying with the "character" of the remedy, the dose should be repeated at intervals that can be thirty days, sixty days, or longer. Given that these intervals were far longer than those of allopathic drugs, which are usually taken at least once a day, the proper moment for the repeat dosage was difficult to schedule. Much worse was that patients are so accustomed to taking medicines daily that they did not have the mental strength to endure long intervals.

A permissible and widely adopted solution to this problem is to prescribe placebos, a practice that Hahnemann explicitly endorsed for drug proving purposes (§91, 96, 281). From an orthodox point of view, it is not possible to cut short the time needed for the medicine to work. Yet during this time, patients can be given psychological reassurance: "What does placebo mean? 'To please'" (Dr. Shah). The best method of doing so was to keep them under regular pseudo-medication, because it makes patients "mentally satisfied" and takes away their anxieties:

[Placebo] is the only way of satisfying the patient, because they are thinking they are taking the medicine. [. . .] I never tell them: "Well, you don't need any medicine," because they would see another doctor. Unnecessary! That's why we close the chapter by giving placebo: sugar and milk. (Dr. Maitra)

Beyond the homeopaths' claim that placebos are exclusively prescribed to satisfy patients who lack the necessary self-control to wait, the doctors also have a vested interest in keeping up patients' expectations of regular medication. Placebos can provide steady revenue both to them (more consultations than necessary) and to homeopathic medicine shops (placebos cost the same as the real remedies).

On the prescription handed over to the patient, the code for a placebo is "/o" added to the code for potency. For example, a placebo pretending to be an extract of Nux Vomica potentized two hundred times is written as "Nux Vomica 200/o." Other codes for placebo are "nihilum" or "plano." Hence placebos are easy to make out once this "secret" is known. That this masquerade works with a patient population that allegedly knows homeopathy's "ins and outs" (Dr. Bannerjee) is surprising. One explanation is that placebos (as "empty" globules of nothing but milk and sugar) are not written down as prescriptions, but dispensed in unmarked vials during consultations.

For the homeopathic drug industry, placebos create an ambiguous situation. Mr. Mitra, sales director of Schwabe pharmaceuticals, confessed how much placebo prescriptions confused him. Like other manufacturers, Schwabe does not produce placebos for sale because "placebo is not really medicine." Doctors only used placebos to "take care of the psychology of the patient," not for "real" healing effects. Only a few outstanding homeopaths could convince patients of the efficacy of their remedies without resorting to placebos. In this perspective, frequent placebo uses were a serious weakness of homeopathy. Most placebos were dispensed by homeopaths themselves, whereas shops only rarely sold them. At what price placebos were sold was entirely up to the medicine shops to decide, but the sales manager felt that placebos should never be sold, especially not under the brand name Schwabe. In the company's sales audits, placebo sales could never be recorded. This meant that a number of remedies were sold by shops as placebos under companies' brand names without the companies making any profit from the sales.

The owner of a reputable homeopathic medicine shop in southwest Calcutta, who also happened to be trained as a homeopathic doctor, said that around 10 percent of prescriptions were for placebos. Doctors obviously tried to conceal placebos as much as possible, and to keep up the facade, his shop charged the same price for a placebo as for a proper homeopathic remedy. Doctors consciously prescribed "brand name placebos" to augment patients' faith in the efficacy of the globules. For example, they might write "Nux Vomica (Schwabe) 30/0." Placebo prescriptions posed a particular problem to his shop, because his was the only one in Calcutta where customers could see, through a window behind the sales counter, how the compounder takes out a brand name bottle, puts a few drops into a vial of globules, and shakes them up to potentize them. To maintain the impression that a proper medicine is prepared, his compounder kept bottles with empty brand name labels to prepare placebos from them. Sometimes the compounders could not be bothered to perform the entire charade, so prepared placebos are kept ready in vials: "We have a placebo bottle ready. But often we're too busy to make this in front of the customer, so we always keep placebo at the ready."

Perilous Polypharmacy

Placebos were also employed to avoid what orthodox homeopaths saw as a homeopath's worst lapse into sin: polypharmacy, the prescription of multiple remedies at once. Polypharmacy can take two forms: either a doctor combines several single remedies, or he prescribes a patent medicine produced by a homeopathic manufacturer that contains various remedies in one prepackaged dose. For example, Schwabe markets formulations such as Alpha™-TS, "a drug that lowers tension and stress without side effects." Each of these contains, in undeclared potencies, a combination of remedies. Today's patients were so busy that they did not want to wait for single-remedy regimes to take out the root of the illness, and they were so accustomed to biomedical prescription patterns that they always expected to get at least five different drugs at once: "Here, people have got the idea: 'If I take more drugs, I will get better,' because they are habituated to taking many allopathic medicines. Like, when they take antibiotics, they take vitamins also" (Dr. Pakrasi). Polypharmacy also reflected a lack of homeopathic expertise and a lack of confidence in identifying the proper single remedy: "Combination drugs are done by people who either don't know homeopathy, or they don't have the guts or confidence in the drugs" (Prof. Thakur).

No homeopath stated openly that Hahnemann's principles were outdated and had to be revised so that multiple remedies were acceptable. All homeopaths claimed that they only prescribed according to Hahnemann. Especially elite homeopaths, with flourishing private chambers, prominent academic positions, and membership in governmental committees, declared steadfast allegiance to the orthodoxy. Although they also complained about patients being illiterate, impatient, and noncompliant, they felt confident about the power of their professional charisma: "I maintain a professional ethics with that and say: 'I am the doctor and you are the patient. So what I am giving is my decision'" (Dr. Bannerjee). The better-off homeopaths could even choose whom to see and whom not to see. Several of them said that they refused to treat any patient who could not accept that homeopathic remedies took longer to work than allopathic ones. One even stated that all low-class people only ever wanted quick relief, and that he would rather turn them away than compromise his homeopathic principles:

[Poor people] have an idea that homeopathic medicine takes time, but they have to be cured within a short time, otherwise they will not be able to join their work. So they don't come at all to the homeopathic doctor.

Even if they do come, even with their babies, I do not like to treat them, because they will not follow my advice. [. . .] So I also don't like that those people come to me. They are illiterate, they are crude. A temperature is there, they want a cure in one hour! (Dr. Gose)

By writing a single "active" remedy and a series of placebos, a homeopathic doctor can stay true to Hahnemann's single-remedy principle without alienating patients anticipating a cocktail of drugs. But the question of whether polypharmacy could still have therapeutic advantages over single-remedy treatments remains open.

The veneer of an uncompromising rejection of polypharmacy peeled off when homeopaths were asked in roundabout ways. Some of them mentioned that they had experimented with polypharmacy, but that they were disappointed with the results and happily returned into the fold of Hahnemannian orthodoxy: "If you want to cure a person in a true sense, you have to give a single medicine. Two, three, four drugs mixed together, you cannot cure a person. I also have experimented with giving them mixtures, but I came to the conviction that it is simply not possible" (Prof. Thakur). There were a few situations where polypharmacy was permitted. For example, if there was a patient whom the doctor could not cure, such as terminally ill patients, polypharmacy could be used: "In most cases, I use single medicine, but in cases in the dying stages, I give combinations of drugs. Just to ease the pain and other things" (Dr. Barman).

A distinction between "curing" patients and "alleviating" patients' suffering was increasingly extended to all patients. The idea was that homeopathic remedies act like allopathic remedies when prescribed in combination with each other, and are given in multiple doses. Even if a doctor secretly frowned upon his patients, he could be pressured to prescribe multiple remedies for quick-fix effects: "Here, the people are illiterate, they don't give it any time: 'Uh! Oh! I have to work, so give me that medicine! From tomorrow morning I have to be back in my factory!' Not patient enough, that's the problem! So in India, we give six doses, seven doses, ten doses at a time, so they feel relieved, so they feel: 'I'm OK'" (Dr. Pakrasi). Polypharmacy may not take out the "roots" of the disease and give permanent cure, but at least the patient was happy. Even if it gave only a superficial cure, it was still better to use homeopathy instead of allopathy, because homeopathic medicine cost less and was free of side effects.

According to a small-time homeopath, patients started to have far more "faith" in homeopathy because of these changes. He did not say openly that an allopathic style of prescribing homeopathy was the reason for this, but he strongly believed that it was the biomedicalization of homeopathy, in teaching and in practice, that enabled this change. Patients now had more faith in homeopathy because there were more rigorous—more biomedical—standards in the education: "Anatomy, surgery, physiology, gynecology, these the homeopaths have to learn. [. . .] Basic knowledge, basic study of these fields is needed. *Bioscience*, the same as the allopaths" (Dr. Siva). More importantly, new homeopathic remedies and prescribing methods had greatly shortened the time needed for the medicines to work. Whereas homeopathy was previously only good for chronic illnesses, now it could deal with acute problems as effectively as biomedicine: "Before, it used to take time. Now we are getting it done quickly. For example, sunstroke, fever, influenza, dysentery, diarrhea, many, many diseases. Acute pain. For these things we have quick relief medicines" (Dr. Siva). Significantly, this doctor belonged to the "lower class" of homeopaths, those who struggled to survive. He did not have his own chamber and shuttled back and forth among several homeopathic centers on his scooter. He barely eked out a living from practicing homeopathy, but was optimistic about the future. From his point of view, the influence of biomedicine on homeopathy was a positive development. It promised to decrease the status of older homeopaths in favor of recent college graduates trained in biomedicine, and the promise of "quick relief" brought in more patients.

Bigger profits from prescribing multiple remedies seemed to be a decisive argument for many homeopaths, especially those who dispensed themselves. As Prof. Thakur pointed out sarcastically, it was impossible to say how homeopathic cocktail medicines were having an effect on the vital force, but it was possible to say that if he charged twenty rupees for one remedy and then added another remedy for twenty rupees, he earned forty rupees. Homeopathic retailers said that they rarely ever saw prescriptions for single remedies. One of them estimated that only 2 or 3 percent of the prescriptions that patients brought to his shop were ever for single remedies. Up to 60 percent of prescriptions were for different remedies combined with each other, the rest for formulations. This tallied with data from the sales manager of Schwabe, who stated that about 50 percent of his company's remedies sold in West Bengal were for single remedies, and the other 50 percent for formulations. He reminded me that "50 percent single-remedy products sold" did not mean that they were actually used as single remedies by prescribers. When I pointed out to him that almost all the doctors I had talked to rejected polypharmacy, he was genuinely surprised that so many of them pretended to be orthodox Hahnemannians when the evidence from sales statistics showed that they were not: "I don't want to mention names. But if someone says that he is not using combinations if he does, that is a different story" (Mr. Biswas).

Typically, the homeopaths who claimed to be pure Hahnemannians added that they were among a dying breed of true believers. They said that it was impossible to counter the corruption within the body of homeopathic doctors. Modernity spoiled health through environmental degradation, urbanization, and industrialization. Modern allopaths further spoiled health by treating patients with drugs that had uncontrollable side effects. Allopathy's promise to give quick relief spoiled patients' expectations about what medicine can realistically deliver. Now modern corruption even took possession of homeopathy, the last defender of unspoiled health, by diverting the doctors from the path of truth shown by Hahnemann.

When greed for fame and money ruined the homeopath's self-discipline, he became responsible for producing side effects that are even worse than those produced by allopaths. The bleakest view was that modernity, allopathy, and allopathic homeopathy produced diseases so bad that not even orthodox homeopathy could cure them. One purist follower of Hahnemann held the most pessimistic opinions about the future of the discipline:

> Now it's total degradation. [. . .] The days of Hahnemann are gone. Nowadays, in the modern era, it is said that single remedy, single dose does not work. If you want to achieve quick reputation in the society, you have to prescribe multiple remedies. You have to cure fast, life is very fast, so they prescribe multiple remedies. But ultimately, what do they do? They neither cure the patient, nor give relief. They just jumble up the

case. They make a hotchpotch inside. [. . .] Allopathic medicines work
on the physical, organic level. They damage the physical-organic level of
the organ. But our [homeopathic] medicine alters the nature of the vital
force, which is more injurious. [. . .] The effect on the vital force, it takes
a long time to understand. By that time, it's too late. Sometimes patients
come to me after all this, and I tell the patient: I cannot cure you, you are
incurable. (Dr. Chodhuri)

Such despair sat side by side with greater hopes for the future.
Even if many felt that polypharmacy and other malpractices adapted
from allopathy had compromised the integrity of homeopathy, most
of them reassured themselves that "the day will come" (Dr. Maitra)
when the true principles had been reestablished and when they could
match allopathy in social prestige, economic reward, and scientific
recognition.

4

Psychiatry

Medicating Modern Moods

"Depression Awareness"

Psychopharmaceuticals have been generically produced by Indian companies for decades. Between 1972 and 2005, India's laws only covered the
mechanical processes of drug manufacturing, but not the active pharmaceutical ingredients (APIs). In practice, this meant that any molecule, even if protected by patents in the originating countries, could
be reverse-engineered and generically produced in India. Over the past
decades, this patent regime allowed the Indian pharmaceutical industry
to become the world's leading producer of generic medications (Chaudhuri 2005). Indian companies have taken up psychopharmaceuticals as
a major segment in both domestic and export markets. With India's full
accession to Trade-Related Intellectual Property Rights (TRIPS) under
the World Trade Organization (WTO) in 2005, Indian manufacturers
now must respect product patents. In the psychopharmaceuticals market, however, the full effects of TRIPS will not be felt for several years to
come, since so many molecules are already available in India. As a professor of psychiatry pointed out to me in 2005, there is an abundance of
pharmaceuticals generally, and of psychopharmaceuticals particularly:
"There are sixty thousand drugs in the market. You can live without
the latest Western drugs for fifteen years" (Prof. Chatterjee). There are
several new drugs available in India that are not even available in all

European or North American countries. For example, the drug tianep-
tine (Stablon) is sold in India but neither in the United States nor in the
United Kingdom: "We get *all* the molecules" (Dr. Burman).

Until the 1990s, the Indian market was dominated by benzodiazepines and tricyclic antidepressants (TCAs) such as amitriptyline
(Elavil). Since the mid-1990s, Indian companies are also producing newer generations of drugs, such as the selective serotonin reuptake inhibitors (SSRIs), serotonin-norepinephrine reuptake inhibitors
(SNRIs), and selective serotonin reuptake enhancers (SSREs). The
most famous molecule in the SSRI group is fluoxetine, licensed in 1987
and best known by its American brand name, Prozac. Amitriptyline
and other TCAs had long been prescribed by specialist psychiatrists,
but had only limited use among general physicians and other nonpsy-
chiatric consultants. With the rise of the SSRIs, antidepressant drugs
became popular among a far wider group of Indian prescribers because
they were perceived as innocuous compared to TCAs or tranquilizers.
In the first decade of the twenty-first century, the Indian market for
antidepressants is characterized by fierce competition among dozens
of generic producers, who all promote practically identical products.
Antidepressants are seen as extremely lucrative because a patient is
expected to be buying medicines for several months, if not years. That
is why these drugs can be very profitable for companies, and in return,
pharmaceutical companies reward doctors for prescriptions.

Three phases of antidepressant prescribing in India can be distinguished: use by specialists, use by licensed nonspecialists, and use by
quacks. First, the drugs are promoted to the obvious specialists in the
field: psychiatrists in private practice. In the second phase, antidepressants are promoted to nonspecialists. This group includes GPs and all
allopathic prescribers who deal with chronic illness, such as cardiologists
and gastroenterologists. Targeting these nonspecialists is the crucial step
to increase sales. In India, as in all developing countries, there are few
psychiatrists and most of them practice in the large cities only (Kumar
2011). Out of the roughly 360 members of the West Bengal branch of the
Indian Psychiatric Society, the majority lives and practices in Calcutta.
In the third phase, antidepressants reach even untrained rural "quack"
doctors, who learn about these drugs chiefly through ready drug reckon-
ers, through prescriptions that doctor-shopping patients show to them,

and through medical representatives from companies that promote their products to anyone who can prescribe them.

By now, antidepressants have gone through at least the first two phases of their market life cycle, and even SSRIs are now also used by quacks (Ecks and Basu 2009). Generic antidepressants are easily available across all West Bengal districts. For example, at least one brand of fluoxetine could be bought in 77 percent of all Bengali shops in the mid-2000s (Tripathi, Dey, and Hazra 2005), and the SSRI fluoxetine was more widely available than amitriptyline, the leading drug among the "old" tricyclics. All the larger and more established Indian companies have already moved away from promoting SSRIs aggressively. Instead, they try to launch newer molecules. In the mid-2000s, duloxetine from the SNRI group was the drug *du jour*—only to go out of fashion by the late 2000s. Companies also work on maintaining their market shares through nurturing "good relations" with the doctors they already know. If anything can be said about antidepressants in India with absolute certainty, it is that there are no prescribers left who would not have heard of them, and that even small-time GPs are using these drugs routinely.

In parallel to targeting prescribers, Indian corporations also try to change popular notions of depression. In India, direct-to-consumer advertising of prescription drugs, including all forms of antidepressants, is not allowed. But campaigns to "raise awareness" about disease conditions are legal. One form this kind of marketing takes is distribution of leaflets that invite people to take a "self-test" for depression (Ecks 2005). These self-tests do not advertise a specific product but aim to grow the market for antidepressants generally. For example, a leaflet distributed by a Mumbai-based company is entitled "The Depression Self Test." On the front, there is a big "smiley" face encircled by the words "Defeat Depression—Spread Happiness," and the text underlines that the test is "FREE!" (implying that people usually pay for diagnostics like this). On the back, a list of ten items for self-diagnosis is presented. Whoever experiences "five or more" of the following ten symptoms is advised to see a doctor:

1. a persistent sad, anxious, or "empty" mood;
2. sleeping too little or too much;
3. reduced appetite and weight loss or increased appetite and weight gain;

4. loss of interest or pleasure in activities once enjoyed;

5. restlessness or irritability;

6. persistent physical symptoms that don't respond to treatment;

7. difficulty concentrating, remembering, or making decisions;

8. fatigue or loss of energy;

9. feeling guilty, hopeless, or worthless;

10. recurrent thoughts of death/suicidal attempt.

The leaflet was produced and distributed by Ipca Labs Ltd., a company that produces a range of psychopharmaceuticals and promotes them through a division for "therapy-focused marketing of neuropsychiatric drugs." Creating consumer awareness of mental health problems is one of this division's main activities.

Corporate attempts to change popular perceptions are, however, of only marginal importance and have never been a focus of Indian companies, in stark contrast to U.S. firms. More substantial is the industry's influence on the media. The last decades have seen an increase in newspaper and TV reports on mental health problems, especially on common disorders such as depression. Typical are articles like this in the Calcutta newspaper *The Telegraph* of March 2, 2008, which headlines depression as "that secret disease" and highlights the World Health Organization prediction that depression will be the second most prevalent health problem in the world by 2020. The newspaper further quotes a range of experts, among them an associate professor of psychiatry at the All India Institute of Medical Sciences: "Depression is grossly underdiagnosed and undertreated in India." Bengali newspapers also have regular columns devoted to mental health problems, which are written by eminent Calcutta doctors. Local TV stations feature podium discussions among experts and invite viewers to phone in and discuss their problems live on air. Whether or not increased media attention to mental health is directly sponsored by corporations is difficult to say. What is clear is that the psychiatrists who feed the media stories are heavily sponsored by the industry. It is also certain that the Indian media coverage of psychiatric topics is almost identical to that in the United States. For example, health sections in Calcutta's English-language newspapers feature syndicated articles from the *New York Times* and other U.S. media.

Psychiatrists generally saw "awareness" as still far away from what it could be. Many said that more awareness about the scope of psychiatric drugs was one of the discipline's most important tasks for the next years. Dr. Roy was particularly keen to extend the reach of psychiatry, to include not only clearly pathological states but also cognitive and emotional enhancement to the highest possible level:

> In the U.S. today, they go to psychiatrists and ask, "How can I be my best?" What has not yet come to India is the transformation from patienthood to personhood. I would like to see that more and more people come to psychiatry saying, "I want to function at my best, I want to contribute my best, so tell me: in what way can I make improvements? What nutrition do I require for my brain and what do I require so I can give the best to my family, my society, my country?" That sort of awareness, that you are performing slightly below your par of awareness, "come and meet a mental health professional." (Dr. Roy)

Dr. Roy envisioned nothing less than a co-constitution of pharmaceuticals, citizenship, and Indian nationalism. Taking psychotropic drugs is framed not just as a right but as every Indian citizen's duty. The low demand for psychotropics in India—compared to Western countries—is turned into a call for a utopian politics of national development *and* self-development through drugs. For him, psychotropics should be used like food supplements, not only to treat disease but also to help patients become "better than well." And the aim should be to think not just of individual betterment but of the improvement of the whole society.

Looked at closely, much of the marketing to "raise patient awareness" in India is, in fact, targeted at doctors (Ecks 2010b). This became strikingly clear to me during a "depression awareness workshop" organized by Pfizer Inc., the world's largest pharmaceutical company. Invited to the workshop were twelve general physicians who practiced in a middle-class area of South Calcutta. The event took place in the back rooms of an expensive restaurant and lasted for around three hours. After a note of welcome, Pfizer representatives showed a fifteen-minute video introducing PrimeMD. Then a buffet lunch was served, lasting for about forty-five minutes. Afterward, a Calcutta psychiatrist gave a PowerPoint presentation on the epidemiology of depression and on available treatments, with Pfizer's Indian brand of sertraline described as the best drug. The presentation given by the hired "thought leader" (Elliott 2010) was supplied by Pfizer reps upon his arrival at the venue, and his formal presentation consisted only of reading out bullet points. In the final session of the day, the GPs were given case vignettes and asked to identify who should be labeled "MDD" (major depressive disorder) and be given antidepressants.

The stated aim of the "awareness" workshop was not to advertise Pfizer's products but to teach the GPs how to use a particular diagnostic questionnaire, called PrimeMD Today™ (short for *Primary Care Evaluation of Mental Disorders*). Pfizer suggests that this questionnaire should be given to patients in the waiting room and be filled in by them before they speak to the doctor. Together with the patient, the doctor would go over the answers and make a diagnosis. The video that opened the workshop showed that leading American psychiatrists developed this questionnaire in order to "enhance the ability of busy physicians to diagnose mental health problems." Because GPs were heavily pressured for time, they needed a "quick, easy-to-use" diagnostic tool to determine whether a patient should be given antidepressants. PrimeMD promised to give them an "advanced algorithm" with which a diagnosis would not take longer than one or two minutes. The Pfizer material stressed the pivotal role of GPs in the global fight against depression: most patients first contacted GPs and other nonspecialists, but since they often did not recognize it, depression remained badly undertreated. The video underlined that "depression *should* and *can* be treated by GPs" and called on the doctors to use it daily: "Believe it or not, it is easy to learn, and you can diagnose depression in less than one minute." The video went on to state that PrimeMD, while based on American diagnostic criteria, was now also available in eleven Indian languages (Hindi, Marathi, Bengali, etc.). Translations were tested with three hundred patients in each language to adjust them perfectly to local idioms.

One of the case studies enacted in the video is the story of Mrs. Rao. A general physician introduces Mrs. Rao as a patient who is "not well educated." She has to support the whole family because her husband is an unemployed alcoholic. Mrs. Rao complains of backaches and headaches and has previously undergone an operation. When the GP gives

Mrs. Rao the PrimeMD questionnaire to fill in, he detects an "underlying depression." The video shows how the doctor and the patient interact (slightly abridged here):

> PATIENT: What is the cause of this?
> DOCTOR: We will come to that. First let's go over some of your answers in the questionnaire. . . . You are not feeling so well . . . you are responsible for the whole family. . . . I think your symptoms are caused by depression.
> PATIENT: No, no, no! I just have a headache! I am not going mad!
> DOCTOR: You are not going insane. Depression is treatable. It will take six months to cure.
> PATIENT: Six months! Oh no! A few days, and I will be all right.
> DOCTOR: Depression is a medical condition. You wouldn't let a medical condition go without treatment, would you?

The fictional patient, despite being resistant to a depression diagnosis, is being educated by her physician and made to understand that her problems did not come from her family problems, but from depression. The message conveyed by the video is that the GPs' educational mission is greatly enhanced if an awareness-raising questionnaire like PrimeMD is put at the center of the doctor-patient encounter. Moreover, Pfizer claims not to push as many pills as it can, but to be a "good citizen" and to fulfill a public service by raising awareness about medical conditions. In the teaching video, a voice off-camera states that "Pfizer's commitment goes beyond developing effective therapies. The company works closely with patient groups and opinion leaders to increase awareness, as well as creating disease management programs. Part of this program is the development of one diagnostic tool, PrimeMD Today."

The drive to raise "awareness" is symptomatic of biomedicalization (Clarke et al. 2010), which wants patients to become flexible, self-caring consumers who take upon themselves the responsibility for being healthy. While PrimeMD was meant by Pfizer's headquarters to "empower" patients, everything said and done during the Calcutta workshop aimed to undermine this. In his lecture, the invited Calcutta psychiatrist told the GPs that they *might* try giving the questionnaire directly to patients, but that this was likely to increase patients' resistance to drug prescriptions. Instead he recommended *not* to share the questionnaire with patients. The Pfizer representatives were happy with this message even though it clearly subverted the goal of increased "patient awareness." At no point during the workshop or afterward were local-language versions of the questionnaire handed out to the GPs. When I asked one of the reps if I could have a look at the Bengali version of PrimeMD, he said that he did not bring any, because giving the questionnaire to patients was not really the point. Patients might misunderstand the questions and misdiagnose themselves. PrimeMD was a "strictly scientific" tool and could never be used properly by patients.

Both the local Pfizer representatives and the lecturing psychiatrist discouraged the GPs from using PrimeMD as designed by Pfizer's headquarters because they already knew that this questionnaire would irritate patients. They knew that GP chambers do not provide the level of privacy that PrimeMD assumes. Most importantly, insinuating to general patients that they might be "mental" cases upsets them. Pfizer local reps knew that private GPs have no time for or interest in "educating" patients. Instead, GPs prefer to not even tell patients anything about antidepressants and try to avoid labeling them as suffering from "depression" as much as they can (Ecks 2008). Instead of confronting patients with questionnaires, the doctors avoided any mention of "depression" or "antidepressant." Patients had too many superstitions about mental disorders to make it possible for GPs to talk straight with them. All in all, Pfizer's depression awareness workshop was more about making the doctors happy with a nice buffet lunch than about helping to spread psychiatric enlightenment for all.

"Bowel Obsession"

If Indian patients are as resistant to antidepressants as both doctors and the industry suggest, what are the "superstitions" that seem to hinder their efforts? One of the answers that the doctors give to this question is that Bengali patients are "bowel obsessed." Psychiatrists—and indeed all allopaths I interviewed, irrespective of specialization—share the notion that Bengalis are too focused on their digestion (Ecks 2010a). Even if other ethnic groups in Calcutta were also concerned with their stomachs and livers, it is a general opinion among local physicians that

Bengalis take this concern to the extreme. What psychiatrist Dr. Desh-pande says here could have been said by any allopath:

> In our culture, most problems are tummy-related problems: "I don't get a clear bowel movement." This is, I think, a state characteristic of Bengalis. If you ask someone in the morning, "How are you?" the first thing he will say is "I didn't get a good motion this morning." Or he is looking very satisfied: "Yes, I got a good motion in the morning."

For the doctors—almost all of whom are Bengalis themselves—"bowel obsession" is a cluster of ideas and practices that are centered on the fixed notion that if the belly is healthy, the whole body will be healthy, too. Bengalis were even more concerned about food than other groups in India: "Bengalis are a very gastronomic community. Give them a chance to eat and they will never finish! So they are mostly occupied with *gas*, which happens in the tummy" (Dr. Bose). Bengalis also loved to talk about digestion, be it their own, their relatives', their neighbors', or even random acquaintances'. Far from being a dark and shameful part of the body, the bowels were a topic of everyday discussion, wide open to public scrutiny. Bengalis paid great attention to their digestive processes: how they feel at various times of the day, their appetite before meals and sensations after meals. Bowel-obsessed patients interpreted most—or even all—illness symptoms as caused by disturbed digestion. Even illnesses that are not, for the doctors, evidently linked to digestion, such as hair loss, headaches, or heart disease, were explained as symptoms of a disturbance lurking in the bowels. Typical of Bengali bowel obsession was a fixation on exactly one motion per day, not one more or less, and that it had to happen right after getting up in the morning. Any deviation from this norm was interpreted as a sign of illness.

Bowel obsession was, for Calcutta physicians, an archaic leftover from humoral traditions such as Ayurveda (Weiss et al. 1988). From the Ayurvedic corpus, only a few elements had survived. Ayurveda's *tridosha* principle had been stripped of *kapha* and *pitta*, to leave only *vata*. Then, the "wind" principle had morphed into *gas*. Psychiatrist Dr. Nandi retraced this history as follows:

The Ayurveda system that was prevalent here over the past thousand years, and all old medicine systems, were all based on bodily fluids. So *gas* was one of the most common Ayurvedic explanations of this. And this has been carried on as folklore. And they try to explain all bodily symptoms in terms of that. Why they don't explain in terms of other bodily fluids and concentrate it all on this one, I have no explanation. [*Question: You mean the three doshas?*] Yes, *doshas*. Basically, of these three doshas, two are forgotten. Only the *vata* part remains. And *vata* is very easily translated as *gas*. So *gastric* becomes *gas* and is related to *vata* from the Ayurvedic system, and all is explained in its terms. (Dr. Nandi)

Comparing his experiences in Calcutta, Bangalore (Karnataka), and Ranchi (Jharkhand), Dr. Nandi said that Bengalis complain more about *gas* than others, and that the expression is "probably specific to this region." The focus on bowels was, however, pan-Indian. Ignorance about anatomy was also to be found across India. People knew so little about their bodies that they did not even have vernacular terms for "liver": "In the original Hindu or Muslim physiology, there was nothing called 'liver.' The whole body was a huge cylindrical structure with fluids in it. The only thing there was the stomach" (Prof. Chatterjee).

The humoral obsession with digestion was "timeless," but to some extent exacerbated by historical transformations, above all urbanization. All Bengalis were obsessing about their bowels, but for city dwellers, regular and healthy digestion was far more problematic than for rural folks. This opened up a juxtaposition between an idealization of traditional peasant life and modern city life. Living in the countryside and working in farming was an ideal way of having regular motions. Living in the city, however, caused all kinds of digestive disturbances, from the constipation of sedentary life to the diarrhea of drinking contaminated water.

The problem with bowel obsession was not that patients lacked knowledge of how the human body truly works, because that was the prerogative of physicians anyway. Instead, the problem was that bowel-obsessed patients suffered from the false illusion of knowing how the body works, and that they were so convinced of what the doctors regarded as crazy ideas that they resisted professional views to the contrary. No matter whether a patient's problem was hair loss, impotence, headaches, skin disease, or fatigue—at the root of it all was digestive imbalance.

Most of the time, this overattribution of symptoms was only a harmless obstruction of practice that required a bit of time for clarification: "Especially those from the rural background, when I give them my prescription, they might ask me: 'But you have not touched my belly!' So I need to tell them that I don't need to touch their belly to treat their depression" (Dr. Nandi). But "bowel obsession" could also become a serious point of disagreement that brought unnecessary suffering or could even be fatal. This was particularly the case with heart problems "mimicking" digestive discomforts. As a Calcuttan psychiatrist said, "Bengalis insist on bowel functions. [. . .] It comes from alternative medicine culture, this stress on diet and food. This is a cultural notion. Here people die of heart attack and say it's *gas!*" (Dr. Chawla). Asked about how Bengali patients present complaints, a professor of psychiatry at one of Calcutta's medical colleges joked that "India has more *gas* than West Asia. We are floating on *gas!*" (Prof. Chatterjee). Along with "headaches," digestive problems were among the most common symptoms presented in clinical encounters.

It was also a common view among allopaths that depression and anxiety take "somatoform" expressions, especially in female and "uneducated" patients. Depression and anxiety were frequently "masked" by gastrointestinal complaints. "There is a belief that a person who has a very good GI tract is very healthy. When you are ill, there is always a chance to express your illness in terms of GI symptoms" (Dr. Mukharji). But the allopaths also often point out that there is no inevitable link between depression and digestive complaints, since Bengalis experienced *all* health problems in the first place as digestive problems. Hence it was impossible to directly translate irregular bowel movements, flatulence, or indigestion into psychiatric categories. A psychiatrist underlined that *gastric* complaints must be accompanied by other symptoms to justify psychiatric treatment: "If someone complains of gas, you have to see if it's only GI or is it just the tip of the iceberg: is there also lack of energy, loss of energy, lost interest in things? When getting up, don't like doing anything? Disturbance of sleep, appetite, libido? *Then* only will you call it depression."

Once a psychiatrist had "unmasked" depression, it was still very difficult to convince patients that digestive troubles were not the root of suffering. A female psychiatrist, Dr. Sinha, pointed out how exasperated she sometimes got with patients' ideas of *gas* causing havoc in the body:

> They have a lot of concepts of gas. Some of them are extremely unscientific. For example, if they have some headaches, some discomfort in the head, they think it's because the *gas* is traveling upwards to the head. So sometimes I tell them: "Don't confuse me with your very unscientific views!" I tell them. I *do* tell them! Because whether that actually does change their views or not, at least next time I don't have to hear this again, because I'm not going to listen to it [*laughs*].

More often than general allopaths, psychiatrists bemoaned that digestive problems were such common presentations that they tended to disregard them altogether: "Abdominal discomfort is so common, we usually ignore that. Everybody says 'I have some flatulence' or 'sluggish bowels'" (Dr. Ghosh). Whereas other doctors still try to find out first if digestive complaints are really about a digestive disease, psychiatrists are prone to take little notice of them. Like other specialists within biomedicine, psychiatrists look at patients from their own discipline's viewpoint and tend to disregard problems that are *not* psychiatric.

There are several somatoform presentations that are not visibly related to "bowel obsession" yet can also be retraced to this notion. One cluster of expressions refers to diffuse burning pain all over the body. For example, patients said that their "body is burning" (*ga jhala kora*). Another common term is *bish*, meaning "poison," but also a diffuse all-body pain. *Bish* is so common that the term has even become a recognized category among UK doctors treating South Asian patients, especially Bangladeshis. That "pain travels all over the body" and causes havoc in the head and elsewhere is another version of the concept of *vata*. A Calcutta psychiatrist (Dr. Mittal) said that "headache" was the most common physical complaint because patients anticipated that psychiatrists always looked for a "head"-based problem. Even if they felt that the source of illness was unquestionably in the bowels, they talked about headaches first. But these headaches were, to them, nothing other than *gas* pushing upward.

A few psychiatrists said that "semen loss" could also be traced to Ayurvedic notions of digestion. *Dhat*, which Calcutta psychiatrists defined as "ejaculation without willingness," was seen as a digestive problem, both because semen was a digestive product and because semen loss was caused by an excess of internal wind that pressed it outwards. Women also thought they suffered from *dhat* when they had leucorrhea, or discharge of white mucus from the vagina. Nowadays, however, *dhat* was mostly a complaint by uneducated patients, and generally less frequent than is usually described in the psychiatric literature.

Echoing Pfizer's PrimeMD marketing material, all psychiatrists agree that somatization was strongest among patients who were not well educated. To diagnose them, there was no other route than relying on physical symptoms. Dr. Basu said that uneducated patients could only ever report physical changes, such as decreased appetite, disturbed sleep, or lack of concentration. Moods independent of bodily sensations were not something they usually spoke about. Poor patients labored under so much daily misery that they found it impossible to distinguish between acute depressive symptoms and everything else that was awful about their lives: "Illiterate people cannot express their mood properly, there are so many negative things in their life that they cannot separate the depressive symptoms. Depression is there for a particular time period, but they cannot separate that particular period from their general life story."

"They Can Express Very Nicely"

Although Calcutta psychiatrists felt that somatization was particularly challenging to their daily practice, they did not hold that all Bengalis somatize all the time. Instead, the psychiatrists mentioned several reasons why the notion of excessive somatization among Indian patients was inaccurate. Mind and body were not separate entities, neither for lay folk nor for state-of-the-art biochemical psychiatry, hence physical presentations were continuous with mental anguish and vice versa. That meant, for the psychiatrists, that there is no form of somatization that does not have some physical basis as well. Some psychiatrists cited research that showed that somatization might be more common among "Third World people" (Dr. Mittal), but it was *not* specific to them.

"Everyone somatizes," Dr. Mittal said, quoting a study he had once read that showed that Indian patients somatize depression to the same extent as Italians (see Jadhav 2007).

In biomedical consultations, Indian patients tended to present bodily instead of "psychological" symptoms to allopaths because they see biomedical treatments as best suited for physiological symptoms. Problems of the heart-mind are not seen as its specialty area (see Jadhav, Weiss, and Littlewood 2001). Dr. Deshpande paraphrased a Bengali poem that encapsulated popular notions of sadness as a state of isolation that one must suffer without any help from others, least of all from doctors:

> We had to learn this poem. [. . .] It starts off by saying, "The land where the largest roses are blooming, and where the butterflies flitter about, and where the sky is always blue, that is the land that I will visit with all my friends and relatives. Whereas the land where there is no color, no flower, where there is only tears and sadness, this is the land I will visit alone." This has been our philosophy for centuries. That sadness is something that you have to suffer alone. So a lot of people do not even know that this can be treated, that it is a treatable disorder.

Time-pressured doctors generally discourage patients from talking about anything other than physical problems. This was particularly the case in general practice, but also applied to psychiatry. For example, Dr. Sanyal, who had worked many years in government hospitals in North Bengali districts, said that general physicians were never interested in patients describing their feelings, and that even psychiatrists wanted quick and simple physical presentations:

> We are so burdened with patients that we *want* to get physical symptoms. I've worked in hospitals where I had to see 250 patients a day. So you have to be very fast. So if a patient goes whining about *mon bhalo lagchena* and so on, I will not listen, even though I am a psychiatrist. "Come to the point!" and I am already writing a prescription [*laughs*]. So people have become primed to that, that you go to a doctor with physical symptoms. You don't go to a doctor with psychological stuff. (Dr. Sanyal)

Bengalis suffered too often from bowel obsession not because they thought too little but because they thought too much. This excess of thinking occurred not only in relation to the belly but in all spheres of life. Bengalis always prided themselves on being the intellectual avant garde of Indians, on being more cultured and more artistic. This made them more sophisticated than other ethnic groups in India, but such sophistication came at a price. One psychiatrist, Dr. Lahiri, compared "obsessive" Bengalis to "psychotic" Hindi-speaking North Indians and hypothesized that the Bengalis' excessive intellectualism made them lean toward obsessive-compulsive disorders, of which bowel obsession was the most prominent example: "We can say that Bengalis, as a race, are intellectually higher. They will be more self-punitive. They will be individually aiming at higher perfection. Once they are very self-punitive, they might develop obsessive-compulsive disorder. That may be socially inherited. Perfection of any sort." He alluded to what Sigmund Freud (1924) summarized as the "anal" character: so orderly and so opinionated that obsession develops easily. Psychiatrists see Bengali bowel obsession less as a somatization based on a lack of psychological self-reflection and more as a problem of thinking, feeling, and worrying too much (Karasz 2004). Bengalis used their "gastric brain" (Dr. Lahiri) more than other people.

Most Bengali patients were well aware of psychological moods and able to "express very nicely" (Dr. Barman), if only they were given enough opportunity to do so. This was particularly the case with "educated" people. Asked what the most common expressions of mental suffering are, the psychiatrists agreed that this was *mon kharap* and that it was the closest approximation to "depression" in Bengali. Other ways in which Bengalis often talked about depressive moods were in terms of *udash* (indifference, loss of interest), *bishad* (feeling morose), *manushik obhashad* (mental fatigue), and *kamla lagche* ("feel like quitting"). On a scale of severity, *kamla lagche* was fairly serious because it already entailed suicidal ideation. "Depression" was also increasingly used by educated patients, although they did not know how it was properly defined by psychiatry. Another term borrowed from English was "nerves," which Bengalis used to speak primarily about anxiety: "'Nerves,' 'chair,' 'table,' these words have all come into Bengali language . . . they have become incorporated, they are not considered English as such" (Dr. Choudhury).

Psychiatrists said that *mon* was more commonly used by educated patients and that less educated people simply said *bhalo lagchena*, which can stand for almost any negative feeling: "That can be used in hundreds of different ways: bored, or have a headache, or anxiety. Everything can be expressed this way" (Dr. Nandi). *Bhalo lagchena* is so impersonal that it does not even specify the "I" of the patient as the locus of suffering. While *bhalo lagchena* was the most generic term, a higher degree of severity could be expressed by saying *kharap lagche* ("feeling bad") or *kicchu bhalo lagchena* ("nothing feels good"). To say that one does not like anything anymore was more clearly understood by relatives than other expressions, because it captured subjective alienation even from the people and things that one usually enjoyed: "People around them lecture them about how good their life is. For example, they have a husband, a house, material comforts. 'You just shut up and feel good, there is nothing to feel bad about.' But *kicchu bhalo lagchena* is different, it's more accepted by others" (Dr. Mukharji). The psychiatrists roughly agreed on the usual sequence of terms that they would hear during a consultation: "First somatic symptoms, then *bhalo lagena*, then *mon kharap lage*" (Dr. Chawla). One of his colleagues explained it similarly: "In my experience, first they say *bhalo lagchena*. Then *kharap lagche*, then they become more specific and say *mon kharap lagche*" (Dr. Nandi).

The origins of various Bengali expressions for depressed moods are harder to trace than those for organic body parts. A professor of psychiatry (Prof. Chatterjee) hypothesized that words for body and belly were among the oldest layers of language. Even in the earliest Sanskrit texts one could find many metaphors of eating-as-destroying and digesting-as-cooking. By contrast, the language of moods was more recent, and more influenced by English terms: "You would not see *mon kharap* in Bengali literature two hundred years back. That means that *mon kharap* came into the language much later. In Bengali we have tons of words that are direct translations of English words, over the past one hundred years." Just as there was no obvious equivalent to "depression" in older texts, there was also no portrayal of "depressed" characters in the classic literature: "Even in classic Sanskrit literature, you would not come across pure literal concepts of 'depression.' The characters are nostalgic, not 'depressed.' I can't think of a Hamlet-like character in Indian literature" (Prof. Chatterjee).

Good Headside Manners

The way patients express illness symptoms toward psychiatrists depends on how diagnostic questions are asked. It was clear both from interviews and from my own observations of clinical practice that Calcutta psychiatrists prefer to phrase their initial questions in an open-ended form. Popular opening questions with patients that they saw for the first time were simply "What happened?" (*ki holo?*) or "How are you doing?" (*apni ki rokom lagen?*). Specific psychiatric terms were avoided, and indeed the opening questions invited patients to talk as much about physical symptoms as about mental problems. Common forms of probing for mental symptoms were questions such as "How is your mind feeling?" (*mon ki rokom lagche?*) or "Is your mind not well?" (*mon bhalo lagchena?*).

Stigmatization of psychiatric illnesses had become less over the past decade, but remained a problem to reckon with (see Priest, Vize, and Roberts 1996; Bridges and Goldberg 1987; Yang et al. 2007). Psychiatrists also felt that much of the stigma was already overcome at the stage when patients reached them. They only saw the "tip of the iceberg" (Dr. Samaddar) of all those who suffered, but those who came had accepted treatment by a psychiatrist. Nevertheless, psychiatrists avoided a too-confrontational style with patients. Dr. Samaddar, a psychiatrist in his sixties who had worked many years for the Indian army, said that one had to word one's questions carefully to avoid alienating patients:

> Straight away we don't tell them, "look, you are suffering from depression." What we try to explain is, "Look, you are going through a difficult phase, mental tension, your current situation, you are at the end of your tolerance, so that is why you are having these problems. I'm giving you some medicine, but you also have to change your coping style, how to manage your stress in a different way." That's the language they understand and that is how we treat them.

Calcutta psychiatrists said that diagnoses and medications should be explained to patients as much as possible. For the doctors, making patients understand what was happening increased compliance with the prescribed treatments. This obligation for explaining was sometimes phrased explicitly in terms of citizenship and rights. Dr. Basu, for example, stated that the ultimate role of psychiatry is to allow full rehabilitation to a patient, which meant "to give full personhood": "Not only freedom from illness, but to reintegrate into society." On the other hand, this was only the ultimate aim and could not be implemented with all patients: "*We* have these notions in our mind but *they* are not prepared for that." Not one psychiatrist stated that *all* patients had the right to be educated under *all* circumstances. There was a consensus that different kinds of patients needed different ways of talking to them, and that comprehensive explanations were reserved to only the most educated patients, those who actively inquired about diagnostics and treatments. Categories of persons usually suspended from proper explanations were the "illiterate," the "rural," and "children," often also "women" and "the elderly." One psychiatrist saw a dividing line between an urban, educated elite and everyone else. For the elite, "what we do is the same what is done for the Western world" (Dr. Nandi). By contrast, rural and illiterate people did not have enough education to understand anything about what psychiatry is and how its drugs work:

> Trying to explain to them how medicine works is almost impossible. Maximum I can do is to mention side effects. If I start with brain chemistry, even in basic terms, that whole story is totally over their heads. They might listen to it, but then they come back again and say: "No, this boy was jilted in love, *that's* why he has that problem." So it's very difficult to bypass their stories and to implement our stories. (Dr. Nandi)

There were several metaphors that psychiatrists used to make patients understand their diagnoses. Some drew on comparisons with nature. For example, one psychiatrist (Dr. Mittal) was fond of comparing changing moods to the weather. He told patients that the sky (here, the mind), is never *only* sunny or *only* cloudy. Similarly, moods are changing all the time. What distinguishes normal low moods from pathologically low moods is for how long they stay the same. A cloudy sky is not a problem; but if the sky is always cloudy, that is a problem.

Another psychiatrist (Dr. Chawla) compared the changing fortunes of life to the Ganges River (here, the soul): it yearns to be reunited with the ocean (here, blissful union with the Absolute) and hence always flows into that direction. But it can never flow in a straight line because it encounters obstacles everywhere. Meandering around these obstacles makes the river so beautiful to behold. All of life's most serious obstacles should not be fought. Instead, one should change one's own direction. The idyllic comparison with the Ganges also helped to convince patients that psychopharmaceuticals did not alter the essence of the person, but only gave it the necessary energy for natural progression: "When you hit an obstacle, don't stop there. Accept it and change your direction. Do not fight it. Medicine is there to help you change directions. But you have to change yourself. The medicines themselves will not change you" (Dr. Chawla).

Yet another way to make patients accept medication is to compare them to everyday over-the-counter drugs, such as "simple painkillers" (Dr. Deshpande). Physical pain is felt when you get hit on the head with a hammer, and taking a pill for headaches is a rational response to this pain. Similarly, mental pain is a healthy reaction of the mind to something sad happening in one's life, and it made good sense to take a pill against that kind of pain. The "hammer" comparison also tied in with popular perceptions of mental anguish as a "shock" or "blow" from outside: "'Shock' is a major explanation. They use the Bengali term. Illness as a reaction" (Dr. Chawla). This explanation locates the source of the anguish firmly beyond the patient, which minimizes stigma.

Explanations for medications do not need to say anything about the exact effects that drugs produce but need only to convince patients that they help to overcome the problems. Dr. Roy drew on popular stories and Hindu mythology to win over patients for his prescriptions. For example, he liked to tell patients a fairy tale. Once upon a time, the king of India wanted to go out and visit all dominions of his realm. But he was afraid that dust could stain his feet once he went outside the palace. His ministers thought about covering the grounds of the entire kingdom in leather, so that the king could tread safely everywhere. When this was deemed impossible, they asked people far and wide for a better idea. Then, one day, a poor cobbler came to the palace and asked to see the king. When his audience was granted, he bowed down, touched the king's feet, and then tailored a pair shoes. The point of the story was, according to Dr. Roy, that highly specific interventions could solve an otherwise intractable problem: "Similarly, with depression, there are a lot of changes in your mind. I don't want to change every thought, I just want to change the nutrition that is lacking in your brain, in your mind. I'm giving you the nutrition and your mind will be clear." Accepting the humble cobbler's shoes (here, psychopharmaceuticals) made the one tiny change that made such a difference overall for the king (here, the patient).

Comparing medicines to glasses for poor eyesight was another method of trying to convince patients to take them. One psychiatrist said that people who wear glasses often start wearing them in childhood and need to keep wearing them until old age. Sometimes one could stop wearing glasses, but it was never possible to say in advance when this might happen. Glasses are so everyday that they feel like an integral part of the body, hence one soon stops noticing that they are there at all: "These medicines are like that, you have to be on them, and nobody knows for how long. Medical science doesn't know for how long. But for the longer, the better" (Dr. Kar).

The textbook explanation for depression now most current in psychiatry emphasizes neurotransmitter imbalance. Since this process cannot be observed in a live brain, a good amount of artistic freedom is necessary to demonstrate how it is supposed to work. In one of the defining textbooks, neurotransmitter imbalance is illustrated by little trains taking neurotransmitters on a ride in and out of the synapse (Stahl 2008). But this kind of explanation hardly featured in Indian doctors' justifications for patients. Some patients could be told that depression is "brain chemistry out of balance" and that "certain chemicals are not secreted in the right amount, that's what is causing the problem" (Dr. Ram). The scientific explanation could be used with "sophisticated" patients: "If a person is educated, knows neurotransmitters and so on, I talk to him in that language. The real science" (Dr. Barman). But the number of patients who could make sense of neurotransmitters was extremely limited, the doctors said. Indeed, in all the hundreds of doctor-patient interactions that I have seen in Calcutta, I have only once heard a psychiatrist use the word "neurotransmitter" (see Jenkins 2010: 35-36; Pickersgill, Cunningham-Burley, and Martin 2011: 356).

If neurochemical imbalance was talked about at all, then it was in comparison to food metabolism. Diabetes and the intake of insulin was a common way to make patients understand neurochemical imbalance. Just as diabetic patients needed a regular supply of insulin, so did a depressed brain require a regular supply of substances to keep it balanced:

I try to explain to them, in their own language. Like, when you have a bit of diabetes, there is some substance in your body that is lacking. So if you have diabetes, you maintain with insulin, to keep on an optimal level. Similarly here, serotonin and norepinephrine are two important brain chemicals, which are essential for your psychomotor activity, for your mood, and that might be a little bit lacking, so we give it. Not only give it, but maintain it. (Dr. Sanyal)

The parallels to diabetes were convincing to patients because that disease has become so rampant among South Asians over the past decades. Everyone had at least one family member who suffered from "sugar." Also, since everyone was aware of the need for regular insulin injections, this made insulin the best example for maintenance drugs— which Joseph Dumit (2012) analyzes as "drugs for life." Diabetes typically struck more affluent people, so it is seen as part of an affluent lifestyle everyone aspires to. Because diabetes is one of the least stigmatized chronic illnesses, a comparison between depression and diabetes promised to minimize the stigma of mental depression. Above all, diabetes is a nutrition-related disorder, which connects it seamlessly with the imagery of antidepressants as *moner khabar*, "mind food" (as discussed in chapter 0). With the model of diabetes, it was also easier to mobilize patients' relatives to keep a watch on daily medication intake. For Dr. Roy, the diabetes example motivated relatives to supervise drug intake: "Suppose someone suffers from diabetes, then I suggest: 'Have you asked in your family if you are taking your medicine, you should not miss your medication.' Similarly, if you have depression, you should ask: 'Have you taken your medication? If you haven't taken, please take it'" (Dr. Roy).

Managing Patient Adherence I: Drug Choice and Dosage

Even with the most folksy explanations for how depression occurs and what the medicines can do, psychiatrists generally complained about incomplete adherence to the course of medicine prescribed.

Compliance was said to be either "so-so" or "poor." Adherence hinged on how long the treatment lasted, how much it cost, how the medications made patients feel, and how supportive their family members were of the treatment.

Poor adherence is one of the reasons why doctors try to select drugs that are as "free from side effects" as possible. In the first decade of the twenty-first century, the molecules most consistently regarded as "safe" were the SSRIs and SNRIs, whereas tricyclic antidepressants and tranquilizers were seen as fraught with risks. Among Indian doctors, drugs such as fluoxetine had been around for long enough to inspire near-complete confidence in their safety. Even the fierce debate about SSRIs causing higher suicidality among teenage patients, which rocked Western psychiatry in the mid-2000s (Rose 2007: 219; Liebert and Gavey 2009; Healy 2006), barely had an impact in Calcutta. Every psychiatrist I interviewed said that SSRIs were safe for patients, including children and adolescents. Dr. Sinha, a female psychiatrist who had worked in England between 2002 and 2005, confirmed her general preference for SSRIs: "I start them off with fluoxetine. Seventy percent, we know that, will respond to that. If they don't, then we start with another drug. Most studies are done on this. We don't want to fool around. At first, why not fluoxetine?" Similarly, Dr. Roy said that SSRIs were the best first-line drugs available. Only when they failed would he resort to SNRIs or TCAs: "To begin with, I prefer SSRI. But if SSRIs fail, I go for dual-action antidepressants, like venlafaxine or duloxetine." There were exceptions to this rule: for example, if a patient showed severe depression combined with suicidal intent, the best clinical results came from prescribing SNRIs in a high dose. SSRIs also worked wonders with a range of other illnesses, such as anxiety, panic, phobias, or obsessive-compulsive disorders. Alcoholism responded well to SSRIs because they reduced the craving. Examination anxieties and academic stress could be helped with a light dose of fluoxetine or sertraline. One additional advantage was that SSRIs were relatively cheap, and so most patients could easily afford them. SNRIs, by contrast, were expensive and prescriptions for them had, therefore, to be limited to more affluent patients.

Tranquilizing benzodiazepines, such as alprazolam (Xanax) or lorazepam (Ativan), were still best for patients who suffered from anxiety and disturbed sleep: "Cases of subclinical depression also come to us.

By examining them we find they don't suffer from major depressive disorder. In that case we don't give antidepressants but we might give some days alprazolam for sleep disturbance" (Dr. Mukharji). The problem with tranquilizers was that they created strong withdrawal symptoms and so patients got addicted to them. However, this did not prevent nonpsychiatrists from using them frequently: "What's bad is that doctors from other fields, like cardiology, also prescribe alprazolam. I have seen a few *thousand* patients who are taking lorazepam for years and when I ask them why, they say that the cardiologist prescribed this" (Dr. Ram).

The older types of tricyclic antidepressants still had a firm place in psychiatry, especially when SSRIs and SNRIs do not improve symptoms. A few doctors, especially older ones, also mentioned that there was no good evidence that tricyclics were any less effective than SSRIs or SNRIs. On the contrary, with obstinate symptoms, tricyclics worked best. But the main problem with TCAs was that they had many side effects and required regular monitoring with blood tests and other diagnostics, making them risky to use with outpatients:

First-line treatment is SSRI. I have hardly used any TCAs in the past ten years, very rarely, only for very resistant cases. These SSRIs have made our lives much easier, because of the side effects. I think that tricyclics are effective, but if I have to give amitriptyline 250mg, most of the time I would like the patient admitted to hospital, because with this dose he can fall down any time. (Dr. Nandi)

The prototype of a patient who receives tricyclics as a first-line drug is the "rural somatizer": someone from the villages, with a low level of education, who presents physical problems such as all-body pain. As Prof. Chatterjee explained, "In rural areas I commonly use amitriptyline. Because the profile is different, more somatization, and in my experience then amitriptyline works better." In Calcutta, on the other hand, where patients are better educated, SSRIs worked fine.

For Calcutta psychiatrists, bowel obsession could be treated directly with antidepressants. One had only to be careful with gastric side effects associated with some molecules. If gastrointestinal complaints responded to antidepressants, it was clear that it was a case of gastric somatization from the start: "I saw one girl, she had long been in treatment for gastric, but now only started on antidepressants. But the gastric lifted quickly, so that was part of the depression" (Dr. Ram). If the drugs worked, it meant that digestive troubles did not originate in the belly, but in the patients' mind. She went on to explain that psychiatric drugs could unmask underlying depression: "They go to gastroenterologists and general physicians for this treatment, and only after years of treatment with them they come to us. [. . .] And immediately, I would say, almost with 75 percent of patients, there is tremendous improvement." For her, making the fog of somatization disappear was part of the "magic" of antidepressants.

A hidden strategy of managing patients' adherence was to reduce the dosage. For example, in cases where both marketing materials and evidence-based medicine recommended a dose of fluoxetine 20mg, Calcutta psychiatrists frequently lowered the dose to 10mg. Lowering dosages for most patients was standard advice by senior psychiatrists during clinical training: "Some of our seniors told that our patients need lower dose" (Prof. Chatterjee). Only a few psychiatrists said that doses should be exactly the same as for Western patients. Lower doses were routinely used in the maintenance phase. Experience showed that, even where the initial four- to six-week dose could be administered according to textbook advice, the maintenance dose for the following months had to be lowered: "The maintenance dose, especially, is much, *much* lower than recommended. Usually it is recommended that patients be maintained on the initial dose. But we find that our patients are maintained on half the dose or one-third of the dose. Most of them remain alright" (Dr. Barman). Calcutta psychiatrists were intrigued by this question and often said that it needed more research. All current clinical guidelines were based on clinical trials among Western patients, whereas no attention had been given to the specific needs of Asians: "There are some pioneers in India, they have shown that the requirement of Oriental people, from India, China, and Japan, is lesser than in the US or in the UK" (Dr. Roy).

When asked why a lower dose is needed, psychiatrists mentioned a range of reasons. Indian bodies were smaller than Western bodies, and therefore needed less active substance, or else toxic side effects resulted: "Indians are definitively more sensitive to side effects. There is something in the pharmacogenetics. This is a genuine problem. A lower dose can address that" (Dr. Chawla). Indian food habits were different. Indians ate vegetables and rice, whereas Westerners ate meat and potatoes, so Indians metabolized their food faster, making drug effects more immediate. Westerners also drank far more alcohol than Indians, and higher alcohol intake required higher drug doses. Indians were fond of taking afternoon naps: "Here, even doctors and professionals go home and have a nap and come back to do a chamber. Our lifestyle is very different" (Dr. Ram). Westerners lived on a tight schedule of nine-to-five work and a night's sleep, and Western dosage recommendations were geared toward maintaining this day/night separation. By contrast, Indian sleep rhythms were more fluid. Lower doses were required so that patients could go back and forth between being awake and being asleep. Higher doses, on the other hand, had sedative effects. Many Indian doctors lacked confidence in their own professional abilities. They were more scared of inducing adverse effects than of failing to help patients. Finally, giving lower doses was a strategy to keep patients in continuous treatment rather than to get them out of treatment as quickly as possible. Pharmaceutical companies supported this trend because they wanted long-term use, not complete cure:

> They think that they are going to lose the patient because of side effects from higher doses. So they write lower doses. But I see that patients on lower doses might have some improvement but they don't have full remission of symptoms. There is a big problem. Pharma companies insist on patient response, *not* on remission. Fifty percent improvement of symptoms is fine with them. So we often also follow this. Going for lower dose makes you a chronic depressive. (Prof. Chatterjee)

In other words, longer maintenance on a lower dose was more lucrative than shorter treatment on a higher dose, and that was why psychiatrists colluded with the pharmaceutical industry to suggest that the bodies and lifestyles of Indian patients were so different that they needed different dosages, too.

Closely related to lower dosages is the use of polypharmacy (Martin 2007: 168-73). Psychiatrists use the term "polypharmacy" in at least three ways. "Polypharmacy" means combining different medicines in one prescription. It also stands for combining different molecules from within the same class of drugs on lower doses. For example, doctors might combine the SSRI fluoxetine on 10mg with the SSRI sertraline on 10mg, to produce a 20mg dose. Finally, "polypharmacy" denotes combinations of one group of drugs with another, usually also on lower doses. For example, the SSRI fluoxetine gets combined with the TCA amitriptyline. Polypharmacy was motivated by a trial-and-error ethos among Indian doctors that was forced on them by a lack of proper training in medical school, lack of peer support among psychiatrists, lack of evidence on how best to treat Bengali patients, and conflicting information provided by pharmaceutical companies: "Now so many new drugs are coming, but we don't know the drug-drug interaction. If you can prescribe rightly, there is no need for a number of medicines, definitively you can treat" (Dr. Choudhury). Despite seeing polypharmacy as less scientific than single-drug therapy, many of them justified it as the more successful approach. One of the psychiatrists who said that he routinely combined SSRIs with tricyclics for all cases of major depression legitimized polypharmacy as the best method to tease out patients' individual drug response:

> I prefer polytherapy. If I give a single molecule in a large dose, there is much risk of side effects. So, although it is less scientific for many researchers, here it is a trend. And I also prefer that. We give two or three molecules in small quantity and ask them to come back to the clinic for reporting, after three to four weeks. That's free of charge. Then we ask not the party but the relatives to report if there is any discomfort or side effect. Then I evaluate what drug he cannot tolerate. That one I stop and increase the dose of the others. (Dr. Barman)

This psychiatrist's support for polypharmacy was unusually forthright. More common was that psychiatrists claimed to prefer monotherapy, described polypharmacy as irrational, and put the blame for this malpractice on *other* doctors: "There was one boy who came with *four* medications. I put him on *one* drug, on a higher dose, that worked. There is still little research, but we know that polypharmacy should be avoided. I don't like it" (Dr. Deshpande). Some of the doctors blamed pharmaceutical marketing for the irrational practice of polypharmacy, because it allowed doctors to divide their prescribing loyalties between two or more companies. Others said that patients themselves expected and demanded polypharmacy from all doctors, including psychiatrists, so they were to blame. One psychiatrist felt that questions of polypharmacy were too sensitive to be answered. When I asked Dr. Choudhury why doctors prescribe several drugs at once, he replied, "I don't want to comment on that".

Managing Adherence II: Doctor Shopping and Floating Prescriptions

When psychiatrists try to manage patient adherence (by choosing "safe" drugs, by lowering doses, and by polypharmacy), they also need to keep track of what competing prescribers are doing. All the psychiatrists I interviewed highlighted that adherence was difficult to assess because patients often did not return after the first or second consultation. Adherence is hard to achieve all over the world, not only in India. Outpatient treatments suffer from a lack of supervision in all countries; only those admitted to psychiatric wards can be properly monitored. But the mentality of Indian patients and the dynamics of the Indian medical market make the supervision of adherence even more difficult than elsewhere.

Dr. Ram, a celebrity doctor who writes columns in an English-language newspaper and also appears on TV, said that even her patients, who mostly came from the educated middle and upper classes, showed mixed compliance: "I'd say 50 percent are compliant, in the sense that they don't stop the medication. Because it's a long treatment. Many, three months down the road, will try to stop the medicine." Many patients only returned after a serious relapse, when they realized that they needed to continue with the treatment. The main problem with antidepressants was that they eased symptoms without giving a lasting cure within a short amount of time. As with antibiotics, one must complete the full course to avoid a relapse: "The drugs are so effective that they feel that they are well." The urge to stop taking medicines as soon as possible was driven by relatives, because they did not support long-term medicine use. Worst was the "weird philosophy" held by the lay population that to stop taking medicines was the same as to stop being a psychiatric patient. In other words, Indians were still far from accepting a "drugs for life" model.

While the psychiatrists criticized patients' faulty idea that "only when you stop medicines, you are healthy again," they also complained about the *opposite* form of noncompliance: taking medicines far longer than was advised. This was part of the phenomenon of "floating prescriptions," which occurs in a context of out-of-pocket-paying patients, doctor shopping, and the lax enforcement of laws that prohibit the sale of prescription medicines without a valid prescription. Once a prescription is issued, patients can return to medicine shops over and over to refill it, without doctors having any control over it. Where the doctor had specified that a course of medicines should be taken for two weeks and that the patient should then return for a check-up, patients could go on with the same prescription for months or even years:

> The problem is, in our country, there is absolutely no control over sales of medicines. Anyone can go to any medicine shop and buy medicines. I have seen clients six years back: once, on that day, I have given medication for fifteen days. Then *years* later the patient comes back, after continuing medicines for six years, which sometimes has disastrous results. Maybe I prescribed alprazolam and an antidepressant, and the client has continued for six years. (Dr. Nandi)

All the psychiatrists perceived continuous self-medication as troubling, but they also recognized advantages. For example, many of the drugs used were still so little understood that even the psychiatrists did not know what the long-term effects of psychopharmaceuticals were. Even though patients should get themselves checked regularly, especially for damage to the liver and the kidneys, they might well be "just fine" on uninterrupted medication. At least, they said, continuous intake was better than an erratic pattern of starting medications, interrupting them after a few weeks, relapsing, starting again on different drugs, and stopping them again. The doctors also pointed out that all their prescriptions had to be given with the recognition that patients might not adhere to the precise course prescribed. This made them avoid certain drugs and combinations wherever possible: "If I prescribe medicine, it's in my mind that the person won't take the way I prescribe. That's part of the game. And I accept that. And after that I prescribe. I try to avoid medicines that have harmful side effects in the long run" (Dr. Kar).

Avoidance of side effects was, according to a psychiatrist, also the main motivation among general physicians and consultants of other specialties. The rise of SSRI prescriptions outside of psychiatry was largely due to the perception that they were safe and easy to use: "In India, prescriptions of SSRIs mainly come from the GP level. Because they find it difficult to handle non-SSRI antidepressants, because of the side effects" (Prof. Chatterjee). SSRI could be experimented with on different dosage levels without harm to the patient. With other antidepressants, however, one had to be careful about dosage, and this was why they never became used beyond psychiatry (see Greenhalgh 1987: 312). In any case, though, GPs tended to give antidepressants only in "homeopathic" doses (Dr. Sinha) to keep patients in continuous treatment without dangerous side effects. One notable exception to this rule was the prescription of tranquilizers. As discussed earlier, certain specialists, such as cardiologists, seemed particularly guilty of keeping patients on tranquilizers for far too long.

Managing adherence included stopping patients from ditching doctors before a course of treatment was complete. Keeping patients was, first of all, a matter of professional honor. It was also a matter of financial necessity. Strong competition among doctors in private practice, all of whom depend on patients' out-of-pocket payments, has several consequences for the way doctors dealt with patients. A rampant practice with patients who had already been in treatment with another doctor was to stop those drugs and start them on different ones. "Rubbishing" rival doctors took precedence over evidence-based treatment. Dr. Sinha, the psychiatrist who had returned from the UK, was particularly scandalized by this habit. Indian psychiatrists put their own yearning for status and income over patients' interests and best clinical practice: "They want to be bigger doctors, they tend to discontinue whatever patients have been on before. But that is not evidence-based! Doing so is wrongful, it is absolutely unethical" (Dr. Sinha).

Some of the younger doctors felt that such professional rivalries were more common among the older generation, while younger doctors prided themselves on collaborating more. Previously, all forms of doctor shopping caused bad blood, but now it was a marker of professional confidence to support patients in getting a second opinion: "Now the younger generation discusses these cases among themselves. I personally encourage patients to go to another doctor. They only go if they are not entirely satisfied [. . .] another voice helps to reorganize their experience, and I hope they come back to me. In all cases, it is beneficial for both sides" (Dr. Deshpande). The few doctors who declared themselves supporters of doctor shopping mentioned that being friendly even to "unfaithful" patients helped to keep people close to them: "I have a mother-daughter patient couple. The mother didn't have success with me for four years and went to another doctor, but she still brings her daughter to me" (Dr. Deshpande).

There can be financial gain in such collegiality. Referrals among doctors were based on "gentlemen's agreements" about dividing the profits: "If a doctor refers to another doctor, he might charge [the other doctor] a fee of two hundred rupees out of one thousand rupees. This is a cardinal unethical practice; the Medical Council does not allow it. But it's done" (Prof. Chatterjee). Such "fee splitting" was most routinized for referrals among different specialists, for example, for psychiatrists referring patients to a gastroenterologist, or vice versa. The introduction of more stringent consumer protection had effectively helped doctors to legitimate irrational referrals, because they could now say that all they wanted was to be absolutely certain of the diagnosis.

Referrals to psychiatrists from other doctors remained rare, however. Psychiatry was a kind of specialization that chronically received too few referrals, rather than too many. If a patient was referred to psychiatry, he or she tended to be unambiguously "mental." Too much stigma was still attached to psychiatry for general physicians to be prepared to recommend that their patients go to a psychiatrist, because they feared any confrontation about recommending a *pagoler daktar* (madman's doctor). However, other doctors' readiness to refer had much improved over the past years, and now up to 30-40 percent of new patients came by referral. Even faith healers and quack doctors were willing to refer, as one psychiatrist reported from his experiences in rural Bengal:

Awareness is quite satisfactory, even in rural areas. I worked at a district hospital, patients were brought from remote areas. Some of them were tied with chains, violent patients. They said, "We went to the lady who can do black magic, but she told us: 'No, go to the district hospital and see the doctor!'" For they [faith healers] don't want to take the trouble if they cry and scream. (Dr. Bhattacharya)

According to the psychiatrists, the group of doctors most likely to refer patients to them, rather than trying to treat them themselves, were the homeopaths. Several of the Calcutta psychiatrists I talked to mentioned that they had a "good friend" among the homeopaths who regularly sent patients. In the psychiatrists' experience, homeopaths had the least prejudices against their treatments and were most aware of their own limitations: "They don't have that kind of prejudice; they know that they can't handle these problems" (Dr. Bhattacharya).

None of the psychiatrists ever mentioned referring patients to other healers. But many of them were well aware that the number of trained psychiatrists in India continued to be small and that it was important for the future growth of the field to establish good relations with anyone in a caregiving position. Dr. Roy said that he encouraged *all* healers: "Homeopathy, Ayurveda, whatever it is, even the magical healers." He reasoned that unqualified practitioners represented the bulk of all practitioners in India and, for that fact alone, they deserved respect. Dr. Roy also found that validating even quack practitioners who prescribe irrational therapies was worthwhile: "I always respect them a lot. . . . Their treatments might not be 100 percent right, just 25 percent right. But if I also recognize them, they start using my medication. Whenever they see a difficult case, they send it to me. So I don't want to antagonize them or abolish them."

Socioeconomic Change and the "Rise" of Depression

One of the most vexing questions about antidepressant prescriptions is whether there is an actual "rise" of depressive illness that justifies the rise of drug prescriptions. It is certain that far more people are now taking antidepressants than in previous years, but the reasons for this are contested. Epidemiological claims that depressive illness is increasing are a cornerstone of current policies for global mental health. Arguments about this "rise" come in at least three different versions. First, it is claimed that there is a rise in the *absolute* number of people suffering from depression relative to population growth. For example, the U.S.

President's Council on Bioethics (2003) held that up to 20 percent of all Americans were suffering from depression at that time, that this was a rise in the *absolute* number of depressed patients, and that this rise was produced neither by new diagnostic criteria nor by new methods of collecting and analyzing data. The second argument is that depression is rising *relative* to other diseases. This argument about a gradual shift away from infectious diseases toward chronic and lifestyle diseases is strongly promoted by the World Health Organization (WHO), which reckons that depression will be the world's second most prevalent health problem by the year 2020. Evidence for this shift comes from novel ways of analyzing data in terms of disability-adjusted life years (DALYs), which has given far more prominence than earlier calculations to chronic, nonfatal suffering. The third claim is that there is neither an absolute nor a relative rise of depressive suffering, but that more people now seek medical help and get diagnosed because there is greater awareness of mental health and less stigma attached to seeking help.

Globalization, as a set of profound economic, cultural, and political transformations that came with an intensification of world trade and communications, appears in different shapes in all three claims about the rise of depression. For supporters of the hypothesis that there is an absolute rise of depression, globalization is linked to urbanization, migration, and deeper divisions between the rich and the poor, all of which trigger rising uses of antidepressants. Economic change is disrupting traditional forms of social cohesion and stripping cultures of their psychologically protective powers (Bhugra and Mastrogianni 2004: 12). Similarly, the WHO (2001: 27) argues that individual poverty, mental illness, and macroeconomic impacts form a vicious circle. According to the WHO, social inequality leads to a higher prevalence of mental disorders that, along with a lack of appropriate care, decreases economic growth, as people become less productive or become unable to work (but see Das et al. 2007). If it is indeed the case that economic globalization causes more social inequality, then it should be no surprise that antidepressant sales are rising.

The claim that there is no rise of depression but only a rise of awareness and willingness to take drugs also refers to globalization. Globalization is then seen as the very process that disseminates Western notions of "depression" *along with* its pharmaceutical therapies. For example, Kirmayer and Minas (2000) hold that the global spread of psychiatric disease classifications and diagnostic routines accounts for the increase in antidepressant uses. This argument is sharpened by the suspicion that the globalization of antidepressants is, by and large, the work of pharmaceutical marketing. As Healy (2004: 2) points out, even psychiatrists did not see depression as so widespread *before* antidepressants became so easily available since the 1950s. Diffuse states of sadness, which earlier went without therapeutic intervention, are becoming increasingly medicalized and treated with drugs (Clarke et al. 2010; Rose 2006). This "bracket creep" was even stronger in depression than in other diseases because, as Kalman Applbaum points out, their pharmacological effects are so diffuse that "the latitude for the reinterpretation of their value back to the consumer through brand positioning is somewhat flexible" (2006: 107).

In this context, what do Calcutta psychiatrists think about the alleged rise of depression and its purported causes? To begin with, all the doctors I met were fascinated by this question, even if they did not follow the research literature on the topic. Clearly, the rise of depression is not an esoteric academic concern but an everyday topic of discussion. As I have argued elsewhere, less specialized allopathic practitioners in Calcutta, such as GPs and also unlicensed RMPs, strongly support the first claim—that the absolute incidence of depression among the population is rising (Ecks 2008; Ecks and Basu 2009). These allopaths saw a clear causal link between depression and the globalization of India. The GPs highlighted that people felt economically insecure, that good schooling and good jobs were even more competitive than earlier, and that traditional kinship structures, such as the multigenerational household, were crumbling.

GPs switched back and forth between talking about *actual* socioeconomic changes and changes in people's *perceptions* of them. For example, they might first argue that life is hard and, therefore, full of reasons to feel depressed. Then they might say that life has always been hard, but that sensibilities had changed: Bollywood movies and TV programs showing affluent lifestyles created great expectations that could only be disappointed by harsh realities. GPs described depression as a multidimensional problem that could not be reduced to brain chemistry. Deepening social inequality, intergenerational changes, consumer desires, and the impact of the mass media all had to be taken into account. To suffer from depression was clearly a form of *social* suffering. Throughout, the doctors felt that relational changes were as important as absolute changes. Globalization might have helped to uplift poor people in terms of absolute wealth, but their mental suffering still increased because of a *relative* deprivation compared to other people—a typical case of how one's own suffering depends on how other people are doing (see Sax and Ecks 2005).

Psychiatrists held far less definitive views of this alleged epidemic of depression than the nonpsychiatrists. They commonly prefaced any answer with caveats such as that there were "no proper statistics" available in India to either prove or disprove claims about rising depression rates. Like the GPs, psychiatrists also mentioned social and economic transformations, but if pressed on the issue, they shied away from definitive statements. Besides the absence of reliable data, they were so committed to a neurobiological model of brain chemistry that socioeconomic factors seemed unscientific. For the GPs, "globalization" and other large-scale socioeconomic transformations were clearly permitted as evidence for a rise of depression, whereas the psychiatrists were more cautious. It was not the case that the GPs saw links between social suffering and depression that the psychiatrists did not see. The difference was that GPs readily allowed social factors to count as evidence, whereas the psychiatrists only did so with qualifications.

Asked about the influence of social changes, one of the psychiatrists (Dr. Sinha) drew a six-field diagram on all the issues that one needed to consider in making a diagnosis. It squared biological, psychological, and social dimensions with predisposition, precipitation, and perpetuation. Social factors could precipitate mental illness. For example, a life crisis such as unemployment could throw someone into depression; it could hurry someone down a path of depression that had already begun; and it could keep someone in an already existing depression. She went on to explain that the predisposing factors were mostly biological, and that the patient was unable to change them. The proper place of medications was in controlling biological predispositions. On the other hand, precipitating and perpetuating factors, be they biological, psychological, or social, could sometimes be transformed for the better. Her main example was depression in children caused by excessive pressure in schools. In this case, parents could help a child by lowering their hopes for success.

Calcutta psychiatrists perceived an increase of stress levels across all social groups, although there was no consensus on whether some sections of society were more affected than others. Some singled out the poor as most affected by globalization because their consumer cravings had increased faster than their actual buying power: "There are more things that people want, and these things act as a material temptation" (Dr. Mukharji). Others said, in turn, that the poor remained surprisingly resilient to mental suffering even under great adversity. One doctor suggested that this would be a fruitful area for future research: "Why are so many people in India *not* depressed, although they are living in such socioeconomically depressed circumstances? What are the social factors that protect them from depression?" His hypothesis was that Indians are more religious and more community-centered than Westerners, and that this kept them (relatively) sane: "Maybe it's spirituality and group activities" (Dr. Mukharji). That strong community ties are also "healing ties" for the mind is a commonplace in Western mind-body medicine (Harrington 2008: 175-204).

All the psychiatrists' examples for socioeconomic changes touched on changes to family relations. There was now far less "tolerance" among family members. Married women now developed more depression than their mothers because they learned from watching TV and movies how much emancipation was possible. They realized that it was unacceptable of husbands to make them do all the hard work and then beat them up, whereas earlier they had been brought up to treat their husband like a god. Middle-aged women suffered from seeing their own daughters living a much freer life than they themselves had ever enjoyed: "They have daughters who say that 'I won't put up with the amount of shit that you put up with'" (Dr. Ram). This included that it had become far more acceptable than earlier to go for a love marriage rather than an arranged marriage (Donner 2008). The gradual decline of multigenerational joint families in favor of nuclear families was highlighted by many doctors as causing mental distress on levels never seen before. The nuclear family could not provide the affective support that the joint family offered. Mothers were left alone to run the household and look after the children. Instead of chatting with relatives, all they had now was a TV set blaring nonsense day and night. Once the children grew up and left home, parents were sliding into loneliness. One type of patient most affected by depression, in ways not seen earlier, was the elderly woman whose husband had died and whose children lived in another city or abroad (Lamb 2009).

Worst affected by the rise of the nuclear family were the children. A single child was burdened with all the parents' aspirations and hopes for competitive success. Child psychiatry was the fastest-growing specialization. Dr. Roy said, as did several other psychiatrists, that psychiatry needed to catch mental illness as early as possible, and that was only possible by convincing parents to bring children and adolescents routinely to psychiatrists. The common metaphor for early psychiatric intervention came from botany: "Many problems, if you can nip them in the bud, will never become manifest illnesses. Early treatment gives the best prognosis" (Dr. Roy). One psychiatrist, Dr. Deshpande, who said that a large number of his patients were school children, explained how parents brought their children to psychiatrists when they were not performing as well as expected. The behavioral triggers for seeing a psychiatrist were lack of concentration on work and withdrawal. Another common expression of protest was to refuse food: "Yesterday I saw a child of nine who does not want to go to school. She refuses to eat if she cannot watch TV. She goes without food for three days, then the parents give up." The schedule of a middle-class child in Calcutta looked like this: up at 6:00 a.m., start school at 8:00 a.m., come home at 3:00 p.m., have an hour of free time, and then take private tutorials, sports and music classes, and then do their homework until 11:00 at night: "Children are losing out on unstructured play time when no one tells them what they should do. Children are losing their childhood in this way" (Dr. Deshpande). There was a strong rule that children should never be allowed to "waste time." He also reported how parents brought their adolescent children when they fell in love: "The parents go bonkers. They come and say: 'The child is in love. Treat him for love! He is wasting time!'" (Dr. Deshpande). The "academically frustrated teenager" is also the typical suicide reported in Calcutta newspapers.

Psychiatrists' qualified hypothesis of an absolute rise of depression among certain groups was not matched by perceptions of a relative rise of suffering. The Calcutta doctors frequently quoted the WHO's claim that depression will be the second leading health problem by 2020, but they generally had nothing detailed to say about it. Evidently, large-scale epidemiological transitions do not lend themselves to observations from everyday clinical practice.

In turn, many psychiatrists said that there was no absolute rise of depressive suffering. This argument came in three different formulations. First, the doctors said that serious "depression" remained constant among the patient population, whereas related conditions had increased. For example, one doctor argued that he had observed a real rise in "anxiety with depression" and in "dysthymia" (i.e., mild but chronic depressive symptoms), while full-fledged major depressive disorder (MDD) stayed on the same level. MDD was primarily a biogenetic disorder and, as such, remained immune to social change. On the other hand, anxiety and dysthymia were triggered by changes in people's economic situation: "There is a real gap between materialist ambitions and actual achievement, especially in the urban population" (Dr. Nath).

Second, the psychiatrists all agreed that there was far more awareness of both psychiatry and psychopharmaceuticals than earlier. More psychiatrists were now available in India, and psychopharmaceuticals were given more prominence in government facilities. Media attention to mental health had greatly increased. A few of the psychiatrists regularly wrote for newspapers or appeared in local TV shows, spreading the word about the field. Many highlighted that the liberalization of the Indian media since the 1990s had expanded both the range of available media channels as well as the average time spent on media consumption. All that was still missing was an endorsement of antidepressants by "ABCD" celebrities from astrology, Bollywood, cricket, or devotion—India's most marketable segments. Astrologers and gurus were unlikely supporters of biopsychiatry, but cricketers and Bollywood actors would make fine ambassadors: "We need more celebrities coming to psychiatry. If Saurav Ganguly [a cricketer] or Amitabh Bacchan [an actor] would say that they take their children to psychiatry, then the stigma would go down. India has more cable channels than New York, more newspapers than New York. Celebrities could make a big difference" (Prof. Chatterjee).

Third, a minority of psychiatrists decried the excessive influence of pharmaceutical marketing. More awareness was positive, but commercially driven exaggerations about a steep rise of mental illness in India was negative. Mixing depression and suicide created a sense of panic among the population: "Unnecessary, aggressive marketing is causing some kind of panic among the people that depression is increasing, that we should take antidepressants lifelong because there is a risk of suicide—all this is nonsense, all these statistics are manipulated to increase the market" (Dr. Barman). Even though most marketing is only targeted at prescribers and not patients, the panic filtered through to the wider public.

Critical statements about pharmaceutical marketing were nearly absent among Calcutta psychiatrists, however. Dr. Kali, a renegade psychiatrist who turned his back on psychopharmacology in favor of intensive counseling, felt that his colleagues lacked distance from the pharmaceutical industry. Doctors' everyday income depended entirely on their collusion with the industry, and they had no interest in jeopardizing their lucrative relations: "Why should they be eating from their pockets and then criticize them?" (Dr. Kali). In his view, the industry's hegemony was so strong that most psychiatrists took everything they said as scientific textbook knowledge. For Dr. Kali, the general discourse of an acute scarcity of psychiatrists and of an intolerable treatment gap between India and Western countries smothered even the slightest critical engagement with psychiatry and the pharmaceutical industry.

Conclusion

Mood medications are paradoxical things. More people are on these drugs now than ever before, but the disorders they are supposed to treat are also said to be increasing. Those who welcome the rise of psychotropics praise their efficacy and safety. Others say they are no better than placebos and allege that they only benefit pharmaceutical corporations. Subjective experiences of them are ambiguous. To some, it feels as if the drugs are giving them their lives back. Others find that getting a psychiatric prescription labels them as "mad" and alienates them from friends and family. Instead of solving problems, taking these drugs may deepen suffering. Medication blurs the boundaries between medical "things" and one's authentic "self," yet they are marketed as one more consumer commodity among others.

This book has analyzed how people in the Indian metropolis of Calcutta perceive mood medications and the plausibility of treating melancholy with them. Throughout, it has been written from a position of doubt about the immediate and long-term side effects of biomedical psychopharmaceuticals. Still too little is known about how mood medications are working. The fears that people in Calcutta have about pharmaceuticals may be couched in cultural metaphors, but they speak to a globalized anxiety about drugs. If this book describes Bengali anxieties of chronic medication intake, of "heating" effects, and of disturbed digestion, then these anxieties should not be shrugged off as local idioms of distress but should be seen as the starting point for a dialogue between an anthropology of pharmaceuticals and a critical pharmacology of adverse drug effects.

This book began by describing an encounter between a Hindu monk and psychiatrists in a hospital ward. Unconvinced by the paradigm of biomedical psychiatry, the monk challenged the doctors to explain the action of the drugs prescribed to him. Rebutting the monk's reservations, the doctors told him that psychopharmaceuticals are "mind food" for a brain starved of nutrients. This book has unfolded why Indian psychiatrists call antidepressants *moner khabar* and how this metaphor tries to counter patients' resistance to medications.

"Mind food" echoes the popular centrality of digestion (chapter 1). Indeed, Calcuttan doctors of all medical streams talk about digestion during consultations to establish rapport with patients. Ayurveda, and the entire tradition of humoral pathology, is built on the idea that health comes from a healthy, balanced diet that harmonizes an individual's personal constitution with the natural and social environment; as such it is continuous with lay beliefs (chapter 2). Homeopathy was founded in explicit opposition to the humoral paradigm that reigned in European medical practice up to the nineteenth century, yet Bengali homeopaths also foreground food preferences and experiences of digestion to stay in favor with patients (chapter 3). Thus for Indian psychiatrists attuned to local health concepts, it is only a small step from acknowledging the centrality of the belly to describing psychopharmaceuticals as "food." Even psychiatrists discourage patients from talking about moods and mental states and instead prefer them to speak about physical symptoms because this accelerates doctor-patient consultations (chapter 4).

Likening psychopharmaceuticals to food makes these drugs seem innocuous. Instead of confronting patients with frightening brain drugs, "food" is as familiar as it gets. No other form of maintaining health is as embodied as a regular intake of food. And no other practice of staying healthy is as sustainable as eating the right food. Food has all kinds of effects on the body, but these are not conceptualized in terms of toxic side effects (Etkin 1992). One can have food cravings, but a risk of "addiction" is not associated with food in the way that psychopharmaceuticals can be addictive (Bancroft 2009; Saris 2010). One can overeat, but one cannot dangerously "overdose" on food. Likewise, food does not produce withdrawal symptoms when stopped. One never ceases to eat even while one takes medications, which allows "food" to be combined with other drugs. Food is right at the center of everyday life within the household and the wider community. Food is not a superficial "quick fix" for an illness, but a grounded path to health. Instead of merely "suppressing" illness symptoms that would reappear in an even more dangerous form (chapter 3), food promises to rebalance the entire body. Eating "mind food" suggests that the substances support an endogenous healing process rather than forcing the mind to change beyond recognition. Instead of messing up one's whole constitution, food is the safest way to achieve longevity. That a mindful diet is the golden route to health has been evinced by thousands of years of experience; hence it does not seem to require any evidence from laboratory tests or clinical trials. If there ever was a healing substance that was timeless and beyond all classifications of "old" or "new," then it must be food. Indeed, food is so everyday that there are no firm boundaries between healthy living and getting back to health. Bengali psychiatrists mobilize the innocent, quotidian nature of food to counter suspicions about psychopharmaceuticals. Just as taking vitamins for the body is simple and mundane, so is taking vitamins for the brain. Taking good nutrition for the body hardly raises concerns about authentic selfhood.

That biomedical prescribers explain the action of psychopharmaceuticals as "mind food" and that they compare ill moods to a nutritional imbalance is deeply ironical if the paradigmatic opposition between specific etiology and humoralism in the history of medicine is considered. Etiology, as a "science of causes," is not unique to biomedicine, and all forms of healing entail theories of disease causation. But what is different about biomedicine is the drive to determine *specific* causes, on the smallest possible level, in an experimental way. The desire to establish clear causes goes hand in hand with the desire to deliver targeted and speedy therapies. "Specific etiology" is so important that it came to define the emergence of laboratory-based, experimental biomedicine in the nineteenth century.

Humoral physiologies, as present both in Bengali popular ideas and in Ayurveda, are the opposite of the specific etiology paradigm. In humoralism, everything is similar to or different from everything else, and causal relations are constructed on the basis of oppositions and resemblances. Humoral thinking is always open to new associations and new causal chains. For Gaston Bachelard (1967 [1938]), a philosopher of science, humoral synesthesia was the polar opposite of scientific abstraction. For millennia, humoralism was the biggest *obstacle épistémologique* ("epistemological obstacle") to the breakthrough of biomedicine. Bachelard held that science is necessarily removed from commonsense and immediate experience. For him, humoralism fell prey to a prescientific appropriation of the world through food. This style of reasoning was erroneous because the causal relations that science established could never be accessed directly. Bachelard sums up nicely what most Calcuttan allopaths are thinking about their humoral rivals today.

Specific etiology goes hand in hand with a pharmacology that targets the cause of disease in the organism without producing side effects. This is the model of the "magic bullet," a term coined by Paul Ehrlich (1854-1915) for the first effective antibiotic. The most "magic" bullets have a maximum primary effect on the specific disease and minimal secondary side effects. By contrast, humoralism knows no magic bullets. When disease is caused by a multiplicity of factors, such as a patient's basic constitution, food, life habits, and the changing seasons, no one single substance can kill disease. A patient of biomedicine is required to "comply" with a prescribed treatment; a patient of humoral medicine needs to transform his or her diet and way of life.

The principles of specific etiology and targeted drugs are driving biomedical psychiatry as well. Current psychopharmacology is predicated on the same ideals of stable disease entity and specific interventions. In the 1950s, the "magic bullet" theory was transported from laboratory medicine to psychiatry. The standard etiology for mental illness is that it is caused by various neurochemical imbalances in the brain. Depression is said to be caused by insufficient quantities of the neurotransmitter serotonin between the synapses. The drugs for this imbalance are named according to the pathogenic mechanism they target, such as "selective serotonin reuptake inhibitors" (SSRIs). That these drugs do not have diffuse effects but are supposedly "smart" is highlighted by the term "selective." The marketing success of Prozac was not built on claims that the drug is supremely effective against low moods but on the claim that it targets a single neurotransmitter system and avoids the toxic side effects of older types of drugs (Rose 2007: 201). Indeed, the notion of an "antidepressant" only makes sense in relation to an etiological model that sees "depression" as a clearly defined entity and "antidepressants" as drugs that hit their target.

The problem is that there is no definitive proof that depression is caused by a neurotransmitter imbalance, and whether "antidepressants" are acting against depression in any targeted way is hotly contested: "The concept of a specific drug for depression was embraced despite the absence of any evidence that they acted in a disease-specific way" (Moncrieff 2008: 135). The key reason why the etiology of neurochemical imbalance was so widely adopted was that psychopharmacology craved success, and the most obvious avenue to achieve this was to claim the same specific etiology/treatment model that helped establish biomedicine as the dominant form of healing. But to this day, psychiatric disease can only be identified by outward symptoms, and lab-based diagnostics remain elusive. Psychiatry has no visible pathogens, and therapy varies according to symptom definitions (which have changed substantially over the past decades), diagnostic styles, and even local clinical traditions.

So it is ironic when psychiatrists call psychopharmaceuticals *moner khabar* and rhetorically merge the idea of "neurochemical balance" with the paradigm of humoral balance. "Mind food" is intuitively convincing because it works with, rather than against, older ideas. One could even argue that current biopsychiatry, with its profound materialism of neurotransmitters and its references to neurochemical "balance" and "imbalance," is far closer to humoral pathology than any approach dominant in psychiatry since the era of psychoanalysis. Humoralism does not assume a fixed state of "inherent health" from which "illness" is merely a temporary deviation. Instead, "health" is in flux and chronically at risk. In the same way, biopsychiatry emphasizes the inherent fluidity of mental states and the need for a long-term modulation of moods once a disorder has been diagnosed. Instead of promising a quick cure through drugs, it highlights that drugs need to be taken for a long time, possibly for life.

The proximity between neurochemical balance and humoral balance even makes promises of becoming "better than well" through psychopharmaceutical enhancement more plausible for Indians than for Europeans or North Americans. For example, the much-debated question in bioethics, whether drugs can and should be used as mood brighteners and cognitive performance enhancers (e.g., President's Council on Bioethics 2003), is to a large extent anticipated by humoral ideas of superhealth (chapter 2). For an Indian audience, achieving a level of mental functioning beyond "normal" capabilities is possible and also desirable (chapter 1). Much stigma is still attached to drugs for "mad" people, but the growth of Indian child psychiatry alone evidences that many parents prefer to put their children on psychiatric medications than to see them fail in school (chapter 4).

Moner khabar does not clash with popular Bengali notions of the mind. As discussed in chapter 1, *mon* straddles both monist and dualist body concepts. On a basic level, *mon* is part of a monist cosmology that draws no fundamental difference between the mind and the body, and the mind is seen as affected by what the body ingests and experiences. At the same time, a powerful mind is able to direct the body into any direction it wants. As the Hindu monk pointed out through reciting Vivekananda, true health can only be achieved if the mind *remembers* the body *into* a state of health, and the body follows the mind's lead (see Benson and Friedman 1996). Accordingly, the mind is both monist and dualist. It is monist because the mind is perishable and affected by the body. *Atman* is either reborn in another body or released from the cycle of rebirths, but *mon* dies. Yet it is also dualist, in that the mind is ontologically distinct from the body and, ideally, ruling over the body without the body ruling over the mind. Mind power is a dominant theme in the whole Hindu tradition: a concentrated mind can substitute all outward action with inner action. It can, for example, perform an entire ritual in honor of a deity in the mind (*moner puja*) and conjure mantras that are as potent as any medication. The transcendent power of the mind is also evoked to explain how Hindu gods can eat the food offered to them in worship: gods can either physically eat the offering or only partake of it on such a subtle level that it cannot be measured in gross materiality.

When Bengali psychiatrists speak of *moner khabar,* they play on these notions: *atman* is separate from both mind and body, hence nothing one eats will change one's soul. It will, however, change one's *mon.* This change will not replace one's true character with an alien, inauthentic character, but rather give a starved mind the nutrition that it needs to be strong again. Against the popular contention that biomedical drugs could never bring a *mon kharap* back to a happy mood, psychiatrists propose that there is no essential difference between the mind and the body. If the body can be hungry and needy of a daily intake of food, so can the mind be hungry and needy of nutrition. If biomedicine can treat the body, it can also treat the mind. Psychiatrists suggest that both the belly's hunger and the mind's hunger are for life.

As intuitively convincing as "mind food" may seem, there are metaphorical glitches. For example, *moner khabar* describes the typically "cool" mind in terms of the typically "hot" belly (chapter 1). The mind is not supposed to be craving for food all its life, but to be still and to take in as little as possible. The mind is not meant to be affected by gross material substances such as biopsychopharmaceuticals. If the mind was as "hot" as the belly, it would be raving mad—which is not something that the psychiatrists try to suggest. The objection that biomedical psychopharmaceuticals are not the best substances to "cool" the mind can, however, be countered by suggesting that the sick mind is a "starving" mind and that "mind food" quells the excessive heat of the mind's hunger.

Furthermore, equating psychotropic drugs with food might make them look so banal that patients think that they can increase or decrease the dosage without a doctor's advice, or stop taking them when they feel like it. Psychiatric drugs have already left the small domain of psychiatrists and have come into the hands of inexperienced or even untrained prescribers (chapter 4). Even rural quack doctors took up prescribing SSRI antidepressants because pharmaceutical marketing has positioned them as completely "safe" and "easy" to use. A few psychiatrists may welcome "floating prescriptions" and speak in favor of quack practices, but most have serious reservations against psychotropics on the loose. That senior psychiatrists describe their drugs as simple "brain vitamins" risks the expansion of irrational uses.

It could be expected that the chief rivals of biomedicine in India, Ayurveda and homeopathy, might provide ammunition against chemical psychopharmaceuticals, but the picture is murky. Ayurveda often targets allopathic drugs in general, and psychopharmaceuticals in particular, as faulty and dangerous (chapter 2). Ayurvedic medicine, and with it the entire humoral tradition, stresses that true health can only be achieved and maintained by mindful everyday self-care and a balanced way of living: "*You* are the medicine," as one Calcutta *kaviraj* pointed out. Mental disturbances reflect deeper disturbances of the body, and without strengthening digestion and purging impurities, illness will not be overcome. The shortsighted use of chemical substances without a change in lifestyle seems futile. Fighting disease with unnatural drugs appears doomed.

But on the whole, Ayurvedic critiques of biomedical psychotropics ring hollow. Ayurvedic drug manufacturers are heavily invested in producing ready-made tonics for the mind, making it difficult for Ayurvedic prescribers to condemn the pharmaceuticalization of mental health. Ayurveda argues that food can be turned into subtle energy for the mind, which encourages a "bracket creep" of psychotropics into areas previously seen as "normal" (Lang and Jansen 2009). For India's classic healing tradition, there has always been a continuum from bare survival to godlike power, and all aspects of life are open to enhancement beyond "normal" health. If one adds to this the realization that Ayurvedic humoralism argues for the centrality of food, then it becomes clear that Ayurveda has no critical leverage against psychiatric drugs except that they are "artificial" and "full of side effects."

Similarly, homeopathy also lends less critical ammunition against biopsychiatric drugs than one might expect. Homeopathy was founded as a critique of allopathic medicine, yet much of what Hahnemann wrote was directed against the humoral medicine of his era and is sometimes more critical of Ayurveda than of biomedicine (chapter 3). Homeopathy upholds the principle that all illnesses can be permanently cured and rejects the need for lifelong medication regimes. Homeopathy's dismissal of allopathic drugs, with their heavy side effects and their inability to reach the root of disease, is easily extended to psychopharmaceuticals. However, by foregrounding food and digestion in clinical encounters, Bengali homeopaths also lend their support to humoral ideas of food and "balance." By emphasizing the vital force as a spiritual power that directs the material body, and by conceptualizing homeopathic drugs as acting automatically on the mind as well, homeopaths advance the plausibility of mind medications. Like Ayurvedic drug manufacturers, homeopathic pharmaceutical producers market tonics for better thinking and better concentration, which further deflates homeopathic critiques of psychiatric pharmaceuticalization. Homeopathy adds credibility to long-term medication regimens by priming patients to believe that there is no quick-fix relief for serious problems and that remedies take months to bear fruit.

Both Ayurveda and homeopathy relinquish much of their critical potential against allopathic psychopharmaceuticals because they propagate the same vision of defective modernization that justifies the alleged rise of depression both in India and around the world. The consensus across all medical disciplines is that people are more stressed and head-heavy than they used to be; that minds and bodies are getting excessively "hot"; that lifestyles are changing for the worse; that chronic illnesses are increasing day by day; and that everyday food is so depleted of nutrients that everyone's health is suffering. Homeopaths and *kavirajs* argue that humankind is being "broken by modern life" (Harrington 2008: 139–74). For both groups of healers, it seems a given fact that it is increasingly "normal" to be mentally disturbed. They hold that modern bodies are overcomplicated and that healthy constitutions are difficult to find. This discourse of desolation makes it more plausible that modern brains are in need of nutritional supplements. Although doctors from these rival systems do not hold that biomedical drugs are the answer to modern imbalances, almost everything they say lends support to a biopolitical regime that sees mental illnesses in urgent need of medication.

Popular notions, Ayurveda, and homeopathy all present various reservations against biopsychiatric prescriptions. But perhaps the greatest obstacle is biomedicine's own promise that diseases can be fixed with targeted chemicals within a few days. It is biomedicine's magic-bullet paradigm with which psychiatrists grapple. Indian patients do not need to be convinced that maintaining health requires constant attention. What they are not convinced of is that biomedical medications can and should be used *chronically* without causing severe side effects. The way Indian doctors try to convince patients to take psychopharmaceuticals is a moment in the global paradigm shift toward "drugs for life" (Dumit 2012).

When Indian doctors call psychopharmaceuticals *moner khabar*, they could be called plain liars. These drugs are surely not as innocent as food supplements. They have a range of serious side effects and even increase the risk of suicide among some patients. They have withdrawal symptoms and should never be experimented with as one might experiment with vitamins. Patients who are told that their drugs are "food" might feel cheated and take the doctor to court. To mislead patients is part of an Indian culture of medical paternalism that sees patients as uneducated and as unable to challenge the experts.

Calcutta doctors tend to evade explaining diagnoses and therapies when this causes resistance from patients, and there is no regulation that stands in their way. Thus the hypothesis of "biomedicalization" in North America and Europe (Clarke et al. 2010), where patients are turned into consumers who get actively engaged in the health-seeking process, only partially applies to India (chapter 4). Arguably, the Indian market has long been more "biomedicalized" than markets in most Western countries because the majority of treatments are taking place in the private sector where patients are automatically "active consumers" by virtue of having to pay for treatments and medications out of pocket. But this consumer-driven market emerged from a *lack* of free services and has not gone together with doctors seeing patients as educated equals. If anything, patients' entitlement to informed consent is quickly suspended wherever the desire to prescribe without being challenged gets the upper hand. Given that most allopaths prefer not to tell patients anything about stigmatized conditions and do not say that the drugs are psychotropics, *any* explanation of how the drugs are working may appear ethically superior to a doctor who uses this language. But whether misleading patients is ethically superior to not telling them anything is debatable.

Indian doctors might argue that simplistic explanations of drug effects are used by prescribers the world over. In the UK, for example, psychiatrists illustrate the action of antidepressants in reference to metabolic disorders such as diabetes (Moncrieff 2008: 5-11), because diabetes bears little stigma and because it legitimates life-long drug intake. If Western doctors compare antidepressants to insulin, then someone might argue that Indian doctors should not be chided for calling them "mind food." If there is a conflict between openness toward patients on the one hand and quick intervention on the other, all the Indian doctors I have met would prefer to treat rather than debate. Alienating patients by aiming at patients' "enlightenment" might be seen as less ethical than convincing them to take the drugs they need by any means necessary.

One of the most problematic side effects of calling psychotropics "*moner khabar*" is that this fudges the difference between autonomous self-care and a commodification of health in the form of biomedical drug taking. With a mindful diet, a patient stays in control over his or her body and does not become a slave to medications. Mind food promises to strengthen patient agency rather than to undermine it. The wholesome, homey, and handmade connotations of food shield psychopharmaceuticals from suspicions of doctors prescribing drugs for financial gain. To equate psychotropics with food suggests that the patient's agency in health seeking is not threatened but reaffirmed. Nothing could be further from the truth, however.

In humoralism, causal links between bodily and cosmic states are open to embodied experience, and becoming and staying healthy is primarily the patient's own responsibility. Where biomedicine tends to emphasize submission to prescriptions, humoralism engenders self-care. In humoral medicine, linkages among food, climate, individual constitution, and social ties are open to self-care beyond biomedical expert knowledge. Even where humoralism is scientifically "wrong," it allows a degree of freedom that biomedicine never does (Foucault 1986). Bengali "bowel obsession" may go way beyond physiological facts, but it is better to be intensely preoccupied with one's digestion than to rely on biomedical knowledge as the only arbiter of truth.

In North America and Europe, psychopharmaceuticals are widely debated in the public sphere. Prozac, as one of the most recognized brand names in history, has grown the market for all psychopharmaceuticals. Rising prescriptions and public anxieties about mind medications have provoked a soul-searching debate about the bioethics of enhancement. The headlines on mood-altering medications may not always be good, but every marketer knows that even bad news is better than no news. By obscuring the effects of their drugs, Bengali psychiatrists are creating not only an "epistemological obstacle" but also a potential marketing obstacle that limits the potential growth of psychopharmaceutical sales in the longer run. For anyone critical of rapidly rising prescriptions in India, the fact that doctors are either keeping silent about the drugs or are describing them as "mind food" might be a blessing in disguise.

Bengali script is difficult to transliterate. Most commonly, words are transliterated by treating Bengali letters as if they were Devanagari (Sanskritic) letters, and then using the standard key for transliterating Sanskrit. This method is not very satisfying, because some elements of the Bengali alphabet have no equivalent in Devanagari, and because it does not convey proper pronunciation. For example, *kavirāj* (Ayurvedic physician) is pronounced *kobiraj*. A number of terms have taken on common English spellings, e.g., *bustee* ("slum") would be transliterated as *bastī* (and sound like *bosti*). Bengalis themselves have never adopted a standard system. Generations of Bengali scholars could not agree on a good system. For want of a better way of doing it, I also treat Bengali letters mostly like Devanagari letters. However, I make a few exceptions when correct pronunciation is more important. For example, *mon* ("mind") would be transliterated as *man* (and is spelled in Bengali only *mn*, with the "a" being an inherent vowel). Because of the closeness to the English term "man," I prefer the spelling that follows Bengali pronunciation.

The following glossary only contains selected key words. Anyone familiar with the complexity of concepts like *darshana* or *dosha* will realize that the English translations are only meant to give a rough orientation. Quotation marks around English words signal that the translation is even more inexact and reductive than in most other cases. The more complex meanings of these terms are explained in the main text.

Bengali terms are marked with "(B)," Sanskrit terms with "(S)." All the Sanskrit terms that appear here are also used in (learned) Bengali, sometimes with a different spelling; and most of the words marked "Bengali" have similar or related Sanskrit forms. Therefore the differentiation between Bengali and Sanskrit is not categorical at all.

agni (agni) (S) – fire
agun (āgun) (B) – fire

akasha (ākāśa) (S, B) – *sky, ether*

antra (antra) (B) – *intestines*

asukh (asukh) (B) – *disease*

atman (ātman) (S) – *soul*

bhadralok (bhadralok) (B) – *"respectable people," educated middle class*

bhagavan (bhagavān) (S, B) – *God*

bhat (bhāt) (B) – *cooked rice*

bhut (bhūt) (S) – *"element"*

brahmacarya (brahmacārya) (S) – *chastity*

bustee (bastī) (B) – *slum*

byatha (byathā) (B) – *pain*

chele (chele) (B) – *boy*

cinta (cintā) (B) – *thought, tension*

cokh (cokh) (B) – *eye*

darshana (darśana) (S) – *sight, seeing*

deri (derī) (B) – *late, slow*

dharma (dharma) (S) – *cosmic law of right and wrong*

dhatu (dhātu) (S) – *bodily tissue*

dosha (dośā) (S) – *fault, defect, humor*

durbol (durbol) (B) – *weakness*

garam (garam) (B) – *hot*

garib (garib) (B) – *poor*

hajam kara (hajam karā) (B) – *to digest*

haoya (haoyā) (B) – *to become, to happen*

haoya (hāoyā) (B) – *air, wind*

jhal (B) – *pungent, spicy*

jor (jor) (B) – *power*

jvala (jvala) (B) – *burning*

jvar (jvar) (B) – *fever*

kaj (kāj) (B) – *work*

kaliyuga (kaliyuga) (S) – *fourth and last of the cosmic ages (the present age)*

kapha (kāphā) (S) – *"phlegm"*

kara (karā) (B) – *to do*

karma (karma) (S) – *action and its consequence in the future (present or next life)*

katha (kathā) (B) – *word*

khabar (khābār) (B) – *food*

khaoya (khāoyā) (B) – *to eat*

kharap (khārāp) (B) – *bad*

khide (khide) (B) – *hunger*

kora (korā) (B) – *strict, hard, having side-effects (medicine)*

lobhi (lobhī) (B) – *greedy*

lok (lok) (B) – *people*

ma (mā) (B) – *mother*

mantra (mantra) (S) – *sacred formula, magic spell*

masala (māsālā) (S) – *mixture*

matha (māthā) (B) – *head*

mon (man) (B) – *mind, heart-mind*

mukh (mukh) (B) – *mouth*

neem (nīm) (S) – *Azadirachta indica tree*

nunta (nunta) (B) – *salty*

osudh (osudh) (B) – *remedy, medicine*

pākā (paka) (B) – *cooked, ripe*

pakhasthali (pākasthali) (B) – *place of cooking, stomach*

panchakarma (pañcakarma) (S) – *Ayurvedic purge*

parishkar (pariskar) (B) – *clean*

pathya (pathya) (B) – *healthy food (for healing purposes)*

patla (pātlā) (B) – *thin*

pet (peñ) (B) – *belly*

pitta (pittā) (S) – *"bile"*

pliha (plīha) (B) – *spleen*

prakriti (prakçti) (S) – *nature; bodily constitution*

puja (pūjā) (S) – *Hindu worship*

rajasik (rājasik) (S) – *energizing, agitating*

rakta (rakta) (B) – *blood*

rasa (rasa) (S) – *juice, taste*

roga (rogā) (B) – *ill*

sab (sab) (B) – *all*

sadhana (sādhanā) (S, B) – *meditation, religious exercise*

sattvik (sattvik) (S) – *cool, pure*

shakti (śakti) (S, B) – *power, especially of a female goddess*

shanti (śānti) (S, B) – *peace, tranquility*

sharir (śarīr) (B) – *body*

shastra (śāstra) (S) – classic Sanskrit teaching

sukra (śukra) (S) – radiant, pure; semen

svada (svāda) (S) – taste

svami (svāmī) (B) – husband

taka (ñākā) (B) – money

tamasik (tamasik) (S) – dark, stale

tapas (tapas) (S) – (ritual) penance, heat of asceticism

teto (teto) (B) – bitter

thakur (ñhakur) (B) – God

thanda (ñhāndā) (B) – cool

totka (totkā) (B) – home remedy

tridosha (tridośā) (S) – three "humors"

vaidya (vaidya) (S) – Ayurvedic physician

vata (vātā) (S) – "wind" humor (tridosha)

vayu (vāyu) (S) – wind (element)

Veda (Veda) (S) –"knowledge" (revealed, sacred)

virya-nirodha (vīrya-nirodha) (S) – semen loss

visvas (vīśvās) (B) – faith

yakrit (yakçt) (B) – liver

yog (yog) (S) – "link"

BIBLIOGRAPHY

Alter, Joseph S. Seminal Truth: A Modern Science of Male Celibacy in North India. *Medical Anthropology Quarterly* 11, no. 3 (1997): 275–98.

Alter, Joseph S. Heaps of Health, Metaphysical Fitness: Ayurveda and the Ontology of Good Health in Medical Anthropology. *Current Anthropology* 40 (1999, Supplement): 43-66.

Appadurai, Arjun. Gastro-Politics in Hindu India. *American Ethnologist* 8, no. 3 (August 1981): 494-511.

Appadurai, Arjun, ed. *The Social Life of Things: Commodities in Cultural Perspective.* Cambridge: Cambridge University Press, 1986.

Applbaum, Kalman. Educating for Global Mental Health. In A. Petryna, A. Lakoff, and A. Kleinman, eds., *Global Pharmaceuticals*, pp. 85-110. Durham, NC: Duke University Press, 2006.

Ariely, Dan. *The (Honest) Truth about Dishonesty: How We Lie to Everyone—Especially Ourselves.* New York: Harper, 2012.

Arnold, David, and Sumit Sarkar. In Search of Rational Remedies: Homoeopathy in Nineteenth-Century Bengal. In Ernst Waltraud, ed., *Plural Medicine, Tradition, and Modernity, 1800-2000*, pp. 40-57. London: Routledge, 2000.

Babb, Lawrence A. The Physiology of Redemption. *History of Religions* 22 (1982): 293-312.

Bachelard, Gaston. *La formation de l'esprit scientifique: contribution à une psychoanalyse de la connaissance objective.* Fifth edition. Paris: J. Vrin, 1967 [1938].

Bagchi, Asoke K. *Rabindranath Tagore and His Medical World.* Delhi: Konark, 2000.

Bakhtin, M. M. *Rabelais and His World.* Bloomington: Indiana University Press, 1984.

Bancroft, Angus. *Drugs, Intoxication, and Society.* Cambridge, UK: Polity, 2009.

Bandyyopadhyaya, Tarasankara. *Arogyaniketan.* Translated by Enakshi Chatterjee. New Delhi: Sahitya Akademi, 1998.

Banerjee, D. D. *Augmented Textbook of Homoeopathic Pharmacy.* Second edition. New Delhi: Jain, 2006.

Banerjee, Madhulika. Ayurveda in Modern India: Standardization and Pharmaceuticalization. In Dagmar Wujastyk, ed., *Modern and Global Ayurveda: Pluralism and Paradigms*, pp. 201-14. Albany: State University of New York Press, 2008.

Barrett, Ron. *Aghor Medicine: Pollution, Death, and Healing in Northern India.* Foreword by Jonathan P. Parry. Berkeley: University of California Press, 2008.

Beck, Brenda. Colour and Heat in South Indian Ritual. *Man* (n.s.), no. 4 (1969): 553-72.

Benson, Herbert, and Richard Friedman. Harnessing the Power of the Placebo Effect and Renaming It "Remembered Wellness." *Annual Review of Medicine* 47 (1996): 193-99.

Bergdolt, Klaus. *Wellbeing: A Cultural History of Healthy Living.* Cambridge, UK: Polity, 2008.

Bernard, H. Russell. *Research Methods in Anthropology: Qualitative and Quantitative Methods.* Third edition. Walnut Creek, CA: Altamira, 2002.

Bhagavad-Gita, The. With a Commentary Based on the Original Sources by R. C. Zaehner. Oxford: Oxford University Press, 1969.

Bhardwaj, S. M. Medical Pluralism and Homoeopathy: A Geographic Perspective. *Social Science and Medicine* 14B (1980): 209-16.

Bhugra, Dinesh, and A. Mastrogianni. Globalisation and Mental Disorders: Overview with Relation to Depression. *British Journal of Psychiatry* 184 (2004): 10-20.

Biardeau, Madeleine, and Charles Malamoud. *Le sacrifice dans l'Inde ancienne.* Paris: Presses Universitaires de France, 1976.

Biehl, João G. *Will to Live: AIDS Therapies and the Politics of Survival.* Princeton, NJ: Princeton University Press, 2007.

Biswas, Arun Kumar. *Gleanings of the Past and the Science Movement in the Diaries of Drs. Mahendralal and Amritalal Sircar.* Calcutta: Asiatic Society, 2000.

Bloch, Maurice. *How We Think They Think: Anthropological Approaches to Cognition, Memory, and Literacy.* Boulder, CO: Westview, 1998.

Blumenberg, Hans. *Paradigmen zu einer Metaphorologie.* Frankfurt am Main: Suhrkamp, 1999.

Bode, Maarten. *Taking Traditional Knowledge to the Market: The Modern Image of the Ayurvedic and Unani Industry, 1980-2000.* Hyderabad: Orient Longman, 2008.

Bonnerjea, Biren. *L'éthnologie du Bengale.* Paris: Librairie Orientaliste Paul Geuthner, 1927.

Borghardt, Tilman. *Homöopathie in Indien.* Berg: Barthel & Barthel, 1990.

Bottéro, Alain. Consumption by Semen Loss in India and Elsewhere. *Culture, Medicine, and Psychiatry* 15, no. 3 (1991): 303-20.

Bray, Francesca. *Technology and Gender: Fabrics of Power in Late Imperial China.* Berkeley: University of California Press, 1997.

Breggin, Peter R. *Medication Madness: A Psychiatrist Exposes the Dangers of Mood-Altering Medications.* New York: St. Martin's, 2008.

Brhlikova, Petra, Ian Harper, Roger Jeffery, Nabin Rabal, Madhusudan Subedi, and M. R. Santosh. Trust and the Regulation of Pharmaceuticals: South Asia in a Globalised World. *Globalization and Health* 7, no. 10 (2011): 1-13.

Bridges, K. W., and D. P. Goldberg. Somatic Presentations of Depressive Illness in Primary Care. In P. Freeling, L. J. Downey, and J. C. Malkin, eds., *The Presentation of Depression: Current Approaches*, pp. 9-11. London: Royal College of General Practitioners (Occasional Paper no. 36), 1987.

Britten, Nicky. *Medicines and Society: Patients, Professionals, and the Dominance of Pharmaceuticals.* Houndmills, UK: Palgrave Macmillan, 2008.

Broom, Alex, Assa Doron, and Philip Tovey. The Inequalities of Medical Pluralism: Hierarchies of Health, the Politics of Tradition, and the Economies of Care in Indian Oncology. *Social Science and Medicine* 69, no. 5 (2009): 698-706.

Burton, Robert. *The Anatomy of Melancholy.* H. Jackson, ed. New York: New York Review Books, 2001 [1621].

Busfield, Joan. "A Pill for Every Ill": Explaining the Expansion in Medicine Use. *Social Science and Medicine* 70, no. 6 (2010): 934-41.

Cant, Sarah, and Ursula Sharma. *A New Medical Pluralism? Alternative Medicine, Doctors, Patients, and the State.* London: UCL Press, 1999.

Carstairs, G. Morris. *The Twice-Born: A Study of a Community of High-Caste Hindus.* Preface by Margaret Mead. London: Hogarth, 1957.

Carsten, Janet. *The Heat of the Hearth: The Process of Kinship in a Malay Fishing Community.* Oxford: Clarendon, 1997.

Chadarevian, Soraya, and Harmke Kamminga, eds. *Molecularizing Biology and Medicine: New Practices and Alliances, 1910s-1970s.* Amsterdam: Harwood Academic Publishers, 1998.

Chaudhuri, Sudip. *The WTO and India's Pharmaceuticals Industry.* New Delhi: Oxford University Press, 2005.

Cipolla, Carlo M. *Miasmas and Disease: Public Health and the Environment in the Pre-Industrial Age.* New Haven, CT: Yale University Press, 1992.

Clarke, Adele, Laura Mamo, Jennifer Ruth Fosket, Jennifer R. Fishman, and Janet K. Shim. *Biomedicalization: Technoscience, Health, and Illness in the U.S.* Durham, NC: Duke University Press, 2010.

Cohen, Lawrence. *No Aging in India: Alzheimer's, the Bad Family, and Other Modern Things.* Berkeley: University of California Press, 1998.

Conrad, Peter. *The Medicalization of Society: On the Transformation of Human Conditions into Treatable Disorders.* Baltimore, Johns Hopkins University Press, 2007.

Cross, Jamie, and Hayley MacGregor. Knowledge, Legitimacy, and Economic Practice in Informal Markets for Medicine: A Critical Review of Research. *Social Science and Medicine* 71 (2010): 1593-1600.

Csordas, Thomas J. *Embodiment and Experience: The Existential Ground of Culture and the Self.* Cambridge: Cambridge University Press, 1994.

Csordas, Thomas J. *Body/Meaning/Healing.* New York: Palgrave Macmillan, 2002.

Danesi, M., and Paul Perron. *Analyzing Cultures.* Bloomington: Indiana University Press, 1999.

Daniel, E. Valentine. *Fluid Signs: Being a Person the Tamil Way.* Berkeley: University of California Press, 1984.

Das, Anirban. *Toward a Politics of the (Im)Possible: The Body in Third World Feminisms.* London: Anthem, 2010.

Das, Jishnu, Quy-Toan Do, Jed Friedman, David McKenzie, and Kinnon Scott. Mental Health and Poverty in Developing Countries: Revisiting the Relationship. *Social Science and Medicine* 65, no. 3 (August 2007): 467-80.

Das, Veena. *Structure and Cognition: Aspects of Hindu Caste and Ritual.* Second edition. Delhi: Oxford University Press, 1992.

Das, Veena, and Ranendra K. Das. Urban Health and Pharmaceutical Consumption in Delhi, India. *Journal of Biosocial Science* 38, no. 1 (2005): 69-82.

Dawson, Ann, and Andre Tylee, eds. *Depression, Social and Economic Timebomb: Strategies for Quality Care.* London: BMJ Books, 2001.

Degele, Nina. On the Margins of Everything: Doing, Performing, and Staging Science in Homeopathy. *Science, Technology, and Human Values* 30, no. 1 (Winter 2005): 111-36.

De Neve, Geert, and Henrike Donner, eds. *The Meaning of the Local: Politics of Place in Urban India.* Abingdon, UK: UCL Press, 2006.

Desjarlais, Robert R. *Body and Emotion: The Aesthetics of Illness and Healing in the Nepal Himalayas.* Philadelphia: University of Pennsylvania Press, 1992.

Donner, F. Henrike. *Domestic Goddesses: Maternity, Globalisation, and Middle-Class Identity in Contemporary India.* Aldershot, UK: Ashgate, 2008.

Dreyfus, Hubert L. *Being-in-the-World: A Commentary on Heidegger's "Being and Time," Division I.* Cambridge, MA: MIT Press, 1991.

Dumit, Joseph. *Drugs for Life: How Pharmaceutical Companies Define Our Health.* Durham, NC: Duke University Press, 2012.

Dundes, Alan. "Wet and Dry, the Evil Eye": An Essay in Indo-European and Semitic Worldview. In Alan Dundes, ed., *The Evil Eye: A Case Book,* pp. 257-312. Madison: University of Wisconsin Press, 1992.

Dwarakanath, C. *Digestion and Metabolism in Āyurved.* Calcutta: Shree Baidyanath Āyurved Bhawan, 1967.

Ecks, Stefan. Bodily Sovereignty as Political Sovereignty: "Self-Care" in Kolkata, India. *Anthropology and Medicine* 11, no. 1 (April 2004): 75-99.

Ecks, Stefan. Pharmaceutical Citizenship: Antidepressant Marketing and the Promise of Demarginalization in India. *Anthropology and Medicine* 12, no. 3 (December 2005): 239-55.

Ecks, Stefan. Three Propositions for an Evidence-Based Medical Anthropology. *Journal of the Royal Anthropological Institute* (Special Issue, 2008): S77-S92.

Ecks, Stefan. Spectacles of Reason: An Ethnography of Calcutta Gastroenterologists. In Jeanette Edwards, Penelope Harvey, and Peter Wade, eds., *Technologized Images, Technologized Bodies: Anthropological Approaches to a New Politics of Vision,* pp. 117-36. Oxford: Berghahn, 2010a.

Ecks, Stefan. Near-Liberalism: Global Corporate Citizenship and Pharmaceutical Marketing in India. In Aihwa Ong and Nancy Chen, eds., *Asian Biotech: Ethics and Communities of Fate,* pp. 144-66. Durham, NC: Duke University Press, 2010b.

Ecks, Stefan, and Soumita Basu. The Unlicensed Lives of Antidepressants in India: Generic Drugs, Unqualified Practitioners, and Floating Prescriptions. *Transcultural Psychiatry* 46, no. 1 (2009): 86-106.

Eliade, Mircea. *Le Yoga: Immortalité et liberté.* Paris: Payot, 1975 [1954].

Elliott, Carl. *Better Than Well: American Medicine Meets the American Dream.* New York: Norton, 2003.

Elliott, Carl. *White Coat, Black Hat: Adventures on the Dark Side of Medicine.* Boston: Beacon, 2010.

Etkin, Nina L. "Side Effect": Cultural Constructions and Reinterpretations of Western Pharmaceuticals. *Medical Anthropology Quarterly* 6 (1992): 99-113.

Farquhar, Judith. *Appetites: Food and Sex in Postsocialist China.* Durham, NC: Duke University Press, 2002.

Fassin, Didier. Another Politics of Life Is Possible. *Theory, Culture, and Society* 26 (2009): 44-60.

Foster, George M. Peasant Society and the Image of the Limited Good. *American Anthropologist* 67 (1965): 293-314.

Foster, George M. *Hippocrates' Latin American Legacy: Humoral Medicine in the New World.* Langhorne, NJ: Gordon and Breach, 1994.

Foucault, Michel. *The History of Sexuality.* Volume 1, *An Introduction.* Translated by R. Hurley. New York: Pantheon, 1978.

Foucault, Michel. *The History of Sexuality.* Volume 3, *The Care of the Self.* Translated by R. Hurley. London: Allen Lane/Penguin, 1986.

Frank, Robert. *Globalisierung "Alternativer" Medizin: Homöopathie und Ayurveda in Deutschland und Indien.* Bielefeld: Transcript Verlag, 2004.

Frank, Robert, and Stefan Ecks. Towards an Ethnography of Indian Homoeopathy. *Anthropology and Medicine* 11, no. 3 (December 2004): 307-26.

Freud, Sigmund. Charakter und Analerotik. In Anna Freud, Otto Rank, and J. S. Storfer, eds., *Gesammelte Schriften Band 5,* pp. 261-67. Vienna: Internationaler Psychoanalytischer Verlag, 1924 [1908].

Fuller, Christopher J. *The Camphor Flame: Popular Hinduism and Society in India.* Princeton, NJ: Princeton University Press, 1992.

Gose, Sarat Chandra. *Life of Dr. Mahendra Lal Sirkar, M.D., D.L., C.I.E.* Calcutta: Hahnemann, 1935.

Graeber, David. *Debt: The First 5,000 Years.* Brooklyn, NY: Melville House, 2011.

Greenhalgh, Trisha. Drug Prescription and Self-Medication in India: An Exploratory Survey. *Social Science and Medicine* 25, no. 3 (1987): 307-18.

Greenough, Paul R. *Prosperity and Misery in Modern Bengal: The Famine of 1943-1944.* New York: Oxford University Press, 1982.

Gupta, Bina. *Cit: Consciousness.* New Delhi: Oxford University Press, 2003.

Gutschow, Kim. A Study of "Wind Disorders" or Madness in Zangskar, Northwest India. In T. Dodin and H. Raether, eds., *Recent Research on Ladakh 7.* Ulm: Ulmer Kulturanthropologische Schriften, 1997.

Hacking, Ian. Kinds of People: Moving Targets. *Proceedings of the British Academy* 151 (2007): 285-318.

Hahnemann, Samuel. *Organon of Medicine.* Translated from the fifth edition, with an appendix by R. E. Dudgeon, M.D. With additions and alterations as per sixth edition translated by William Boericke, M.D., and introduction by James Krauss, M.D. Calcutta: Modern Homoeopathic Publication, 1994 [1833].

Halliburton, Murphy. *Mudpacks and Prozac: Experiencing Ayurvedic, Biomedical, and Religious Healing*. Walnut Creek, CA: Left Coast Press, 2009.

Hannaway, Caroline. Environment and Miasmata. In W. F. Bynum and Roy Porter, eds., *Companion Encyclopedia of the History of Medicine*, vol. 1, pp. 292-308. London: Routledge, 1993.

Hardiman, David, and Projit Bihari, eds. *Medical Marginality in South Asia: Situating Subaltern Therapeutics*. London: Routledge, Chapman & Hall, 2012.

Harrington, Anne. *The Cure Within: A History of Mind-Body Medicine*. New York: Norton, 2008.

Hausman, Gary. Making Medicine Indigenous: Homeopathy in South India. *Social History of Medicine* 15, no. 2 (2002): 303-22.

Healy, David. *The Antidepressant Era*. Cambridge, MA: Harvard University Press, 1997.

Healy, David. *Let Them Eat Prozac: The Unhealthy Relationship between the Pharmaceutical Industry and Depression*. New York: New York University Press, 2004.

Healy, David. Did Regulators Fail over Selective Serotonin Reuptake Inhibitors? *British Medical Journal* 333, no. 7558 (2006): 92-95.

Heesterman, Jan C. *The Broken World of Sacrifice: An Essay in Ancient Indian Ritual*. Chicago: University of Chicago Press, 1993.

Helman, Cecil G. "Feed a Cold, Starve a Fever": Folk Models of Infection in an English Suburban Community, and Their Relation to Medical Treatment. *Culture, Medicine, and Psychiatry* 2 (1978): 107-37.

Helman, Cecil. *Culture, Health, and Illness*. London: Hodder Arnold, 2007.

Henare, A., M. Holbraad, and S. Wastell, eds. *Thinking through Things: Theorising Artefacts Ethnographically*. London: Routledge, 2007.

Holtzman, Jon D. Food and Memory. *Annual Review of Anthropology* 35 (2006): 361-78.

Homoeopathic Medical Association of India. *XI All India Homoeopathic Seminar and Silver Jubilee Celebration 1999, Calcutta*. Under the auspices of Homoeopathic Medical Association of India. Organized by West Bengal Branch, on 24-26 December 1999, at Dr. J. N. Kanjilal Nagar, Calcutta, West Bengal (Millennium Issue), 1999.

Honigberger, Johann Martin. *Fruechte aus dem Morgenlande: Oder Reise-Erlebnisse, nebst naturhistorisch-medizinischen Erfahrungen, einigen hundert erprobten Arzneimitteln und einer neuen Heilart dem Medial-Systeme*. Vienna: Carl Gerold und Sohn, 1853.

Hsu, Elisabeth, and Chris Low. *Wind, Life, Health: Anthropological and Historical Perspectives*. Malden, MA: Blackwell/Royal Anthropological Institute, 2008.

Huwer, Elisabeth. *Das Deutsche Apotheken-Museum Im Schloss Heidelberg*. Regensburg: Schnell & Steiner, 2008.

Indian Ministry of Health and Family Welfare. *Annual Report, 2006-2007*. New Delhi: Government of India, 2007.

Jadhav, Sushrut. Dhis and Dhat: Evidence of Semen Retention Syndrome amongst White Britons. *Anthropology and Medicine* 14, no. 3 (2007): 229-39.

Jadhav, Sushrut, Mitchell G. Weiss, and Roland Littlewood. Cultural Experience of Depression among White Britons in London. *Anthropology and Medicine* 8, no. 1 (2001): 47-69.

Jain, Sumeet, and Sushrut Jadhav. A Cultural Critique of Community Psychiatry in India. *International Journal of Health Services* 38, no. 3 (2008): 561-84.

Janeja, Manpreet K. *Transactions in Taste: The Collaborative Lives of Everyday Bengali Food.* New Delhi: Routledge, 2010.

Jeffery, Roger. *The Politics of Health in India.* Berkeley: University of California Press, 1988.

Jelliffe, D. B. Social Culture and Nutrition: Cultural Blocks and Protein Malnutrition in Early Childhood in Rural West Bengal. *Pediatrics* 20 (1957): 128-38.

Jenkins, Janis H., ed. *Pharmaceutical Self: The Global Shaping of Experience in an Age of Psychopharmacology.* Santa Fe, NM: School for Advanced Research Press, 2010.

Johnson, Mark. *The Body in the Mind: The Bodily Basis of Meaning, Imagination, and Reason.* Chicago: University of Chicago Press, 1987.

Jütte, Robert. *Geschichte der alternativen Medizin: Von der Volksmedizin zu den unkonventionellen Therapien von heute.* Munich: Beck, 1996a.

Jütte, Robert. Eine späte homöopathische Großmacht: Indien. In M. Dinges, ed., *Weltgeschichte der Homöopathie: Länder, Schulen, Heilkundige,* pp. 355-81. Munich: Beck, 1996b.

Kaelber, Walter O. Tapas and Purification in Early Hinduism. *Numen* 26 (1979): 192-214.

Kaelber, Walter O. *Tapta-Marga: Asceticism and Initiation in Vedic India.* Albany: State University of New York Press, 1989.

Karasz, Alison. Cultural Differences in Conceptual Models of Depression. *Social Science and Medicine* 60 (2004): 1625-35.

Khan, L. M. Pleasure of Prescribing. New Delhi: Jain, 2003.

Khan, Shamshad. Systems of Medicine and Nationalist Discourse in India: Towards "New Horizons" in Medical Anthropology and History. *Social Science and Medicine* 62, no. 11 (June 2006): 2786-97.

Khare, R. S. *The Eternal Food: Gastronomic Ideas and Experiences of Hindus and Buddhists.* Albany: State University of New York Press, 1992.

Kirmayer, Laurence J. Healing and the Invention of Metaphor: The Effectiveness of Symbols Revisited. *Culture, Medicine, and Psychiatry* 17, no. 2 (1993): 161-95.

Kirmayer, Laurence J. Psychopharmacology in a Globalizing World: The Use of Antidepressants in Japan. *Transcultural Psychiatry* 39, no. 3 (2002): 295-322.

Kirmayer, Laurence J., and H. Minas. The Future of Cultural Psychiatry: An International Perspective. *Canadian Journal of Psychiatry* 45, no. 5 (2000): 438-46.

Kirmayer, Laurence J., and Norman Sartorius. Cultural Models and Somatic Syndromes. *Psychosomatic Medicine* 69 (2007): 832–40.

Kirsch, Irving. *The Emperor's New Drugs: Exploding the Antidepressant Myth*. London: Bodley Head, 2009.

Kitanaka, Junko. *Depression in Japan: Psychiatric Cures for a Society in Distress*. Princeton, NJ: Princeton University Press, 2011.

Kleinman Arthur. *Patients and Healers in the Context of Culture: An Exploration of the Borderland between Anthropology, Medicine, and Psychiatry*. Berkeley: University of California Press, 1980.

Kohrt, Brandon, and Ian Harper. Navigating Diagnoses: Understanding Mind-Body Relations, Mental Health, and Stigma in Nepal. *Culture, Medicine, and Psychiatry* 32 (2008): 462–91.

Kövecses, Zoltan. *Metaphor and Emotion: Language, Culture, and Body in Human Feeling*. Cambridge: Cambridge University Press, 2000.

Kramer, Peter D. *Listening to Prozac: A Psychiatrist Explores Mood-Altering Drugs and the New Meaning of the Self*. New York: Viking, 1992.

Kumar, Anant. Mental Health Services in Rural India: Challenges and Prospects. *Health* 3, no. 12 (December 2011): 757-61.

Kundu, A. K., and Prithvish Nag. *Atlas of the City of Calcutta and Its Environs*. Calcutta: National Atlas and Thematic Mapping Organisation, Ministry of Science and Technology, Government of India, 1990.

Laderman, Carol. *Taming the Wind of Desire: Psychology, Medicine, and Aesthetics in Malay Shamanistic Performance*. Berkeley: University of California Press, 1991.

Lakoff Andrew. The Mousetrap: Managing the Placebo Effect in Antidepressant Trials. *Molecular Interventions* 2, no. 2 (2002): 72-76.

Lakoff, Andrew. *Pharmaceutical Reason: Knowledge and Value in Global Psychiatry*. Cambridge: Cambridge University Press, 2005.

Lakoff, George. *Women, Fire, and Dangerous Things: What Categories Reveal about the Mind*. Chicago: University of Chicago Press, 1987.

Lakoff, George, and Mark Johnson. *Metaphors We Live By*. Chicago: University of Chicago Press, 1980.

Lamb, Sarah. *White Saris and Sweet Mangoes: Aging, Gender, and Body in North India*. Berkeley: University of California Press, 2000.

Lamb, Sarah. *Aging and the Indian Diaspora: Cosmopolitan Families in India and Abroad*. Bloomington: Indiana University Press, 2009.

Lang, Claudia, and Eva Jansen. Depression und die Revitalisierung der ayurvedischen Psychiatrie in Kerala, Indien. *Curare* 32, nos. 3 and 4 (2009): 14-20.

Langford, Jean M. Medical Mimesis: Healing Signs of a Cosmopolitan "Quack." *American Ethnologist* 26, no. 1 (1999): 24-46.

Langford, Jean M. *Fluent Bodies: Ayurvedic Remedies for Postcolonial Imbalance*. Durham, NC: Duke University Press, 2002.

Latour, Bruno. *Science in Action: How to Follow Scientists and Engineers through Society*. Cambridge, MA: Harvard University Press, 1987.

Latour, Bruno. *The Pasteurization of France*. Cambridge, MA: Harvard University Press, 1988.

Latour, Bruno. *We Have Never Been Modern.* Cambridge, MA: Harvard University Press, 1993.

Latour, Bruno. *Reassembling the Social: An Introduction to Actor-Network-Theory.* Oxford: Oxford University Press, 2005.

Laws of Manu, The. With an Introduction and Notes. Translated by W. Doniger, with B. K. Smith. Harmondsworth, UK: Penguin, 1991.

Lemke, Thomas. *Biopolitics: An Advanced Introduction.* New York: New York University Press, 2011.

Leslie, Charles. The Ambiguities of Medical Revivalism in Modern India. In C. Leslie, ed., *Asian Medical Systems: A Comparative Study,* pp. 356-67. Berkeley: University of California Press, 1976.

Leslie, Charles. Interpretations of Illness: Syncretism in Modern Āyurveda. In Charles Leslie and Alan Young, eds., *Paths to Asian Medical Knowledge,* pp. 177-208. Berkeley: University of California Press, 1992.

Lévi, Sylvain. *La doctrine du sacrifice dans les brâhmanas.* Preface by L. Renou. Second edition. Paris: Presses Universitaires de France, 1966 [1898].

Lévi-Strauss, Claude. *The Savage Mind.* Chicago: University of Chicago Press, 1966.

Liebert, Rachel, and Nicola Gavey. "There Are Always Two Sides to These Things": Managing the Dilemma of Serious Adverse Effects from SSRIs. *Social Science and Medicine* 68, no. 10 (2009): 1882-91.

Lindenbaum, Shirley. The "Last Course": Nutrition and Anthropology in Asia. In T. K. Fitzgerald, ed., *Nutrition and Anthropology in Action,* pp. 141-55. Assen/Amsterdam: van Gorcum, 1977.

Lock, Margaret M., and Vinh-Kim Nguyen. *An Anthropology of Biomedicine.* Chichester, UK: Wiley-Blackwell, 2010.

Majumdar, R. C. Medicine. In D. M. Bose, S. N. Sen, and B. V. Subbarayappa, eds., *A Concise History of Science in India,* pp. 213-73. New Delhi: Indian National Science Academy, 1971.

Malamoud, Charles. *Cuire le monde: Rite et pensée dans l'Inde ancienne.* Paris: La Découverte, 1989.

Malinowski, Bronislaw. *Coral Gardens and Their Magic: A Study of the Methods of Tilling the Soil and of Agricultural Rites in the Trobriand Islands.* New York: Paul R. Reynolds, 1935.

Mallory, J. P., and D. Q. Adams, eds. *Encyclopedia of Indo-European Culture.* London: Fitzroy Dearborn, 1997.

Maloney, Clarence. "Don't Say 'Pretty Baby' Lest You Zap It with Your Eye": The Evil Eye in South Asia. In Clarence Maloney, ed., *The Evil Eye,* pp. 102-48. New York: Columbia University Press, 1976.

Mandelbaum, David G. Transcendental and Pragmatic Aspects of Religion. *American Anthropologist* 68 (1966): 1174-91.

Marriott, McKim. Hindu Transactions: Diversity without Duality. In Bruce Kapferer, ed., *Transactions and Meaning,* pp. 109-42. Philadelphia: Institute for the Study of Human Issues, 1976.

Marriott, McKim. Constructing an Indian Ethnosociology. *Contributions to Indian Sociology* (n.s.) 23 (1989): 1-39.

Martin, Emily. *Bipolar Expeditions: Mania and Depression in American Culture*. Princeton, NJ: Princeton University Press, 2007.

Metzl, Jonathan, and Anna R. Kirkland, eds. *Against Health: How Health Became the New Morality*. New York: New York University Press, 2010.

Michaels, Axel. *Der Hinduismus: Geschichte und Gegenwart*. Munich: Beck, 1998.

Miller, Daniel, ed. *Materiality*. Durham, NC: Duke University Press, 2005.

Mintz, Sidney W. *Tasting Food, Tasting Freedom: Excursions into Eating, Culture, and the Past*. Boston: Beacon, 1996.

Moncrieff, Joanna. *The Myth of the Chemical Cure: A Critique of Psychiatric Drug Treatment*. Basingstoke, UK: Palgrave Macmillan, 2008.

Mukharji, Projit Bihari. *Nationalizing the Body: The Medical Market, Print, and Daktari Medicine*. London: Anthem, 2009.

Naraindas, H. Of Spineless Babies and Folic Acid: Evidence and Efficacy in Biomedicine and Ayurvedic Medicine. *Social Science and Medicine* 62 (2006): 2658-69.

Nichter, Mark. *Anthropology and International Health: South Asian Case Studies*. Dordrecht: Kluwer, 1989.

Nichter, Mark. The Political Ecology of Health in India: Indigestion as a Sign and Symptom of Defective Modernization. In L. H. Connor and G. Samuel, eds., *Healing Powers and Modernity: Traditional Medicine, Shamanism, and Science in Asian Societies*, pp. 85-106. Westport, CT: Bergin & Garvey, 2001.

Nichter, Mark. *Global Health: Why Cultural Perceptions, Social Representations, and Biopolitics Matter*. Tuscon: University of Arizona Press, 2008.

Nutton, Vivian. Humoralism. In W. F. Bynum and Roy Porter, eds., *Companion Encyclopedia of the History of Medicine*, vol. 1, pp. 281-91. London: Routledge, 1993.

Obeyesekere, Gananath. The Impact of Āyurvedic Ideas on the Culture and the Individual in Sri Lanka. In C. Leslie, ed., *Asian Medical Systems: A Comparative Study*, pp. 201-26. Berkeley: University of California Press, 1976.

O'Flaherty, Wendy Doniger. *Ascetism and Eroticism in the Mythology of Shiva*. London: Oxford University Press, 1973.

Oldani, Michael. Uncanny Scripts: Understanding Pharmaceutical Emplotment in the Aboriginal Context. *Transcultural Psychiatry* 46, no. 1 (2009): 131-56.

Organization for Economic Cooperation and Development. OECD Economic Surveys: India 2011. Paris: OECD Publishing, 2011, available at http:/dx.doi.org/10.1787/eco_surveys-ind-2011-en; last accessed 22 August 2012.

Panjika. Guptapress Directory Panjika 1407 (2000-2001). Calcutta: Shrianadicaran, 2000.

Parker, Robert. *Miasma: Pollution and Purification in Early Greek Religion*. Oxford: Clarendon, 1996.

Parry, Jonathan P. Sacrificial Death and the Necrophagous Ascetic. In Maurice Bloch and Jonathan P. Parry, eds., *Death and the Regeneration of Life*, pp. 74-110. Cambridge: Cambridge University Press, 1982.

Parry, Jonathan P. Death and Digestion: The Symbolism of Food and Eating in North Indian Mortuary Rites. *Man* (n.s.) 15 (1985): 612-30.

Parry, Jonathan P. The End of the Body. In M. Feher, with R. Naddaff and N. Tazi, eds., *Fragments for a History of the Human Body: Part 2*, pp. 490-517. New York: Zone, 1989.

Parry, Jonathan P. The Hindu Lexicographer? A Note on Auspiciousness and Purity. *Contributions to Indian Sociology* (n.s.) 25, no. 2 (1991): 267-85.

Parry, Jonathan P. *Death in Banaras*. Cambridge: Cambridge University Press, 1994.

Petryna, Adriana, Andrew Lakoff, and Arthur Kleinman, eds. *Global Pharmaceuticals: Ethics, Markets, Practices*. Durham, NC: Duke University Press, 2006.

Pickersgill, Martyn, Sarah Cunningham-Burley, and Paul Martin. Constituting Neurologic Subjects: Neuroscience, Subjectivity, and the Mundane Significance of the Brain. *Subjectivity* 4, no. 3 (2011): 346-65.

Pinto, Sarah. Cultures of the Psyche, Politics of Illness. In Isabelle Clark-Deces, ed., *A Companion to the Anthropology of India*, pp. 482-99. Chichester, UK: Wiley-Blackwell, 2011.

Pool, Robert. Hot and Cold as Explanatory Model: The Example of Bharuch District in Gujarat, India. *Social Science and Medicine* 25 (1987): 389-99.

Porter, Roy. *The Greatest Benefit to Mankind: A Medical History of Humanity*. New York: Norton, 1997.

Pound, Pandora, Nicky Britten, Myfanwy Morgan, Lucy Yardley, Catherine Pope, Gavin Daker-White, and Rona Campbell. Resisting Medicines: A Synthesis of Qualitative Studies of Medicine Taking. *Social Science and Medicine* 61, no. 1 (2005): 133-55.

President's Council on Bioethics, The. *Beyond Therapy: Biotechnology and the Pursuit of Happiness*. Washington, DC: President's Council on Bioethics, 2003.

Priest, R. G., C. Vize, and A. Roberts. Lay People's Attitudes to Treatment of Depression: Results of Opinion Poll for Defeat Depression Campaign Just before Its Launch. *British Medical Journal* 313, no. 7061 (1996): 858-59.

Raman, S., and R. Tutton. Life, Science, and Biopower. *Science, Technology, and Human Values* 35, no. 5 (2010): 711-34.

Rashid, Sabina Faiz. 2007. *Durbolata* (Weakness), *Chinta Rog* (Worry Illness), and Poverty: Explanations of White Discharge among Married Adolescent Women in an Urban Slum in Dhaka, Bangladesh. *Medical Anthropology Quarterly* 21, no. 1 (March 2007): 108-32.

Ray, Dhirendra Nath. *The Principle of Tridosa in Āyurveda*. Calcutta: Chikitsa Prakash, 1937.

Rig Veda, The. Translated by Wendy Doniger. London: Penguin, 2005.

Róheim, Géza. The Evil Eye. In Alan Dundes, ed., *The Evil Eye: A Case Book*, pp. 212-22. Madison: University of Wisconsin Press, 1992 [1952].

Rose, Nikolas S. Disorders without Borders? The Expanding Scope of Psychiatric Practice. *BioSocieties* 1 (2006): 465-84.

Rose, Nikolas S. *Politics of Life Itself: Biomedicine, Power, and Subjectivity in the Twenty-First Century*. Princeton, NJ: Princeton University Press, 2007.

Roy, Parama. *Alimentary Tracts: Appetites, Aversions, and the Postcolonial.* Durham, NC: Duke University Press, 2010.

Rubel, A. J., and M. R. Hass. Ethnomedicine. In C. F. Sargent and T. M. Johnson, eds., *Handbook of Medical Anthropology: Contemporary Theory and Method,* pp. 113-30. Westport, CT: Praeger, 1996.

Safranski, Rüdiger. *Romantik: Eine Deutsche Affäre.* Munich: C. Hanser, 2007.

Saris, A. Jamie. The Addicted Self and the Pharmaceutical Self: Ecologies of Will, Information, and Power in Junkies, Addicts, and Patients. In Janis H. Jenkins, ed., *Pharmaceutical Self: The Global Shaping of Experience in an Age of Psychopharmacology,* pp. 209-30. Santa Fe, NM: School for Advanced Research Press, 2010.

Sax, William S. *God of Justice: Ritual Healing and Social Justice in the Central Himalayas.* New York: Oxford University Press, 2009.

Sax, William S., and Stefan Ecks, eds. "The Ills of Marginality: New Perspectives on Subaltern Health in South Asia." Special issue of *Anthropology and Medicine* 12, no. 3 (2005).

Saxena, K. G. *Struggle for Homoeopathy in India.* New Delhi: Jain, 1992.

Schumann, U. *Homöopathie in der modernen indischen Gesundheitsversorgung: Ein Medium kultureller Kontinuität.* Münster: Lit-Verlag, 1993.

Shorter Oxford English Dictionary. Sixth edition. Oxford: Oxford University Press, 2007.

Sigerist, Henry E. *A History of Medicine, Vol. 2.* New York: Oxford University Press, 1961.

Singer, Milton. *When a Great Tradition Modernizes: An Anthropological Approach to Indian Civilization.* Foreword by M. N. Srinivas. Chicago: University of Chicago Press, 1972.

Singh, Ramjee. *Textbook of an Introduction to the Study of Homoeopathic Materia Medica.* Calcutta: Homoeopathic Publications, 2003.

Stahl, Stephen M. *Stahl's Essential Psychopharmacology: Neuroscientific Basis and Practical Applications.* Third edition. Cambridge: Cambridge University Press, 2008.

Sujatha, V., and Leena Abraham. Medicine, State, and Society. *Economic and Political Weekly* 44, no. 16 (April 18, 2009): 35-43.

Sumathipala, A., S. H. Siribaddana, and Dinesh Bhugra. Culture-Bound Syndromes: The Story of *Dhat* Syndrome. *British Journal of Psychiatry* 184 (2004): 200-209.

Sutton, David E. Food and the Senses. *Annual Review of Anthropology* 39 (2010): 209-23.

Taylor, Charles. *Philosophical Arguments.* Cambridge, MA: Harvard University Press, 1995.

Thompson, Jennifer Jo, Cheryl Ritenbaugh, and Mark Nichter. Reconsidering the Placebo Response from a Broad Anthropological Perspective. *Culture, Medicine, and Psychiatry* 33 (2009): 112-52.

Tripathi, S. K., D. Dey, and A. Hazra. *Medicine Prices and Affordability in the State of West Bengal, India: Report of a Survey Supported by World Health Organization and Health Action International,* 2005, available at http://www.haiweb.org/medicine-prices/surveys/200412IW/survey_report.pdf; last accessed 15 April 2013.

Tyrer, Peter. The End of the Psychopharmaceutical Revolution. *British Journal of Psychiatry* 201 (August 2012): 168.

Unschuld, Paul. *Medicine in China*. Berkeley: University of California Press, 1992.

Van der Geest, S., S. R. Whyte, and A. Hardon. The Anthropology of Pharmaceuticals: A Biographical Approach. *Annual Review of Anthropology* 25 (1996): 153-78.

Vigarello, Georges. *Concepts of Cleanliness: Changing Attitudes in France since the Middle Ages*. Translated by J. Birrell. Cambridge: Cambridge University Press, 1988.

Vuckovic, Nancy. Fast Relief: Buying Time with Medications. *Medical Anthropology Quarterly* 13, no. 1 (1999): 51-68.

Wahlberg, Ayo. Pathways to Plausibility: When Herbs Become Pills. *BioSocieties* 3 (March 2008): 37-56.

Walens, Stanley. *Feasting with Cannibals: An Essay on Kwakiutl Cosmology*. Princeton, NJ: Princeton University Press, 1981.

Warren, Donald. The Bengali Context. *Bulletin of the Indian Institute of History of Medicine* 21, no. 1 (1991): 17-60.

Weiss, Mitchell G. Cultural Epidemiology: An Introduction and Overview. *Anthropology and Medicine* 8, no. 1 (2001): 5-25.

Weiss, Mitchell G., Amit Desai, Sushrut Jadhav, Lalit Gupta, S. M. Channabasavanna, D. R. Doongaji, and Prakash B. Behere. Humoral Concepts of Mental Illness in India. *Social Science and Medicine* 27, no. 5 (1988): 471-77.

Whitaker, Robert. *Anatomy of an Epidemic: Magic Bullets, Psychiatric Drugs, and the Astonishing Rise of Mental Illness in America*. New York: Crown, 2010.

Whitmarsh, Ian. Medical Schismogenics: Compliance and "Culture" in Caribbean Biomedicine. *Anthropological Quarterly* 82, no. 2 (2009): 447-75.

Whyte, Susan Reynolds, Sjaak van der Geest, and Anita Hardon. *Social Lives of Medicines*. Cambridge: Cambridge University Press, 2002.

World Health Organization. *Mental Health: New Understanding, New Hope; The World Health Report 2001*. Geneva: World Health Organization, 2001.

World Health Organization. *mhGAP Intervention Guide for Mental, Neurological, and Substance Use Disorders in Non-specialized Health Settings*. Geneva: World Health Organization, 2010.

Wujastyk, Dominik. *The Roots of Āyurveda: Selections from Sanskrit Medical Writings*. Selection, translations, and introduction by Dominik Wujastyk. New Delhi: Penguin, 1998.

Wujastyk, Dominik. Interpreting the Image of the Human Body in Premodern India. *International Journal of Hindu Studies* 13, vol. 2 (2009): 189-228.

Yang, Lawrence Hsin, Arthur Kleinman, Bruce C. Link, Jo C. Phelan, Sing Lee, and Byron Good. Culture and Stigma: Adding Moral Experience to Stigma Theory. *Social Science and Medicine* 64, no. 7 (2007): 1524-35.

Zimmermann, Francis. *The Jungle and the Aroma of Meats: An Ecological Theme in Hindu Medicine*. Berkeley: University of California Press, 1987.

Zimmermann, Francis. Gentle Purge: The Flower Power of Āyurveda. In Charles Leslie and Alan Young, eds., *Paths to Asian Medical Knowledge*, pp. 209-23. Berkeley: University of California Press, 1992.

ABOUT THE AUTHOR

Stefan Ecks, MA, DEA, PhD, is Director of the Medical Anthropology Program and Senior Lecturer in Social Anthropology at the University of Edinburgh. Since 1999 he has carried out ethnographic fieldwork on body, illness, and medicine in India.